Future of Business and Finance

The Future of Business and Finance book series features professional works aimed at defining, describing and charting the future trends in these fields. The focus is mainly on strategic directions, technological advances, challenges and solutions which may affect the way we do business tomorrow, including the future of sustainability and governance practices. Mainly written by practitioners, consultants and academic thinkers, the books are intended to spark and inform further discussions and developments.

More information about this series at http://www.springer.com/series/16360

Stefano Gatti · Carlo Chiarella
Editors

Disruption in the Infrastructure Sector

Challenges and Opportunities for Developers, Investors and Asset Managers

 Springer

Editors
Stefano Gatti
Department of Finance
Bocconi University
Milano, Italy

Carlo Chiarella
CUNEF (Colegio Universitario de Estudios
Financieros)
Madrid, Spain

ISSN 2662-2467 ISSN 2662-2475 (electronic)
Future of Business and Finance
ISBN 978-3-030-44666-6 ISBN 978-3-030-44667-3 (eBook)
https://doi.org/10.1007/978-3-030-44667-3

This Springer imprint is published by the registered company Springer Nature Switzerland AG.
The registered company address is: Gewerbestrasse 11, 6330 Cham, Switzerland

Foreword

This is a very timely book. Over the past decade, we have seen a strong increase in both the demand for and supply of infrastructure investments. Although infrastructure remains a relatively young asset class, investors are "sold" on its key features of resilience and cash generation with a moderate risk profile.

At Antin, we eagerly supported the research that constituted the basis for this book. We feel it is a good moment to provide answers to some of the key questions the industry is facing today. What are the key drivers of infrastructure? What are the long-term trends? And most importantly: what are the key challenges of the asset class? Whilst we would have some answers from a day-to-day perspective, we felt nobody was better placed than the renowned team at Bocconi to find answers to these questions looking decades ahead into the future.

Disruption is a key topic we have been observing in infrastructure in recent years. Whereas 15 years ago it was a safe "bet" to invest into car park, the arrival of driverless vehicles, a generation in which sharing counts much more than ownership and an increased awareness of environmental matters all combine to change today's equation. Long-held truths of "safe" assets can suddenly become "stranded assets". We feel it is key to thoroughly understand the changing market environment we live in today and its implications for investing in infrastructure.

This publication fills a gap both for practitioners in the field and for future infrastructure professionals. We hope that the interest in the asset class will persist and that it will continue to attract bright students as human capital is more important than ever.

From a personal perspective, I would like to thank Prof. Gatti for leading this research and for the valuable contributions he and his team of researchers are making to the infrastructure industry in general and to the Investment Team at Antin in particular.

Antin Infrastructure Partners   Angelika Schöchlin
Paris, France

Foreword

Autonomous vehicles. Beyond Meat. Bitcoin. Drones. 3D printing. Netflix. Smart homes. The Green Revolution. Uber. Universal Basic Income. These are all examples of technologies, companies and concepts which have only very recently become mainstream. If we look back only a decade ago, these were very much nascent concepts, some of which would have been inconceivable.

The world population is forecast to reach over ten billion by 2057.[1] Global temperatures are rising and an overall two degrees Celsius increase by 2050 is forecast.[2] Studies predict that 47 per cent of occupations in advanced economies are at high risk of being automated by 2034.[3] Our world's pace of development has increased exponentially.

Where will we be in 20 years' time? What are the unknown unknowns that will dominate our world? How should investors assess and monetise these risks and opportunities? Professor Gatti's book is timely. Disruption is a prevalent theme in the wider economy and in particular infrastructure with the advent of new technologies allied with changing habits creating both new risks and new investment opportunities.

At Antin, we like to say that there were no airports before airplanes were invented. Infrastructure businesses play a key role in enabling many of the trends outlined above. We focus on infrastructure businesses where we see an opportunity to create value during our ownership by transforming and growing our portfolio companies. To create value you need to understand what is important for stakeholders, both today and, more importantly, tomorrow. We typically hold businesses for 7 years and will then sell to new owners with at least a similar time horizon. A lot can change in this kind of time period. Therefore, we pay close attention to disruptive trends and aim to predict how a particular industry might look 10–15 years from now. Many of the chapters in this book delve further into these themes.

---

[1] https://www.worldometers.info/world-population/

[2] https://www.un.org/en/sections/issues-depth/climate-change/

[3] The future of employment: how susceptible are jobs to Computerisation? Carl Benedikt Frey & Michael A. Osborne, Oxford Martin School, University of Oxford, September 2013.

Transport, the exchange of data and the food supply chain are all areas of infrastructure where we have seen disruption in recent times, and this is the heart of our Investment Committee's debates. For example, travel retail is an interesting transport infrastructure sector which is growing strongly due to an ever-growing trend, partly linked to urbanisation and the decline of car usage in cities. Consumers have moved away from the old model of driving to a large out-of-town hypermarket every few weeks in favour of smaller scale but more regular "shopping-on-the-go" in places like train stations, en route to or from the workplace. In 2016, Antin invested in Grandi Stazioni Retail, which operates the long-term leasehold providing exclusive rights to the commercial leasing and advertising spaces of the 14 largest Italian railway stations, serving 750 million visitors per year.[4] Having studied the shopping trends and the increasing passenger flows due to improvements in high-speed rail in Italy, we decided that it represented an attractive investment opportunity. Disruption in the transport infrastructure sector is further explored by Oliviero Baccelli in Chap. 3.

The exponential increase in data flows around the world needs to be supported by certain infrastructures such as fibre-optic cable. Fibre is disrupting the old copper technology and thus we have backed the trend by investing in four fibre providers, serving both businesses and providing fibre to the home across the Netherlands, Belgium, France, Spain, the UK and the USA. The almost limitless capacity of fibre makes it particularly suited to supporting large data flows and enabling the take-up of 5G technologies.

The transition to clean energy, explored by Di Castelnuovo and Biancardi in Chap. 2, is a trend we have focused on for a long time. We made an initial acquisition with our 2018 acquisition of Idex in France and then followed up with our 2019 acquisition of Veolia's District Energy business in the USA. These companies provide district heating and cooling and are well-placed to benefit from the strong trend towards clean energy.

In the media we often read about different demographic groups, such as baby boomers, Generation X and Millennials. Each of these groups has different needs and wants which create both challenges and opportunities. In the social infrastructure realm, we expect to see an increased demand for services related to old age such as elderly care and the prevalence of particular diseases and more chronic conditions due to the ageing population.

Antin has developed strong links with Bocconi University since its inception in 2007. We have numerous colleagues who studied at Bocconi and have since made important contributions to our firm. In 2018, we started sponsoring the Antin IP Associate Professorship in Infrastructure Finance, held by Professor Gatti. As a firm we benefit from the academic research led by Professor Gatti and his world-class team, whilst in the spirit of knowledge-sharing, most of the Antin Partner team has lectured to students at the university. Allying with one of the world's leading

---

[4]GSR estimate

universities enables us to maintain an edge, by benefiting from the results of research, getting access and exchanging views.

We hope you enjoy this insightful publication which serves as a useful compendium for the challenges and opportunities created by disruption in the infrastructure sector.

Antin Infrastructure Partners   Alain Rauscher
Paris, France
Antin Infrastructure Partners   Mark Crosbie
Paris, France

Contents

Introduction

1

Stefano Gatti and Carlo Chiarella

A number of dramatic changes are reshaping infrastructure, a sector that has always been considered by investors and asset managers as a safe harbor in the field of alternative investments. Understanding the future of infrastructure is indispensable for guaranteeing a sustainable future for our planet and the welfare of the world's population. Enhancing our knowledge of this asset class is one important step we can take toward reaching this crucial goal.

This book presents the collected results of the first year of activity in a five-year research plan on the future of infrastructure and how to prepare for the unexpected. This work is being carried out by a group of Bocconi University researchers under the Antin IP Associate Professorship in Infrastructure Finance. Its goal is to improve and disseminate the culture of infrastructure among academics, professionals and policymakers, in order to spark debate on the future of infrastructure and the evolution of the way in which financial markets will support relative investments and financing needs.

This represents a vital and very timely topic. Infrastructure is called to serve as a real catalyst for growth precisely when the industry is undergoing a process of change as it matures. Historically, factors such as regulation, high barriers to entry, rigid demand, and hedges against inflation allowed infrastructure investors to benefit from stable and inflation-linked cash flows for extended periods of time. However, a combination of renewed attention to environmental impact and ESG, world population dynamics and urbanization trends, the impact of the digital revolution, a change in the attitude of society and politicians toward infrastructure—these are only a few examples of the megatrends that investors and asset managers expect to reshape the

S. Gatti (✉)
Department of Finance, Bocconi University, Milano, Italy
e-mail: stefano.gatti@unibocconi.it

C. Chiarella (✉)
Colegio Universitario de Estudios Financieros, Madrid, Spain
e-mail: carlo.chiarella@cunef.edu

© Springer Nature Switzerland AG 2020
S. Gatti, C. Chiarella (eds.), *Disruption in the Infrastructure Sector*, Future of
Business and Finance, https://doi.org/10.1007/978-3-030-44667-3_1

established business model of infrastructure. This poses important questions to industrial developers/utilities, investors and asset managers about the long-term changes that the sector will experience in the next few years. An understanding of these megatrends, how new ecosystems work and how investors can adapt their strategies to the new investment environment are key success factors for lasting and sustainable investment strategies. Indeed, a clear conception of all this is essential for long-term investors wishing to identify the best investment opportunities available and avoid the trap of investing in stranded assets.

To this end, the book collects a series of contributions covering the key megatrends that are expected to reshape the way we think about infrastructure and the implications for infrastructure investors and asset managers. The main focus is on Europe and the European Union, specifically three key sectors: power and energy, transportation infrastructure, telecoms and ICT. However, in many sections of the book, given the magnitude of changes and megatrends, reference to global trends and perspectives is natural and necessary.

The book is organized in six chapters. The first three follow a sectorial approach, in line with the way in which infrastructure investors and asset managers are still used to allocating resources. However, this is shown to be an overly-simplified stance in today's world where the boundaries of traditional sectors are blurring under pressure from technological and sociocultural disruptive forces. In light of this, the rest of the book provides a discussion of the emergence of a new infrastructure ecosystem and the implications for investors and asset managers.

More specifically, Chap. 2, by Matteo Di Castelnuovo e Andrea Biancardi, is focused on the future of energy infrastructures. The chapter starts by providing a detailed account of the global energy balance and its evolution, from oil to natural gas and renewables, and eventually turns its attention to electricity. In particular, six key trends in the electricity ecosystem are identified and discussed: decarbonization, electrification, decentralization, customer activation, digitalization and the convergence of industries. All together, these trends represent the driving force of what is labelled an "R-evolution". The chapter then provides an in-depth analysis of the economics behind such a course, highlighting the role played by offshore wind in the process, as well as the merit order book, and discussing the function of networks and the need for flexibility and storage as both enablers and constraints. The chapter concludes with an assessment of the impact of the "R-evolution" on the financial performance of European utilities and on the demand for rare earth elements and other metals.

Chapter 3, by Oliviero Baccelli, provides insight into future developments in the transport infrastructure sector. First, the chapter describes the three main trends currently influencing transport infrastructure investments across the EU: demographic changes, urbanization and ageing. Then, it highlights the increasing prominence of international tourism and discusses the organizational, technological and regulatory innovations and challenges in three key transport sectors: airports, ports and railways. This analysis is then integrated into the context of the European political agenda by means of a thorough discussion of the EU infrastructure policy, the decarbonization program and the role of the European Investment Bank as early mover in more innovative sectors.

In Chap. 4, Francesco Sacco shifts focus to the telecom infrastructure business and its evolution, as the number of people and devices that are connected constantly grows, and the flow of data escalates at an unprecedented pace. In particular, the chapter highlights the centrality of the telecom network and its value, revisiting its evolution in light of the growth in the demand for connectivity as people change their living and working habits. Moreover, it provides a detailed discussion of the regulatory issues raised by the ever-greater centrality of the network and the potential risks posed by its vulnerability. The chapter concludes by providing an overview of the emerging investment opportunities that originate by the formation of different layers of telecom infrastructure across fixed networks and network evolution, as well as the development of wireless business models centered around 5G.

Considering the disruptive forces reshaping the infrastructure ecosystem in the energy, transport and telecom sectors, in Chap. 5 Markus Venzin and Emilia Konert take a broader view to analyze how investment decisions in the infrastructure world will change and how incumbents can adapt by means of business model innovation through corporate entrepreneurship initiatives. In order to identify where disruption is coming from and why it is so difficult for incumbents to react, the chapter starts by defining small disruptions with big impacts. The discussion then moves on to the creation of industry adaptability through the protection of core investments, the use of core investments to accelerate the business of startups, the improvement of the profitability of core investments with an acceptable risk, or the implementation of alternative investment strategies by learning from disruptors. Narrowing down the argument to infrastructure, this leads the authors to advance a proposal for the development of an "infrastructure radar" to navigate the infrastructure disruption map and give decision makers the tools they need to identify the most promising infrastructure investment opportunities.

Chapter 6, by Stefano Gatti and Carlo Chiarella, looks instead at the disruptive trends reshaping the infrastructure ecosystem with the aim of drawing general implications for investors and asset managers. The chapter starts with an overview of the current state of infrastructure investing and how investors are approaching this alternative asset class. The picture that emerges shows that the aspects which have contributed in the past to the success of the infrastructure asset class are increasingly offset by new elements that pose growing threats to the ability of asset managers to continue offering investors attractive yields. This is followed by a thorough discussion of the technological and socio-cultural trends with the strongest potential impact on infrastructure investment, trends which are shown to affect multiple infrastructure sectors at the same time. This last crucial observation prompts to question the traditional business model of infrastructure asset managers based on sectorial specialization, which may therefore become inefficient and prove unable to capture those transformative trends that would guarantee investors long-term sustainable returns. This leads to the proposal of a new approach to infrastructure investing by which the traditional *silos* strategy, based on sectorial/industry specialization, is replaced by *eligibility criteria*, where infrastructure is no longer defined based on industries but on features/characteristics of the needs served by that same infrastructure. By doing so, the chapter suggests that asset managers adopt a less dogmatic view of infrastructure, stretching the very concept and embracing an investment approach closer to traditional private equity with a redefined balance between reliable income streams and capital appreciation/capital gains. More specifically, two complementary courses of action are recommended to adapt to a changing ecosystem. The first one, which is more short-term oriented and more in line with the investment style of private equity, involves tactical optimization aimed at enhancing performance but not changing the long-term strategic vision. The second one, which is instead oriented on an extended time horizon, involves redefining the selection criteria asset managers use in light of the lasting trends that are reshaping the way modern society works and lives. This would allow them to identify the investments with the best potential in the long run and exploit continuative strategic opportunities by means of "theme" investing.

Chapter 7 summarizes the main results from each contribution and sheds light on future development of research on this field.

The Future of Energy Infrastructure

2

Challenges and Opportunities Arising from the R-Evolution of the Energy Sector

Matteo Di Castelnuovo and Andrea Biancardi

2.1   Introduction

Energy plays a fundamental role in our daily lives, being at the basis of all the economic activities. Transportation, communication, lighting, heating/cooling, conservation and distribution of food, hospital and industrial processes are all examples of activities that need energy (Smil 2017). Electricity, in particular, is fundamental in order to support economic and social progress and to build a better quality of life, especially in developing countries.[1]

Nowadays the energy sector is undergoing major transformations. The rapid deployment and falling costs of clean energy technologies, the growing share of electrification in consumption, climate change awareness and the action of policymakers to decarbonize the economic system: these are some of the trends that will be disrupting the fundamentals of the sector and the status quo of its players over the next few years.

We address this as a "r-evolution".

Indeed, on the one hand the above-mentioned transformations represent the evidence of a much-needed evolution towards a more sustainable, smarter and more flexible energy system. This evolution will take several years to complete as the bulk of our energy technologies are often either the result of long-term investments (e.g. natural gas networks) or represent the dominant solution in the industry (e.g. internal combustion engines). New cleaner technologies like wind, solar PV, biogas and electric vehicles have a long way to go before replacing existing technologies. In fact, according to the International Energy Agency (IEA),

---

[1]According to the International Energy Agency (IEA), over 120 million people worldwide gained access to electricity in 2017, reducing the total number of people without access to below 1 billion.

M. Di Castelnuovo (✉) · A. Biancardi (✉)
SDA Bocconi School of Management, Milano, Italy
e-mail: matteo.dicastelnuovo@unibocconi.it; andrea.biancardi@sdabocconi.it

© Springer Nature Switzerland AG 2020
S. Gatti, C. Chiarella (eds.), *Disruption in the Infrastructure Sector*, Future of
Business and Finance, https://doi.org/10.1007/978-3-030-44667-3_2

in 2017 fossil fuels accounted for 81% of total energy demand, a level that has remained stable for more than three decades.

On the other hand, both the climate change agenda and technological progress have triggered a revolution on an unprecedented time scale for the entire energy industry, with radical implications for all the actors involved. As noted by Helm (2017), it is not just one specific technology; it is a revolution that touches each and every part of energy production and consumption. Developing an understanding of these changes is a fundamental task for all asset managers or financial players who aim to include energy infrastructures in their portfolios.

The purpose of this paper is to identify the key trends of the "r-evolution" which are occurring within the energy sector and to draw some potential conclusions for investors. We start our analysis with an overview of the global energy balance and its evolution over time, highlighting the relevant changes taking place in oil and natural gas markets, the growing electrification and the expansion of renewables. Then, we focus on the electricity industry, describing the key trends that are shaping its fundamentals, especially in Europe. We pay specific attention to electricity because of its greater role in all the decarbonisation scenarios. Moreover, the evolution of the electricity industry is having a great impact on the whole energy sector.

We also highlight the economics behind these changes, describing how they are affecting energy supply and existing infrastructures. In particular, we illustrate the impact of renewables (notably wind and solar) in the electricity generation mix and the challenges and opportunities brought about by their deployment (e.g. the reduced profitability of conventional power plants, like coal). This analysis aims at providing the reader with a broad picture of the main transformations occurring in the sector and the main challenges and opportunities to watch for in the next few years.

Subsequently, we investigate the revenue model and performance of the main European utilities, highlighting the differences between network-only companies (i.e. transmission system operators—TSOs) and other utilities (e.g. energy suppliers). This analysis aims at understanding whether utilities, gas and electricity TSOs represent a worth investment for infrastructure funds. Lastly, the final part of the paper is dedicated to draw some conclusions for financial investors and to provide some indications for their portfolio allocation strategy.

2.2   An Overview of the Global Energy Balance

In order to grasp some of the challenges surrounding the sector we first analyze the evolution of the energy mix over time.

Figures provided by the IEA (2018a) show that fossil fuels (coal, oil, gas) have played a dominant role in global energy systems, and continue to do so. When Arabic countries set up the first oil embargo in 1973, oil accounted for 47% of total primary energy consumption, gas for 16% and coal for 24%. In total, fossil fuels contributed 87% of global primary energy consumption. The oil embargo of 1973–74 caused price hikes, fuel shortages and induced governments to introduce public measures to conserve energy (so-called "Austerity"). All of this generated

Fig. 2.1 Global primary energy consumption fuel mix in 2017 (Source: Authors' elaboration of data provided by IEA 2018)

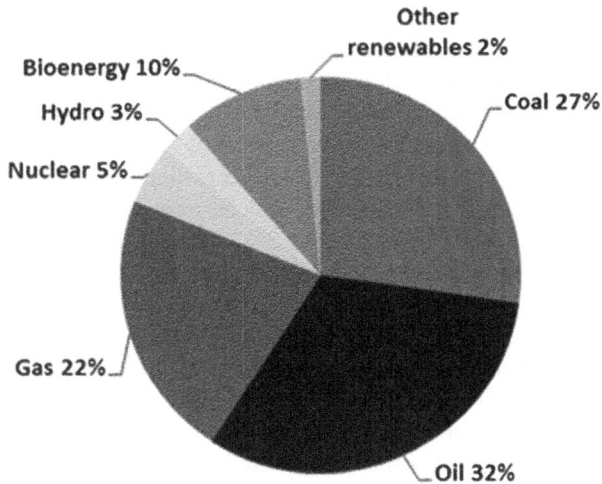

public awareness of dependency on foreign energy resources and spurred the search for alternative sources of energy, especially in the US.

However, more than 40 years later, in 2017, the overall share of fossil fuels in global energy demand was still 81%. Furthermore, this share was calculated on higher demand (14,050 million tons of oil equivalent (MTOE) in 2017, compared to 5681 MTOE in 1973). This means that the consumption of hydrocarbons in absolute terms has significantly increased over the past decades (IEA 2018a). In other words, we can affirm that the entire energy sector currently depends on fossil fuels almost as much as it did in the past, as shown in Fig. 2.1.

Global energy demand is expected to continue growing over the next few years, making the displacement of fossil fuels in the energy mix a tough challenge. According to the last IEA's World Energy Outlook, energy demand will increase by 25%[2] from now to 2040, mainly driven by population growth, urbanization and economic growth in non-OECD countries, especially in Asia (Baccelli 2020). In this regard, for instance, global oil consumption has increased more than 5 million barrels per day (mb/d) since 2015, and it is expected to surpass the threshold of 100 mb/d by the end of 2018.

As a consequence, policy-makers now have a crucial role as they are called to harness the transition towards a sustainable energy system, favoring investments in cleaner, smarter and more efficient energy technologies. To date, after the Paris Agreement on climate change, 187 nations committed to limit global average temperature increases to 'well below' 2° above pre-industrial levels. In particular, each country submitted plans, the so-called 'nationally determined contributions'

---

[2]According to the IEA, energy demand growth would be twice as large in the absence of continued improvements in energy efficiency (IEA 2018).

(NDCs), setting targets for emissions reductions by 2030, relying primarily on increasing the share of renewable energy and of (near) zero-carbon sources (e.g. fossil fuels with carbon capture, utilization and storage).

However, some studies suggest that meeting the NDC emissions targets will not be enough to achieve the well-below 2 °C objective of COP21 (WEF 2017a). Thus we might expect a review of NDCs earlier than expected.

In general, it is necessary to achieve a large-scale shift in our global energy. To put the world on a well-below 2 °C pathway, it is necessary to completely decarbonize power generation and extend electrification to a wider set of activities. This in addition to more effective government policies and large-scale public and private investment. Achieving decarbonisation targets involves scaling up finance, most of all for long-term investment in infrastructure, low-carbon technologies and energy efficiency across all sectors and regions of the global economy (OECD 2017). In particular, according to IRENA (2018), in order meet the climate goals by 2050, a $120 trillion investment is required in all the sub-sectors of the energy system.

2.2.1 Oil

Predictions on oil prices and key fundamental shifts in the oil market have always had a very poor track record. Specifically, the idea of peak oil has been repeatedly reaffirmed throughout the 20th and 21st centuries and every time these predictions failed for several reasons, notably the discovery of new reserves and technological improvements (e.g. fracking).

In this section, we briefly discuss the major challenges that are having a relevant impact upon the sector.

In this regard, one massive technology advance, i.e. fracking, has recently transformed the fossil fuel industry, changed geopolitics, brought new companies into the market and significantly affected oil prices (Helm 2017). Due to the efficient exploitation of vast reserves of shale oil (and shale gas), in fact, the United States has become the world's largest producer of fossil fuels. What's more, this country is now on its way to achieving energy independence within the next few years. The IEA estimates that shale (or tight) oil production in the United States might double by 2025, providing around 75% of the global increase in oil production up until that year.

Shale production is a worldwide game changer and it is already altering the balance of power, especially in the Middle East. Here oil exporter countries, in particular Saudi Arabia, no longer have the ability to rebalance supply and demand. Hence, they are losing some of their political influence.

Another main challenge for the sector is rising awareness of climate change, which particularly among financial investors has created concerns regarding huge stranded assets in the industry (Caldecott 2018). As a result, the financial community is now putting more pressure on the top management of major oil and gas companies, demanding information disclosure and business model adaptation.

Finally, other factors are reshuffling the fundamentals of oil demand for transport, such as the diffusion of electric vehicles (EVs), the introduction of more restrictive fuel efficiency standards for cars and, as illustrated by Baccelli (2020), the use of alternative fuels (i.e. biofuels for road transport or liquefied natural gas—LNG and other fuels for maritime transport).

The actual impact of such changes on the oil industry is subject to a huge degree of uncertainty. However, according to recent IEA forecasts (2018a), oil demand is expected to peak only after 2040 in the absence of additional significant commitments to improve vehicle fuel efficiency and more prohibitive policy measures, especially those aimed at reducing plastic use.

According to the figures provided by IEA (2018), most oil is currently used for transportation, especially by road (i.e. cars, buses and trucks).

Looking at the future, over the next few decades, oil demand will be mostly driven by the petrochemical sector, whose consumption has nearly doubled since 2000. Specifically, this sector is estimated to grow by 5 mb/d despite efforts to encourage recycling (IEA 2018a).

Intuitively, emerging economies are driving demand of many products (e.g. personal care items, food preservatives, fertilisers, furnishings, paints and lubricants for vehicles) whose manufacture require chemicals derived from oil and natural gas. As a result, almost all new refining capacities under development today integrate some petrochemical processes (IEA 2018b). This appears to be part of a long-term strategy both to seek additional margins and to hedge against the perceived risk of a peak in global oil demand.

The use of oil for transport, instead, is expected to peak in the middle of the next decade (IEA 2018a). On the one hand, nearly 90% of the cars, trucks, motorbikes and buses on the road are currently fuelled by oil and the number of vehicles is estimated to grow, as populations in emerging countries become wealthier. On the other hand, oil demand growth in transport will be offset by the rapid electrification of the sector, the development of more fuel-efficient automobiles and the use of alternative fuels (i.e. biofuels and natural gas). In particular, the increasing fuel efficiency of the internal combustion engine will play a major role in containing oil demand growth in the next few decades (IEA 2018a).

New mobility services including leasing, sharing and hailing, as well as the application of new technologies such as platooning (i.e. the linking of two or more trucks in a convoy), automation and connected vehicles, will all likely have a major impact on mobility (IEA 2018a).

Overall, electrification and the digitalization of mobility services and the increase in vehicle and logistics efficiency might eliminate almost 15 mb/d of additional oil demand in 2040 (IEA 2018a).

However, as highlighted by the Carbon Tracker Initiative (CTI), all the predictions about oil demand might be mistaken as the penetration of electric vehicles in the market could be more rapid than most analysts are projecting. The future size of the EV fleet, which is the most significant variable determining the potential displacement of oil demand, is subject to many inter-relating economic, political and behavioral factors. Consequently, there is a wide range across energy industry projections for the growth of the EV fleet.

According to CTI forecasts (2018a), 2 million barrels per day of oil demand could be displaced by EVs in the 2020s, and this number could hit eight mb/d by 2030. This, in turn, may have a disruptive impact on the industry.

In addition to this, a critical issue in the oil industry is represented by the reduction in new upstream oil investments. Due to financial pressures, in fact, oil and gas companies have drastically reduced their exploration activities. In 2018 they represented "just 11% of global upstream spending, the lowest share ever" (IEA 2018b). As a result, there has already been a drop in new oil discoveries, which, in turn, may result in oil spikes, and increased volatility in the coming years, thus further incentivizing the shift from oil.

2.2.2 Natural Gas

Natural gas has been advocated as a potential "bridge fuel" during the transition to a decarbonized energy system, due to the lower carbon dioxide it emits during combustion compared to other fossil fuels (i.e. oil and coal) (Levi 2013). However, natural gas is facing intensified competition from renewables. Moreover, this industry is not exempt from major changes that are challenging the status quo of its players and the fundamentals of the market.

Shale gas deployment in the United States and the rise of liquefied natural gas (LNG) are the most relevant factors driving the transformation.

As already highlighted in Sect. 2.2.1, the United States has experienced significant increases of oil and natural gas production in recent years underpinned by new technological developments, such as hydraulic fracturing and horizontal drilling combined with advancements in seismic imaging and surveying technologies. In particular, the United States was able to unlock vast reserves of "tight" oil and gas found in geological formations "previously thought to be inaccessible and nonviable for conventional development and production" (Newell and Prest 2017).

As a result, shale gas production has increased exponentially over the past few years and the United States is now transitioning from the biggest world consumer and importer of oil and gas into an energy superpower. In fact, according to IEA (2018a), shale gas production, especially in the US, will rise by 770 billion cubic meters (bcm) from now until 2040.

The abundance of cheap gas on the market, made possible by such technological advances, has also prompted the economic viability of LNG trade. LNG trade has, in fact, significantly expanded in volume (i.e. 293.1 million tonnes in 2017) and has reached previously isolated markets. Moreover, higher volumes might be expected as additional liquefaction plants come online over the next few years (IGU 2018).

LNG demand is constantly on the rise, especially in Asia (notably China, South Korea and Japan). In particular, China is on track to become the world's largest gas-importing country, with total gas demand that is expected to triple to 710 bcm by 2040, mainly due to resolute policy efforts in supporting economic growth and improving air quality. In this regard, China is supporting a concerted coal-to-gas switch as part of the drive to "turn China's skies blue again."

With regard to the European Union, it is currently the world's largest importer of natural gas, and continued declines in domestic production will turn into more imports, unless new targets for efficiency and renewables will be able to offset part of the demand. In particular, the combination of domestic resource depletion and the objective of further diversification away from traditional suppliers (i.e. Russia) creates new opportunities for LNG imports.

LNG over the past few years has risen at an annual rate higher than the growth of either global production for indigenous consumption or international pipeline exports. In 2016, in fact, LNG's share of global gas trade was around 9.8%, while pipeline exports counted around 20.8%. LNG and pipelines are considered, to some extent, in competition and perhaps mutual exclusive. However, the presence of a pipeline network is crucial for inland transport of natural gas from the LNG terminal to the demand centers. In addition, many existing pipeline systems require the supply of LNG to face the natural decline of supply from nearby gas fields, or in order to increase the diversification of supply options (Schwimmbeck 2008).

The power sector is currently the largest consumer of gas. Prospects vary widely by region, but retirement of coal-fired capacity and strong demand for electricity create space for gas-fired power generation to expand in many developing economies in the coming years (IGU, Snam, and BCG 2018). Moreover, the resilience of gas in the power sector, especially in the EU, is primarily a result of the closure of 50% of coal-fired capacity by 2030, along with reductions in nuclear power (IEA 2018b).

However, as highlighted by the IEA (2018a), with renewables-based capacity set to almost double by 2040, the business case for building new gas-fired power plants is more and more challenging. As a result, the industry sector, notably the chemical industry, is expected to become the main source of growth in natural gas demand in the next few years.

At present gas is mainly used in energy-intensive industries that require high-temperature heat. According to IEA (2018a) gas demand will rise in light industries where policy impetus is gaining ground to curb emissions. Particularly, natural gas will be utilized more often not only as a source of energy for processes but also as feedstock for chemicals.

Finally, natural gas demand for transport is assumed to increase (i.e. nearly triple by 2040), a result of policy efforts to promote compressed natural gas (CNG) and LNG-fuelled vehicles, especially in China. LNG use in shipping is also expected to grow due to International Maritime Organization regulations to reduce the sulfur content in marine fuels, though its share in the overall fuel mix for shipping is modest (Baccelli 2020).

2.2.3 Renewables

Renewable technologies have grown notably over the past few years. In particular, according to UNEP and Bloomberg New Energy Finance (BNEF), from 2004 to 2017 the additional capacity increased at a rate of 9% and related investments at 14%.

In 2017 investments in renewable technology decreased to $333 billion. On the contrary, as highlighted by (UNEP-BNEF 2018), the total capacity installed in renewables and other low-carbon technologies in the same period increased. This trend is due to a drop in the cost of clean energy technologies; in fact, prices have fallen 83% since 2010. This will be further illustrated in Sect. 2.4.

As a result, in terms of annual capacity, renewable installations now contribute for most of total new capacity installed.

In terms of share of the global energy fuel mix, renewables now account for 10.4%, a figure which has nearly tripled since 1973. The largest consumption of renewable energy in absolute terms is for heating. In particular, bioenergy (mainly biomass) accounted for 10% of global heating consumption in 2017.

As a result, bioenergy is also the main renewable energy source globally (IEA 2018a).

The share of renewables in the transportation sector, which is less significant (i.e. 3.4%), is represented mainly by biofuels.[3]

However most of renewable energy expansion occurred in the electricity sector. Renewables,[4] in fact, have gained a relevant share in the power sector, accounting for almost 25%[5] of global electricity consumption in 2017, as illustrated in Fig. 2.2.

According to the IEA (2018a), the share of renewable technologies is expected to increase to almost 30% by 2023,[6] with hydropower accounting for 16% of global electricity demand, followed by wind (6%), solar PV (4%) and bioenergy (3%). In addition to that, Bloomberg New Energy Finance estimates that almost 50% of electricity will be generated by solar and wind by 2050.

In some countries renewables already in some instances account for 100% of electricity consumption, or even more. For example, energy from renewable sources made up 103.6% of Portugal's electricity consumption in March 2018, according to data from the country's power grid operator REN. Intuitively, excess electricity can represent an additional source of revenues when, like in this case, it can be exported to neighboring countries. Scotland reached record levels in 2017, with renewables contributing to 68.1% of its electricity. Denmark often produces around 100% of its

---

[3]Renewable electricity used for rail and road transport (i.e. electric vehicles) is growing, but is currently low compared to biofuels (IEA 2018a).

[4]Specifically, solar PV and wind are the technologies that saw the greatest growth over the past seven years (IRENA 2018).

[5]In Europe, renewables, including hydro, accounted for 30% of total electricity generation in 2017.

[6]The renewables' share of the electricity fuel mix is also estimated to grow to over 40% by 2040 (IEA 2018). In addition, renewable technologies, mostly solar PV and wind, will supply over 70% of global electricity generation growth in the period 2018–2023.

Fig. 2.2 Global electricity
generation—fuel mix in 2017
(Source: Authors' elaboration
of data provided by IEA 2018)

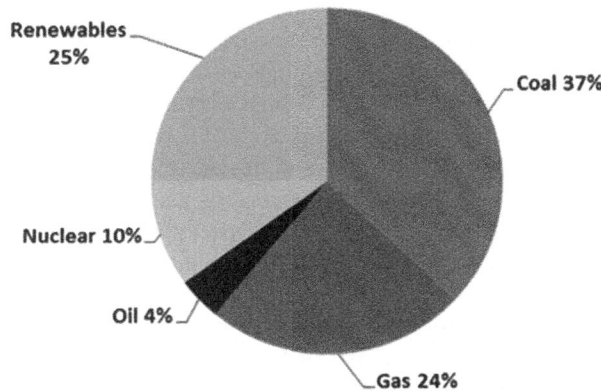

own needs from renewable sources if favorable weather conditions permit. Norway
and Iceland do the same thanks to hydropower and geothermal heat.

In other words, we are definitely moving from an electricity system where most
power is generated by fossil fuels to a system with two-thirds renewable energy by
2050, "ending the era of fossil fuel dominance in the power sector" (BNEF 2018a).

2.2.4   Electricity

Electricity is considered as the source 'of choice' to pursue decarbonization goals
and combat climate change (Helm 2017). Over the past two decades, global electricity consumption has grown by 3% annually, more than any other source, and faster
than the total final consumption. Electric power currently accounts for 19% of total
final energy consumption, compared to just over 15% in 2000. What is more, power
is expected to expand its share of final energy use at least to 24% by 2040 globally
(IEA 2018a).

Demand for electricity continues to grow, especially in developing economies
(notably China and India) even though nearly one billion people still have no access
to electricity. The power sector now attracts more investments than oil and gas
combined. Specifically, in 2017, power sector investments were $750 billion, higher
than investments in oil and gas for the second consecutive year. Moreover,
investments in electricity networks (i.e. transmission and distribution) rose to more
than $300 billion (accounting for 40% of the power sector investment), its highest
level in nearly a decade (IEA 2018b).

With specific regard to the electricity generation mix, the largest share of power is
currently produced from coal but this situation is destined to change.

According to the IEA (2018a), global coal demand actually peaked in 2013/2014.
Indeed, after the Paris Agreement on Climate Change, governments, utilities, industry and financial institutions committed to stop investing in coal (Capgemini 2017).

In Europe, for example, after the UK and France, also the Netherlands, Italy and Portugal announced coal phase-outs. At the time of writing, the debate in Germany, Europe's largest coal and lignite consumer, is still ongoing.

However, we are still far from achieving the total phase-out of coal at a worldwide level. Particularly, while the coal fleets in the USA and Europe are older (i.e. 42 years on average), and nearing the end of their life, Asia's coal plants are just 11 years old on average, "meaning that they still have decades left of operational life" (Hook et al. 2018). Asia, especially China, has 2000GW of new coal-fired power plants that are operating or under construction. This figure is more than 10 times the capacity of the EU. According to the IEA (2018a), these new plants will significantly hamper attempts to achieve emission reduction goals.

As already mentioned in Sect. 2.2.3, renewables have grown significantly in recent years. Hydropower is currently the main renewable energy source of the electricity mix. However, solar PV and wind are growing fast and will cover most of the generation growth of the coming years.

Electricity generated from nuclear, the second-largest source of low-carbon electricity after hydropower, has stagnated over the past two decades. Its share of generation has declined from 17% in 2000 to 10% in 2017 (IEA 2018a). In this regard, the nuclear fleet is ageing. There are currently 413 GW of nuclear capacity in operation worldwide and more than 60% of the fleet is over 30 years old[7] (IEA 2018a). In advanced economies, where most nuclear capacity is located, about two-thirds of the fleet is older than 30 today. In some countries, many projects have already received lifetime extensions on nuclear power plants. Other countries, like Hungary, Czech Republic and France are reviewing plans to prolong the lifetimes of the reactors.

Besides the need to extend the lifetime of most of the reactors, the nuclear industry is facing further challenges. In particular, following the 2011 accident at Fukushima in Japan, and relative safety issues, anti-nuclear public sentiment that now become the major concern for countries. As a direct result, Germany, Belgium and Chinese Taipei have decided to phase out nuclear power.

Furthermore, market dynamics are threatening the financial conditions of both existing reactors and prospective investments in new reactors. Low wholesale electricity prices, due to the increasing penetration of renewables and low gas prices, are making it difficult to justify the additional capital needed to maintain and refurbish reactors (notably in the United States and in the European Union).

These developments are straining nuclear plants that had previously been granted lifetime extensions. Several reactors in the United States announced that they will close prematurely as a result of prevailing financial conditions. According to IEA (2018a), without further lifetime extensions and new builds, the share of nuclear in generation capacity will drop substantially. For instance, in the United States, nuclear power would sink from 20% of electricity generation in 2017 to around

---

[7]The original reactor design lifetimes of most of these plants were between 30 and 40 years.

7% by 2040. In the European Union, although currently the largest source of generation, nuclear would plummet from 25% of generation today to 5% by 2040.

The source of power that could benefit more from the phase-out of coal and from the reduction of nuclear power, at least in the short term, is natural gas. In the UK, for instance, the share of gas in power generation increased from 29.5% in 2015 to 42.4% in 2016 prompted by its increasingly competitive prices and the closure or conversion of some coal-powered plants. Similarly, in Germany, new gas-fired power plants started to operate due to competitive prices and the progressive phase-out of nuclear plants (Capgemini 2017).

Today, cheap gas is also a threat to new nuclear power plants and less efficient, older plants. Recent advances in power plant technology and the currently low price of natural gas have led to increasing efficiency and cost reduction of new natural gas-fired turbines. New natural gas combined cycle power plants can be built for about one-sixth the cost of a new nuclear plant, and run with almost twice the efficiency. What's more, these new plants can be developed in smaller increments, making them easier to finance (Rhodes et al. 2017).

All of this has led to a significant rise in investments in new gas-fired capacity in recent years, especially in the United States. Utilities and independent power plant developers have announced plans to invest over $110 billion in new gas-fired power plants through 2025 (RMI 2018a).

However, natural gas-fired power plants are not the only resource options capable of replacing retiring capacity. Indeed, they are facing increasing competition from renewables, as we will discuss further in Sect. 2.4.

2.3 Key Trends in the Electricity Industry

Electricity systems used to be characterized by centralized control, large "conventional" generation plants and "passive" distribution grids with unidirectional energy flows to final consumers. In the last 15 years, technological innovations, environmental constraints and a changing economic and regulatory setting have resulted in a profound transformation in this structure. All this has significant impacts on the economic viability of current market designs and the business models of market players.

We are witnessing a paradigm shift in power systems. In fact, several sectors and applications are being powered more and more by electricity, switching away from fossil fuels. In addition, an increasing amount of energy is being generated locally and connected directly to distribution networks. Also, energy storage technologies, similarly to solar PV panels, are undergoing dramatic cost reductions. These factors are poised to revolutionize the nature of electricity dispatch and transport. The electricity generation mix is changing considerably in favor of renewables. For example, in the European Union 30% of electricity generation came from renewables, including hydro, in 2017 according to figures provided by Agora (2018). Consumer attitudes are evolving, becoming more active and interested in value-added services. New sectors (i.e. Oil and Gas, Automotive and ICT) are

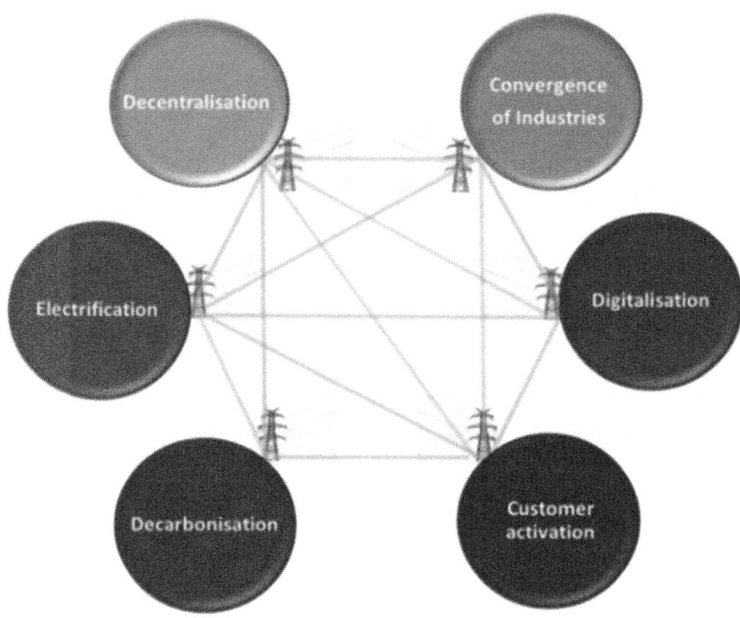

Fig. 2.3 Key trends shaping the electricity industry (Source: Authors)

converging into the electricity industry, creating new opportunities but also multiplying the number of actors and consequently competition (Venzin and Konert 2020).

We have identified six major trends which are reshuffling the industry. These trends are global and as such we provide examples from all over the world, even though our main focus is Europe. Figure 2.3 offers a graphic representation of these six trends, which are often highly interconnected.

We now describe each of them, highlighting how they are affecting the European electricity system (although they are applicable to the US system as well).

2.3.1 Decarbonization

The term "decarbonization" refers to the trend of reducing the presence of fossil fuel in the economy and in particular in the power sector. This trend, mainly driven by policy objectives, is confirmed by the evolution of the EU electricity generation mix. According to Agora (2018), the share of conventional fossil fuels (i.e. coal, lignite, natural gas and other fossil fuels) has decreased by 7.7% over the past 8 years, from 52.1% of 2010 to 44.4% in 2017. Specifically, those with the highest emissions (i.e. coal and lignite) accounted for 24.7% of the EU electricity output in 2017, decreasing from 29.2% in 2010.

Albeit the reduction has not been dramatic so far, the share of fossil fuels in the electricity mix is expected to continue decreasing, especially with regard to coal. This is a result of its phase-out, which has already been planned in some European countries, as illustrated in Sect. 2.2.4.

According to Capgemini (2017), in 2017 in Europe, decommissioned fossil fuel generation capacity was 2.2 GW for fuel oil, 2.2 GW for gas and 7.5 GW for coal.

Several factors prompted the beginning of the decarbonization process in Europe. For example: technological innovations and the reduction of the costs of low carbon technologies, which allowed the development of large renewable power plants and the diffusion of energy efficiency technologies, policy action, changes in consumer behavior.

In particular, policy makers had a fundamental role, introducing subsidies, feed-in tariffs, emissions and efficiency requirements, and incentivizing the diffusion of renewable energy and energy efficiency. Since 2007, the European Union has committed to reaching the so-called 20-20-20 targets. Specifically: (i) to reduce greenhouse gas emissions by 20% compared to 1990s levels, (ii) to achieve the 20% share of renewable energy over energy consumption, (iii) to make a 20% improvement in energy efficiency, when compared to the projected use of energy in 2020.

For the years after 2020, the EU has adopted the following objectives: by 2030: (i) a 40% cut in greenhouse gas emissions compared to 1990 levels, (ii) at least a 32% share of renewable in energy consumption, (iii) at least 32.5% energy savings compared with the business-as-usual scenario. In addition to that, the EU has set itself the long-term goal of reducing by 2050 greenhouse gas emissions by 80–95%, when compared to 1990 levels.

In order to achieve these goals, the EU is leveraging on a combination of different factors, such as: the electrification of sectors which traditionally rely on fossil fuels (i.e. transport and heating); the diffusion of renewable; improvements in energy efficiency, especially in buildings; and the use of alternative carbon-neutral fuels (hydrogen, biofuels, etc.).

In particular, the diffusion of renewables plays a crucial role for achieving the goals of the EU. Besides representing a source of economic growth and job opportunities for Europeans, in 2015 renewables contributed to gross avoided greenhouse gases (GHG) emissions the equivalent of the emissions of Italy (EC 2017).

As illustrated by Staffell et al. (2018), combined capacity of renewables has indeed overtaken total fossil fuel power capacity installed in the UK. In particular, renewables in the UK reached 41.9 GW in the third quarter of 2018. Meanwhile, available capacity from fossil fuels fell to 41.2 GW,[8] with around one-third of plants being retired over the last 5 years. Wind had the largest share of renewable capacity, around 20 GW, followed by solar with 13 GW.

---

[8]The amount of electricity generated from fossil fuels was still greater in the third quarter of 2018, generating around 40% of the UK's electricity, compared to 28% for renewable sources (Husseini 2018).

In terms of share in the European generation mix, in 2017 renewables accounted on average for 20.9% of the electricity consumption. The share of renewables (including hydro) increased to 30% of the total (Agora 2018).

According to Eurostat (2017), in tandem with supply-side policies, the EU has launched a number of initiatives which aim to increase the efficiency of energy use, reduce energy demand and attempt to decouple it from economic growth (i.e. a rise in the GDP). Several instruments and implementing measures are utilized in this field, including the promotion of co-generation, the energy performance of buildings (whether private or public buildings), district heating and cooling (which are expected to play an important role in some regions), and energy labelling for domestic appliances.

In particular, energy efficiency technologies are key players in favoring the decarbonization of the economy, increasing the EU's competitiveness and security of supply. Moreover, energy efficiency technologies are the cheapest way to reduce greenhouse gas emissions. According to WEF (2017a), in fact, avoiding a kilowatt-hour of demand is typically cheaper than supplying that demand by any other available resource. In addition, the IEA estimates that every dollar spent on energy efficiency eliminates the need for more than $2 in supply investments. As such, 90% of the Paris Agreement's NDCs rely on energy efficiency to deliver their commitments.

According to data provided by the European Environment Agency (EEA), between 1990 and 2014, final energy efficiency[9] rose by 28% in the EU-28 countries at an annual average rate of 1.4% per year, driven in particular by improvements in the industrial sector (+1.8% per year) and households (+1.7% per year). In 2015, the European Union energy demand entered into a positive trend and in 2017, energy demand in the EU rose by 1.5%, corresponding to stronger economic growth. However, the increase in energy demand was less pronounced than the rise of the GDP over the same period. As a result, energy efficiency continued to improve (IEA 2018a).

Despite the apparent success, energy efficiency improvements are challenged by long replacement cycles for appliances and equipment (nine or more years). In addition, these improvements are largely dependent on technological innovation and incentives (IEA 2018c). Energy efficiency is also complex to achieve because of cultural habits and due to the fact that decisions are often taken at a local level. Sometimes there is also a high number of parties involved with divergent interests (Capgemini 2017). Moreover, low energy prices penalize investments in energy efficiency related projects, reducing the attractiveness for investors.

Furthermore, the overall impact of energy efficiency on the future of electricity demand is complex because it reduces the cost of powering appliances. This may lead some consumers to buy larger appliances or run them for longer than they

---

[9]Energy efficiency is measured by energy intensity, the amount of energy used to produce a unit of output (i.e. primary energy demand per unit of global GDP).

otherwise would, hence consuming more electricity, a phenomenon known as the 'rebound effect' (Sorrell et al. 2009).

2.3.2 Electrification

The term "electrification" means the trend by which the consumption of energy is increasingly equating to consumption of electricity, as already highlighted in Sect. 2.2.4. At a European level, figures provided by Eurelectric (2018) show that direct electrification represented the 22% of final energy consumption in 2015, varying across different sectors and countries. This rate is expected to rise from at least 38% to 60% in 2050, based on different scenarios (Eurelectric 2018).

Such a process is strongly aligned with the European policy objectives in terms of decarbonization, by enabling a greater proportion of total energy demand to be met by electric power generation from low-carbon energy sources such as solar and wind (WEF 2017b). Indeed, in terms of power generation, the EU production mix is expected to change considerably in the coming years in favor of renewables. For example, according to Eurelectric (2018), removing the barriers to adopting electric technologies together would enable EU to cut emissions by 80–95% between now and 2050.

Among the four economic sectors of energy use: (i) residential, (ii) commercial, (iii) transportation, and (iv) industrial, the one with the highest rate of direct electrification is commercial. In fact, commercial buildings recorded a maximum level of 66% in the Iberian Peninsula (Eurelectric 2018). Nonetheless it is the transportation sector that is undergoing the most disruptive transformation.

The global electric car stock has been growing since 2010 and surpassed 3 million units in 2017, after crossing the 1 million threshold in 2015 and the 2 million threshold in 2016 (IEA 2018d). Particularly, electric cars sales in 2017 were over 1 million units worldwide. China is currently by far the largest electric car market, accounting for more than half of such vehicles sold in the world in 2017. In terms of market share, instead, Norway has achieved the most successful deployment of electric cars with a 39% market share. This result is mainly due to the introduction of government incentives which dramatically boosted the sales of EVs. Norway is followed by Iceland, with an 11.7% electric car market share, and Sweden with 6.3%.

In terms of the outlook for EVs, BNEF (2018b) estimates that 55% of new car sales worldwide will be EVs by 2040. By that date, with around 559 million cars on the road, EVs will represent 33% of the global car fleet. Instead, sales of ICE vehicles (i.e. with internal combustion engines) will slow. According to BNEF (2018b), the number of ICE vehicles sold per year (gasoline or diesel) is expected to start declining in the mid-2020s, as EVs gain shares in the market.

The electrification of transport is also fundamental in order to achieve the EU policy goals in terms of GHG emission reduction. According to data provided by the European Environment Agency, in 2015, the transport sector contributed 25.8% of total EU-28 greenhouse gas emissions. Passenger cars and light-duty vehicles account for the majority of the transport segment GHG emissions.

Switching away from fossil fuels in this sector is crucial for combating climate change worldwide. This is due to the fact that rising incomes in developing countries prompt individuals to seek access to personal mobility. As a result, we might expect that car ownership will significantly increase, augmenting the current fleet of 1.2 billion vehicles (Exxon Mobil 2017). In Sect. 2.2.1 we mentioned that new mobility services (e.g. car sharing) may partially offset this increase, but their overall effect is subject to a great deal of uncertainty.

However, the diffusion of EVs entails both challenges and opportunities. One of the main challenges brought about by the advent of this technology is that, as electric cars on the road continue to multiply, there will be a need for private and publicly accessible charging infrastructure. According to BNEF (2018b), the outlook for EV sales will be influenced by how quickly charging infrastructure will be developed.

According to the IEA (2018c), a relevant aspect related to EV charging stations is that, being integrated in the electricity system, they are subject to power sector regulation.

Depending on the specific regulatory approach of a given country, and whether legislation considers EV charging stations as a retailer or as a distributor of electricity (i.e. network company), the regulatory environment can facilitate or limit the possibilities for utilities to invest or own charging infrastructures. In Germany and the United Kingdom, for instance, network companies are not allowed to operate charging infrastructure (Hall and Lutsey 2017). The rationale is that utilities receive regulated revenues from network operations, and as such they can obtain a regulated revenue stream also from charging infrastructure. This gives these companies an unfair competitive advantage. Relaxing some of these restrictions can promote the expansion of charging infrastructure.

Another challenge related to the diffusion of EVs lies in the fact that higher shares of electric cars represent a potential source of stress for the grid since the capacity required at certain times and locations may have consequences for both adequacy and quality (e.g. if a significant number of EVs were being charged at the same time) (Boßmann and Staffell 2015). Hence, a greater understanding of EV charging patterns and technologies will thus be necessary to ensure their appropriate integration into the grid (especially distribution grid).

On the other hand, according to BNEF (2018b), the diffusion of EVs will contribute to the integration of renewables into the grid. Particularly, the electrification of transport (as well as air conditioning) will allow greater penetration of renewables, since their demand may fit well with the production profile of a solar plant.

Great opportunities also derive from the fact that EVs may draw electricity from the grid or emit stored electricity back into the grid to help balance resources (e.g. through vehicle-to-grid technologies (V2G)). In other words, electric vehicles represent a good example of a potential demand-side revolution (IEA 2018a). The extent of the interaction is technically almost unlimited but, as highlighted by several experts, it also depends greatly on economic evaluations, the efforts for improving customer participation and the supporting policies (Eurelectric 2018; Karlsruhe Institute for Technology 2013).

2.3.3   Decentralization

The term "decentralization" mainly refers to the rapid growth of distributed energy resources (DERs), energy supplies and power sources that tend to be smaller than the typical utility-scale sources. They are usually connected to the lower voltage levels (distribution grids) and close to final customers (demand centers). The importance of decentralization as a game changer is evident if we think about the fact that the expansion of DERs will force a shift away from the centralized, one-way electrical grid.

Traditionally, the electricity system has been characterized by large-scale centralized generation plants, which carried electricity to final customers through the grid. Power flows used to be unidirectional, from the high voltage transmission grid to the final customers connected to the grid. We are now witnessing a paradigm shift in power systems with an increasing amount of energy being generated locally and connected directly to distribution networks, from solar panels on people's roofs to small power plants.

By combining small-scale solar, small-scale batteries and distribution-grid-level demand response, we can obtain a measure of the proliferation of decentralization in the future electricity system (BNEF 2018a). According to Bloomberg New Energy Finance forecasts regarding the decentralization of selected countries, Australia will have the highest rate, with as much as 45% of total capacity located behind the meter by 2040. Germany is the European country with the highest expected decentralization ratio of over 30%.

Decentralization as well as all the other trends represent both opportunities and challenges for the entire electricity system. On one hand, distributed energy resources (DERs) such as storage and advanced renewable technologies can help facilitate the transition to a smarter grid. Theoretically, the overall system could become more resilient and enable small and large power consumers alike to produce most of the electricity they need locally. All of this may also make it possible to defer capital investments to maintain and upgrade grids (WEF 2017b).

On the other hand, the transition makes the real-time balancing of the power system more difficult (ENTSO-E 2019). This in turn means that guaranteeing the security and the quality of supply is more complicated, a task carried out by the transmission system operator (TSO).

The massive deployment of renewables which are connected at distribution level would be beyond the direct control of the TSO. The result would be more uncertainty and volatility, with higher risks of sunk investments over time and potential problems of cost recovery via the tariff system.

For instance, solar PV and wind output is reducing the demand on the transmission system in the UK and due to very high distribution connected generation, the UK system operator National Grid saw day-time minimum demand falling lower than the overnight minimum. This happened on two occasions, on the eighth and ninth April 2017, but this kind of phenomena are likely to reoccur if there are high PV days with wind and high temperatures (National Grid 2018).

Another main feature of this new system is the presence of final users who produce (and soon store) energy on their own, the so-called "prosumers". This is the case of households that installed rooftop PV panels (possibly with integrated battery storage). Instead, for the commercial sector, in most cases we refer to emergency back-up systems that can be used to provide additional electricity in periods of high prices or when there is a need for grid management. Industrial prosumers often have their own plants that deliver electricity and heat at the same time (cogeneration or CHP). These plants can be profitable because of higher efficiency and lower tax burdens.

Besides great opportunities, the shift from consumers to prosumers has also raised some key economic challenges to policymakers and regulators. One of the most pressing ones is how network charging should evolve as more distributed generation is deployed on consumer premises. In particular, network costs (and the policy support charges) tend to be quasi-fixed, i.e. the level is not directly related to the amount of energy being consumed. Since grid tariffs are usually volumetric (kWh charge) and prosumers consume less energy from the grid, network costs will be shifted to other customers when the share of prosumers grows, unless the regulatory frameworks evolve. In other words, the effect of prosumers will lead to rising network charges on remaining users, with re-distributional effects among customers (Friedrichsen et al. 2015). Obviously the more electricity is self-generated and self-consumed, the stronger this effect becomes. Therefore, this relationship is sometimes referred to as the "death spiral effect" (Mountouri et al. 2015). Furthermore, the impact of PV self-consumption may be particularly intensive in some specific geographic areas, leading to regional inequality.

All of this suggests the need to modify network tariffs to take into account higher cost causality in power systems with significant shares of (renewable) decentralized generation (Friedrichsen et al. 2015; RMI 2014).

The economic implications go beyond consumer welfare. In fact, unless network tariff design changes, energy companies may experience a significant drop in revenues. As most of the renewable production is consumed locally, this net offtake of energy can be expected to decrease with increasing penetration of renewables. Reviewing and updating current network tariffs is vital in order to promote the transition towards a more decentralized energy system while fully recovering all grid costs.

2.3.4 Customer Activation

The trend identified as "customer activation" refers to the fact that consumers are evolving: they are becoming more active both as consumers and as producers. Regarding their role as consumers, they are more aware of the possibilities offered by the market in terms of prices and added-value of services. This is proven by the increasing rate of switching and by the greater use of online comparison tools (now available in 22 of the EU countries). The average annual switching rate in the EU28 countries was 6.2% in 2015, higher than the average from 2009 to 2015 which was 5.3%. In the United Kingdom, the first liberalized market in Europe, the switching rate of domestic consumers trended upward from 11% in 2014, to 18% in 2017. At the same time, digitalization and new technologies such as the internet of things and smart meters allow customers to take control of the devices they use. They can monitor their consumption and vary it according to their needs and to market signals (demand-side response). With the huge amount of data on consumer behavior, utilities for their part can formulate energy offers that suit their customers best (i.e. improving customer experience).

In this regard, both residential and institutional customers also more and more often demand products and services that are both "green" (i.e., environmentally friendly) and "smart" (i.e., internet-connected, communicating, and automated) (RMI 2018b).

Customers are also taking on the complementary role of producers. Thanks to the spread of decentralized renewable energy, they can produce power and consume it, store it (through distributed storage technologies) or emit it in the grid. In other words, electricity, together with the digitalization, have made a paradigm change possible.

Changes in consumer behavior (households, energy-intensive industry, heating and the transportation sector) may also add to the flexibility needed by the system (i.e. through demand-side response solutions). Household consumption, in particular, has been highly inflexible so far. However, with the introduction of smart metering and automation, this may change, even if the overall contribution from the demand side will depend principally on technological development.

More broadly, digitalization opens up the opportunity for millions of consumers to sell electricity or provide valuable services to the grid (IEA 2017).

2.3.5 Digitalization

The integration of digital technologies into the electric system is a key change.

According to IEA (2017), investments in digital technologies by energy companies have increased significantly over the last few years. For example, global investment in digital electricity infrastructure and software was USD 47 billion in 2016.

The digitalization of the energy system can bring benefits to all energy players. The so-called Digital Revolution will result in the modernization of the grid, making it smarter and more resilient. This phenomenon can also help reduce the frequency and duration of power outages, restore service faster and prevent damages and problems, lowering operation and maintenance (O&M) costs. Consumers can better manage their own energy consumption and costs because they have easier access to their own data. Grid companies can increase integration of renewables, lowering operational costs that fall within the tariff. Utilities can develop new services, and consequently add new sources of revenues. Moreover, making the demand for electricity 'intelligent' means that capacity can be provided when and where it is most needed. This paves the way for a cleaner, more affordable, and more secure energy system.

More pragmatically, digitalization means data. According to the Boston Consulting Group (BCG), smart meters and other energy management devices, are expected to be installed in 60% of homes by 2019. Eventually, these devices will be capable of generating a massive stream of detailed data about energy consumption patterns, almost in real time, which will be critical to new business models and will facilitate customer engagement (BCG 2014). New digital tools will also enhance customer experience on several dimensions, such as improving customer service through better access to more information and by enabling customers to flexibly manage their electricity demand (WEF 2017b).

Building up digital skills and technology, also through acquisitions, is vital to successfully face the new challenges and to compete in the new arena. According to GTM Research (2016), in the next 5 years, utilities around the world will spend more than $2 billion annually on analytics solutions and service integration.

A critical issue related to digitalization consists in the fact that digital disruption creates new threats, such as the possibility of cyberattacks (see also Gatti and Chiarella 2020). The first confirmed power outage triggered by a cyberattack was in December 2015 in Ukraine. More than 250,000 customers lost power for more than 6 hours. Although its impact was not as widespread, a second power outage in December 2016 was more dangerous since it used a modular, automated cyber weapon capable of inflicting multiple types of damage to a much larger number of power grids.

In that regard, grid companies are far more vulnerable than in the past. This is due to their highly interconnected digital infrastructure, which enables real-time visibility into power outages, lets customers manage electricity consumption from their smartphones, and deploys sophisticated tools for energy management. All this exposes these companies to possible cyber threats, and they must overcome several obstacles in order to minimize this risk. For example, there are continually evolving business and technology requirements, a widespread shortage of qualified personnel, additional risks associated with third-party relationships, and the need to enable the entire workforce to participate in managing cybersecurity risks. In addition, it is vital that power companies intensify their collaboration with third parties to establish appropriate levels of security within the utility ecosystem, and to implement supply chain risk management programs.

2.3.6 Convergence of Industries

More companies currently belonging to other industries are integrating their business models as "energy companies". New industry partnerships are being formed, as large incumbent organizations recognize that they need access to more digital skills in their workforce (WEF 2017b).

This convergence is disrupting the way power companies usually operate and will force a transformation in organizational capabilities, business models, market structure and design (Venzin and Konert 2020). Strategies that may have worked in the past no longer will; there will be a proliferation of new entrants into the market. What's more, in coming years the leading actors in the electricity industry may be companies we have never heard of (Helm 2017). In this regard, one of IDC Energy Insights predicted that by 2020, non-utility companies and digital disrupters will seize 20% of the retail energy market.

One of the most relevant converging trends is impacting the power sector and ICT. According to BCG (2014), by 2020 nearly everything in a home will be capable of generating data that can be monitored online and through a device. We have already seen that digitalization gives rise to huge opportunities for the entire sectors. Besides new opportunities, however, this convergence is also intensifying competition. Energy retailers have demonstrated much less sophistication in their data capabilities than companies in other sectors (BCG 2014). Especially in the US, major technology companies like Amazon, Google, and Apple are competing fiercely for the "smart home" space, fighting for market share to provide home assistants, smart thermostats, and software platforms to integrate many different kinds of devices (RMI 2017). More and more often, established companies including IBM, SAP, Microsoft, Intel and Cisco are offering technologies (such as predictive maintenance) and services. At the same time, numerous start-ups are seeking to exploit the new opportunities in the market. In 2017 there were more than 360 companies offering Internet of Things platforms, according to IOT Analytics, a Hamburg-based research group.

Another relevant converging trend is between the power and automotive sectors. We have already analyzed how electrification is reshaping the transportation sector. EVs are becoming progressively more competitive due to the declining costs of batteries, which have more than halved in the recent years and will result in a relevant upsurge of the electricity demand expected in the coming years. In particular, most major automakers offer at least one electric option or outline plans for electrification.

Another example of convergence between the power and automotive sectors is provided by Tesla, which in 2016 acquired SolarCity, a company specialized in the production of solar panels for the retail market, for $2.1 billion. Tesla made this acquisition at a time when it was believed that the goal of Tesla was to become a mass automobile manufacturer. On the contrary, residential solar is a perfect fit as part of an energy company's offerings, which in addition to electric cars also includes solar PV and battery storage (GTM 2017). In this regard, another Tesla product is the Powerwall 2.0, a powerful battery designed to hang on the wall and provide power to the house, as it is specifically designed to work with Tesla's solar panels and car chargers.

Following the example of Tesla, other automotive companies, including some European ones, have also recently entered into the power storage market. Enel in the meantime has developed a National Plan for the activation of an electric vehicle charging infrastructure, which envisages the installation of around 7000 charging stations by 2020 to reach a total of 14,000 stations by 2022 (Enel 2017).

Another converging trend is leading more companies that identify as "oil and gas companies" today, to integrate their business models as "energy companies" (WEF 2017a). Electrification of transport and heating, for example, may create a bridge between the oil & gas and electric power sectors, a bridge which both collaborators and competitors will cross. Moreover, new technology companies, especially in the power sector, are looking for patient capital. Meanwhile, oil and gas companies, with the capital and longer time horizons, are looking for opportunities to diversify in the face of uncertainty over fossil fuel demand from transportation and broader climate policy. In that regard, several oil & gas companies are more frequently investing in low carbon technologies and renewable projects.

2.4   The Economics Behind the R-Evolution

In the previous sections we analysed the key trends that are reshuffling the fundamentals of the energy sector and, in particular, the electricity industry. One of the most disruptive transformations is the rapid deployment of renewable technologies which is causing major challenges among market players. We now highlight the economics behind these changes, to provide the reader with an understanding of the factors that are prompting this R-evolution.

We start by analyzing how renewables were introduced and how they became fully competitive with other sources of energy. Then, we highlight how electricity is sold in the market (the so-called merit order) and what impact renewables have on other technologies (notably conventional power plants). Finally, we focus on some side effects related to the rising share of renewables in the electricity mix (i.e. negative prices).

2.4.1   The Competitiveness of Renewables

The deployment of renewable technologies has been mainly driven by policymakers (i.e. through the introduction of subsidies and emission reduction targets). According to REN21, last year 87 countries had targets in place for renewables (REN21 2018). Specifically, Europe has led the renewable technology expansion at global level thanks to the introduction in the early 2000s of the first targets for 2020. Policy mechanisms used to provide support for the deployment of renewables, especially at the beginning of their expansion, included: feed-in-tariffs (FiTs), but also market premiums, grants, green certificates and investment tax credits.

Progressively, we moved from more rigid subsidy schemes to competitive auctions with higher levels of competitiveness in the market. To date, incentives for renewable energy sources (RES) are in place only in "new" markets that want to stimulate their development or in markets characterized by specific technologies which are not yet mature.

In recent years, indeed, auctions and other awarding mechanisms based on competition have become the main support mechanisms for renewables (e.g. schemes in which a tendering entity calls for the lowest bid to produce electricity). One of the main advantages of such schemes is to allow governments to specify how much renewable capacity they want to build, and eventually other characteristics of the new plants. This, in turn, allows governments to plan their transition to renewables in line with the targets they have set (Leger et al. 2018).

Moreover, auctions enhance cost transparency and increase competition, especially in contrast to predefined feed-in tariffs. Not secondary, auctions contribute to achieve important savings. For example, in Italy, the cost for supporting wind turbines in 2017 was on average 66 €/MWh, compared to about 180 €/MWh in 2011. Similarly, the cost for solar was on average 41 €/MWh in 2017 compared to 134–289 €/MWh in 2011 (Enel Green Power 2018). Auction mechanisms are also often described as being "capacity-neutral," as bidders can propose coal-or gas-fired power if they want to.

However, in practice, wind and/or solar almost always won the auctions because of their zero fuel cost. In 2017, more than 20% of new solar projects that received support were selected on the basis of competition, together with about 30% of onshore wind and 50% of offshore wind projects (IEA 2018a).

Chile, the second electricity market to be liberalized in 1991, after the UK, represents a case in point for renewable auctions.

As illustrated by IRENA (2018) over the past years, in the Chilean auctions (technologically neutral) renewables plants have been increasingly competitive, replacing conventional generation.

Auctions have also contributed to driving down margins in the value chain (Leger et al. 2018). For example, recent renewable energy auctions have been won by record low solar and wind bids.

If policy support and subsidies had a fundamental role in initially helping renewables come into play, several factors have boosted the competitiveness of renewable technologies in recent years. Technological improvements, for instance, have played a fundamental role, leading to higher performances and cost reductions (IRENA 2018). In this regard, the size of the turbines went from around 2 MW in 2011 to around 3 MW in 2017 while the efficiency of solar panels rose from 14% in 2011 to about 18% in 2017 (Enel Green Power 2018).

Escalating economies of scale in manufacturing, vertical integration and consolidation among manufacturers are also fundamental to cost reductions. Moreover, continuous efficiencies are being achieved through bigger projects. For example, larger and more efficient wind turbines are set to significantly reduce the cost of onshore and offshore wind generation (BNEF 2018a). Competitive procurement and the emergence of experienced large project developers are other recent drivers that are supporting the diffusion of renewable technologies. Real-time data and 'big data' have enhanced predictive maintenance and reduced operation and maintenance (O&M) costs.

All of this is unlocking further performance improvements and cutting O&M costs, hence reducing project risk and significantly lowering the cost of capital

(IRENA 2018). As a result, the levelized cost of electricity (LCOE) for renewable technologies has constantly declined. Now it is close to the lowest level of the fossil fuel cost range, meaning that electricity from renewables might soon actually be cheaper than from most fossil fuels (Lazard 2017).

The learning rate, the cost reduction per doubling of deployed capacity, for the main solar and wind technologies (i.e. the LCOE reduction for every doubling in global cumulative installed capacity) is characterized by remarkable cost declines for the electricity produced by these technologies. For example, as highlighted by BNEF (2018a), the price of silicon PV modules plunged from $79/W to $0.37/W in 2017. This curve describes a learning rate of about 28.5%.

The corresponding figure for wind turbines is about 10.5%.

The enhanced attractiveness of renewables is also proven by the fact that more and more medium-sized Commercial & Industrial (C&I) clients are signing renewable Power Purchase Agreements—(PPAs).[10] There are many different types of PPA structures, based on the regulatory design of the relevant electricity market, the corporate buyer's strategy and the capability of the off-taker (WBCSD 2017, 2018).

Customers choose renewable energy sources for two main reasons. The first is the fact that renewables are becoming cheaper than any other source of energy, as illustrated by Lazard (2017). The second reason is sustainability. Large private companies are moving toward a sustainable business choice by setting targets in terms of renewable energy supply. This situation is convincing more and more customers all over the world: not only large corporations but also even medium-sized companies are participating in the growing market for PPAs through renewable energy.

Meanwhile, developers are diversifying their activities towards C&I to offset the growing competition on the auction price. The most successful market for corporate renewable procurement through PPAs is in the US where volumes rose to 2.9GW in 2017, mostly driven by high-tech companies like Apple, Google and Facebook. However, recent years have seen a growth in corporate renewable PPA deals in Europe (Wind Europe 2018a). Albeit not comparable with the US, the volume and demand for corporate renewable PPAs has tripled in the last 3 years (BNEF 2018a; Wind Europe 2018a).

Companies sourcing renewable electricity in Europe come from various sectors, demonstrating that the trend is widespread and dynamic. All this plays an important role in driving investment in renewables and contributing to global climate objectives (IRENA 2018). Over the period 2017–22, average global generation costs are estimated to further decline by a quarter for utility-scale solar PV; by almost 15% for onshore wind; and by a third for offshore wind (IEA 2018e). Bloomberg New Energy Finance even estimates the levelized cost of an average PV plant will fall 71% by 2050, to around $25/MWh.

---

[10]In general, PPAs are contracts that allow Commercial & Industrial clients to buy electricity produced by renewable technologies.

Thanks to nosediving costs and supportive government policies, IEA forecasts that renewables will account for almost two-thirds of global power capacity additions to 2040 (IEA 2018e).

2.4.2   The Merit Order Effect

In this section we analyze the way electricity is sold in the market, the so-called merit order, and the effect of renewables (and other market forces) on the profitability of conventional power plants in Europe.

Most competitive electricity markets are auction-based, meaning that companies that run power plants participate in the auction in order to provide electricity on the market. In particular, they place bids in the auction to provide electricity at a certain time for a certain price. These bids are collected and arranged in order by price, to make sure that the lowest-cost power plants are dispatched first and the most expensive power plants are last (hence the name "merit order"). This market-based system is designed to deliver the lowest-cost electricity to consumers (Rhodes et al. 2017).

With regard to conventional power plants, they are often categorized by the type of load (energy supply) which they commonly provide: baseload, intermediate or peaking. Generally, different types of plants are used to meet each type of load. Baseload plants are typically lower cost nuclear or coal plants. These technologies generally meet the constant demand on the system and even though their output levels can be altered, "it is usually more economical for them to run at close-to-full capacity at all times" (DOE-EPSA 2016).

Intermediate load plants, often gas-fired and including combined-cycle plants, are sourced to meet the daily variations in demand. More recently, low gas prices are prompting the use of natural gas combined-cycle (NGCC) plants as baseload plants. Where available, hydroelectric units also serve as baseload or intermediate load plants. Finally, peaking generators meet the more extreme spikes in demand and are often used for only a few hours of the year. Peaking generators are typically "simple cycle" gas turbines or older gas- or oil-fired steam generators. Peaking plants are relatively inexpensive to build but are more expensive to run because they are generally less efficient than other types of plants or use more expensive fuel. In planning and daily operations, system operators tend to choose the mix of generators that allows them to meet demand economically (DOE-EPSA 2016).

The impact of renewables on the system is disruptive because sources such as wind, solar and hydro have no fuel costs: the energy they produce is free. In other words, their marginal operational cost is near zero. Since in competitive markets the price for electricity is determined by the marginal cost of the last power plant that has to be switched on to meet demand, a higher renewable penetration leads to a decrease in the wholesale price of electricity.

The other major effect of a higher penetration of renewables is that they push out other generators such as nuclear, natural gas and coal, reducing the dispatchment of their energy into the grid.

Fig. 2.4 EUA prices (€/tCO2) (Source: Authors' elaboration of data provided by EEX 2018)

The merit-order effect is particularly evident for coal. In other words, not only public and private commitment are straining the coal industry but also market dynamics. On one hand, renewables have started to compete with fossil fuels without subsidies. As such, this is significantly lowering the profitability of traditional fossil-fuelled generators (Genoese and Egenhofer 2015). On the other hand, cheap natural gas prices are "pushing out of the market" coal-fired power plants, especially in the United States (Fell and Kaffine 2017). As a result, in 2017, coal was surpassed by natural gas as the main source of energy in the electricity generation mix in the United States. What is more, coal will shrink further as old coal plants retire and are replaced by cheaper renewables and natural gas.

Coal usage for power generation is progressively decreasing in Europe as well. Recent reforms of the EU Emissions Trading System (ETS), adopted by the European Parliament, have contributed to raising the price of European Emission Allowances (EUA). In recent years the price per ton of carbon was too low to encourage carbon-free investment. Now, instead, as shown in Fig. 2.4, the price of carbon emissions entered in a positive trend, potentially driving investments towards cleaner or relatively cheaper sources of energy.

The rising costs of carbon emission allowances, in turn, is reducing the competitiveness of coal generation on the market. This is emphasized by the Clean Dark Spread, the difference between electricity's spot market price and the cost of electricity produced with coal plus the price of related carbon dioxide allowances[11] (Capgemini 2017). While from 2012 until 2015, the Clean Dark Spread was positive, the rising price of carbon negotiated on the EU ETS is driving down coal profitability.

---

[11]The Clean Spark Spread is the same indicator but it refers to electricity produced with gas.

Deteriorating economics and stronger climate policies are squeezing coal generation, closing power plants and threatening huge stranded asset costs (CTI 2018b). The symbolic beginning of the end for coal generation in Europe occurred in April 2017. This was when the United Kingdom, birthplace of the coal-fired Industrial Revolution, ran without coal for 55 hours then for another 76 hours a week later (Bloomberg 2018). Britain's last coal power station will be forced to close in 2025, as part of a government plan to phase out the fossil fuel to meet its climate change commitments.

Despite all the factors undermining the economics of coal power in the EU (falling renewable energy costs, air pollution regulations, rising carbon prices, and the public commitment to phase out coal) only 27% of operating coal units in the EU are planning to close before 2030. According to CTI (2018b), these generation assets could become unusable by 2030 (i.e. stranded assets). Therefore, the EU could avoid €22 billion in losses by phasing out coal power in line with the Paris Agreement. 54% of coal for merchant energy (energy sold in the market), in fact, produces negative cash flows and makes units reliant on lobbying to secure capacity market payments (CTI 2018b). In particular, the coal units operating in Germany could avoid losing €12 billion by retiring early, while units in Poland could avoid losing €2.7 billion. The UK has proportionally lower negative stranded value due to the fact it already has a phase-out policy. Phasing out coal will contribute to preserving the financial interests of utility shareholders by avoiding value destruction. Italy and Slovenia have positive stranded value of €480 million and €740 million, respectively. To a much lesser degree, Portugal, Romania, Ireland and France are also in the same situation (CTI 2018b).

As we have already mentioned, the source of power that could benefit most from the phase-out of coal, at least in the short run, is natural gas.

However, natural gas-fired power plants are not the only resource options capable of replacing retiring capacity. Utility-scale renewable projects, thanks to sharp cost reductions, are becoming increasingly cheaper and have now started to compete with fossil fuels in auctions, based on a pure cost competition (i.e. without FiTs).

Moreover, developers and grid-operators have demonstrated the ability to offer "clean energy portfolios" (i.e. renewable energy, including wind and solar, and distributed energy resources, including batteries). This means they can provide many, if not all, of the grid services typically supplied by thermal power plants, and often at net cost savings (RMI 2018a).

In particular, according to BNEF (2018a), thanks to the ability to switch on and off in response to grid electricity shortfalls and surpluses over periods of hours, stand-alone batteries are starting to compete with open-cycle gas plants.

As highlighted by RMI (2018a), which compared costs of gas-fired power plants against optimized, region-specific clean energy portfolios of renewable energy and distributed energy resources (DERs), in some cases, clean energy portfolios may cost less to build than CCGTs cost.

In other words, the same technological innovations and price declines in renewable energy that have already contributed to early coal-plant retirement are now threatening to strand investments in natural gas (RMI 2018a). This refers specifically to investments in gas-fired power plants currently proposed or under construction, and has significant implications for investors in gas projects, especially utilities.

2.4.3 Negative Prices

A remarkable effect of the deeper penetration of renewables is that it may lead to greater volatility in power prices, because of the higher exposure to weather conditions (even though weather forecasting has significantly improved over the past few years). Moreover, extremely high and extremely low prices are expected to occur, in the absence of a more rapid deployment of storage and other technologies (i.e. demand-side response).

In this regard, another challenge introduced by renewables is more frequent negative prices of electricity sold in the power exchange over time (where allowed). This may happen, for instance, when high renewable power supply exceeds demand and producers bid their electricity for negative prices.

The rationale of this behavior is that most of the renewable energy fed into the grid has a minimum guaranteed price (FiTs). In that case it is opportune to bid a negative price when prices are zero or already negative for other reasons. Since renewable power producers are not paid if they don't feed electricity into the grid, it makes sense to bid a negative price.

From the perspective of social welfare, it might be cheaper if output from windfarms could be curtailed (capped) when it is too high. When intermittent power producers are allowed to bid prices below their (zero) marginal costs, the market becomes very distorted indeed.

In this regard, in 2017 the number of hours with negative power prices in Germany escalated by around 50% to 146 hours. The average negative power price was minus 27 euros per MWh (Amelang and Appunn 2018).

The phenomenon of negative prices also occurred in other markets characterized by a high penetration of renewables, like the United States. According to data provided by CAISO, the California system operator, in that state in 2015 the phenomenon of negative prices was recorded more than 7700 times. Forecasts estimate this imbalance will grow over the next few years, as more electricity enters the grid from renewable sources (WEF 2017a).

At a first glance, negative prices are signaling that there is no more space for conventional generation to be installed in those specific areas where they occur.

Moreover, negative prices can be considered a price signal to owners of traditional coal and gas plants to shut down production for a period, even though many of the facilities are not designed to switch on and off quickly. In this regard, conventional power station operators, which are either losing money or at least losing profits during times of negative prices, may decide to keep their plants running for several reasons. These reasons can be technical, for example the power plant can be too inflexible to change its output, or the cost of shutting down and starting up again can be too expensive.

Conventional power station operators may have the obligation to provide contracted balancing power to keep the grid stable or provide re-dispatch power. Alternatively, in some cases power production cannot shut down because it serves critical infrastructure (e.g. a residential heating network).

Also, those plant operators which have already sold their power on the longer-term futures market face no extra costs when they let their units run. They are merely losing the profit that they could make by buying cheap power to supply their customers instead of producing their own. Looking more closely, negative prices can be also good news, since "they may provide incentives to utilities to make their power stations more responsive to changing conditions on the power market, or to find new business opportunities by adapting demand" (Amelang and Appunn 2018).

According to Capgemini (2017), another relevant counter-effect of the rising penetration of renewables is the increasing need for flexibility caused by the fact that renewables, especially wind and solar, are intermittent. More precisely, there are two main categories of renewables: renewables with storage (e.g. hydropower and biomass) and those without (mainly photovoltaic solar and wind). The non-dispatch nature of renewables without storage, creates grid disturbances (balancing problems, grid overhaul), leading to extra costs. For example, in 2016 in Southern Australia, around 50% of the electricity was produced by solar PV and wind. However, this level was not sustainable, and the state experienced several blackouts and load shedding (Capgemini 2017). Following these events, in March 2017, the Government decided to spend more than 550 million of Australian dollars (i.e. the equivalent of €333 million) to build a new gas-fired power plant and a large-scale storage battery in order to secure the continuity of electricity supply.

The intermittent nature of renewables may also augment the cost of balancing the system. For instance, the cost of balancing the UK electricity system has doubled in the last 4 years. The amount of flexible generation on the system is a key driver. Balancing costs rise when the output from flexible generators such as gas, coal, biomass and hydro, falls below 10GW (this happens when the output from wind and solar rises). More flexible generation, storage and demand-side response will be critical in minimizing system costs in the future (Staffell et al. 2018).

2.5   Some Trends to Look Out for, in the Coming Years

This section aims at highlighting some trends that financial investors should take into consideration for their portfolio allocation strategy. We will pay specific attention to offshore wind. Albeit not yet a mature technology like other renewables, it is attracting rising interest, especially among financial investors.

Then, we focus on one of the main challenges brought about by the R-evolution: the need for flexibility. We discuss battery storage as one of the most suitable potential solutions for coping with this need, as well as a potential option for financial investors. Finally, we investigate the future role of existing gas and electricity transmission infrastructure, highlighting possible threats and opportunities.

2.5.1   Watch this Space: Offshore Wind

Among renewables, wind power is growing rapidly and attracting escalating investments, especially among financial players such as infrastructure funds. In 2017, Europe installed 16.8 GW of additional wind power capacity (onshore and offshore). In particular, wind accounted for the largest percentage of all new capacity installed in Europe in 2017. With a total net installed capacity of 168.7 GW, wind is currently the second largest form of power generation capacity in Europe, closely approaching gas installations (Wind Europe 2018b).

Specifically, the wind energy industry attracted €51.2 billion in Europe with investments in new wind farms which amounted to €22.3 billion.

In terms of investments in new renewable capacity installed in Europe, excluding solar PV, wind had the largest growth. Technological cost reductions and lower offshore wind investments were the two main reasons for the drop in fresh investments for new capacity, in monetary terms (Wind Europe 2018a).

Offshore wind in Europe, in particular, saw a record 3.15 GW of net additional installed capacity in 2017, corresponding to 560 new offshore wind turbines across 17 wind farms. In total, Europe now has offshore wind capacity of 15.78 GW (Wind Europe 2018c).

According to GWEC (2018), Ørsted (formerly DONG Energy) is currently the largest owner of offshore wind power in Europe, with 17% of cumulative installations. Next in the ranking is E.ON with 8% of installed capacity owned, followed by Innogy (7%), Vattenfall (7%), and Northland Power (4%). The top five owners represent 42% of all installed capacity in Europe.

Some of the largest wind developers, like Ørsted, carry out investments with the aim of bringing in an equity partner (e.g. an institutional investor) as soon as the wind farm is operational. The strategy here is to earn a premium on the book valuation of the project.

In this regard, the sector's progressive maturity and technology competitiveness have brought in a more diverse mix of corporate financial and institutional investors as equity partners in projects. In particular, the financial services industry (i.e. infrastructure funds, pension funds, asset managers and diversified financial services) acquired 70%, of onshore wind assets available for sale (i.e. a total of 4.5 GW), compared to 36% in 2016. Financial actors accounted for 35% of the offshore wind capacity traded throughout 2017 (i.e. 2.9 GW), up from only 27% in 2016 (Wind Europe 2018a).

This trend is largely due to progressive sector maturity, adequate asset size and a risk profile that matches the investment profile of financial investors.

Indeed, financial investors are gaining momentum, especially in the equity mix of offshore wind projects in the EU (Wind Europe 2018c).

For example, according to The Crown Estate (2018), in November 2017 Danish pension providers PKA and PFA purchased 50% of Ørsted's Walney 3 project. This consolidated PKA's presence in the market. The financial service industry is also showing more interest in offshore transmission assets (OFTO) (i.e. cables that are necessary to connect offshore wind farms to the mainland's grid). In the UK, for instance, the ownership structure of these assets, which are allocated through a competitive tender process, highlight the heightened interest of institutional investors and infrastructure funds.

Transmission Capital Partners has the largest slice of the OFTO market with almost a third, followed by Blue Transmission and Equitix.

2.5.2   The Need for Flexibility: Storage

The increasing share of intermittent renewables (notably wind and solar) in the electricity generation mix are causing major challenges in terms of balancing supply and demand. In particular, the penetration of these energy sources is augmenting the need for flexibility.

There are several ways to facilitate the integration of a greater share of renewables in the electricity system while providing the flexibility this requires. Examples are: developing more interconnections across regions, promoting demand response (e.g. implementing "time-of-use tariffs" to trigger higher customer demand response when cheap renewable electricity is available), dispatching "peakers" that are typically simple-cycle gas turbines, able to start up and minutes (or other fossil fuel generators), and using storage facilities. Figure 2.5 offers a graphic representation of the main flexibility options.

As more renewables come online, the need for storage becomes increasingly acute (Di Castelnuovo and Vazquez 2018; Chatham House 2017). Without storage, when too much electricity enters the grid, supply exceeds demand and negative pricing occurs. This can be the case of particularly sunny days and windy afternoons, or days when demand is low.

On the contrary, storage adds flexibility to the system, allowing electricity to be stored and discharged later when it is needed, for example in evening hours or during peaks. In this way, storage offers a way to flatten out the peaks and valleys of supply and to prevent disruptive events.

Fig. 2.5 Flexibility options (Source: Di Castelnuovo and Vazquez 2018)

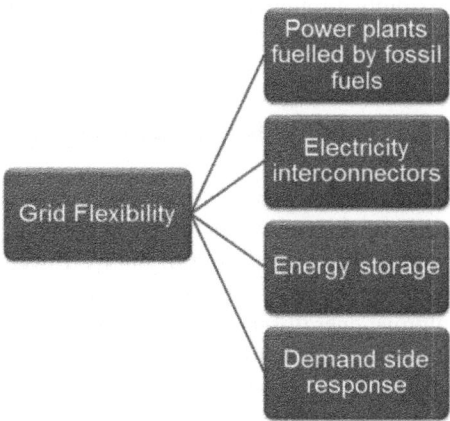

There are different types of storage systems, primarily pumped water, compressed air, magnetic flywheels, batteries and hydrogen. The first two depend on suitable natural sites (i.e. appropriate geology). In Europe, there are adequate sites for pumped storage. However, most of them have been already exploited (Capgemini 2017).

The technology which is attracting far more attention is Lithium-Ion battery storage (Schmidt et al. 2017). In this regard, we should distinguish between (i) utility-scale storage (in front of the meter) and (ii) distributed storage (behind the meter). The former accounts for the majority of installed storage capacity (so far), providing numerous system functions. The latter, instead, allows customers to store the electricity generated by their rooftop solar panels, for instance, and use it later when needed (RMI 2018a).

As highlighted by the Rocky Mountain Institute (2015), batteries can provide up to 13 services and be sited at three different levels: (1) behind the meter, (2) at the distribution level, or (3) at the transmission level. It is not still clear whether storage (and in particular battery storage) is actually a profitable investment. The reason for this uncertainty is that any attempt at storage valuation requires making assumptions on storage regulation (Zucker et al. 2013). However, regardless of the deployment level, battery storage can add value to the grid.

Energy storage will affect the entire electricity value chain, notably replacing peaking plans, altering future transmission and distribution (T&D) investments, and reducing the intermittency of renewables. For utilities, battery storage will become an integral tool for managing peak loads, regulating voltage and frequency, ensuring reliability from renewable generation, and creating a more flexible transmission and distribution system. For their customers, instead, storage can be a tool for reducing costs related to peak energy demand.

As a result, the global energy storage market could significantly expand from now to 2030, rising from less than 5 gigawatt-hours last year, to more than 300 gigawatt-hours and 125 gigawatts of capacity by the end of the next decade. An estimated $103 billion will be invested in energy storage over that time period (BNEF 2018a). Energy storage, both utility-scale and behind-the-meter, will be a crucial source of flexibility throughout this period and will be essential to integrating mounting levels of renewable energy (BNEF 2018a).

2.5.3 Energy Networks as Both Enablers and Constraints

The European Commission aims to enhance the further integration of electricity markets, especially by amplifying the interconnection capacity (measured in terms of net transfer capacity) out of the total installed electricity capacity in place. Indeed, investing in interconnection at several borders and when economically justified will improve energy security, reduce dependency on imports from outside the EU and prepare networks for renewable energy. All of this also applies for gas. In order to create a fully connected internal competitive energy market and to achieve its energy policy and climate objectives, the European Commission published a list of key infrastructure projects it has denominated Projects of Common Interest (PCIs). Most of them are represented by electricity interconnectors and gas infrastructure projects. In particular, in 2017, there were 173 PCIs, of which 53 involved natural gas, 106 electricity, 4 smart grids, 6 oil projects and 4 carbon dioxide transport projects (Ecofys 2018; E3G 2017). In terms of capital expenditure, 66% of the total refers to projects for electricity transmission, followed by gas transmission with 18%.

The huge investments attracted by these projects raise concern. To be specific, investments in gas infrastructures risk becoming stranded assets as the transition towards a cleaner energy system requires the complete decarbonization of the economy, including natural gas. In our study, we observed that natural gas is starting to regain its competitiveness vis-à-vis coal (see Sect. 2.2.2). In addition, reforms to the emissions trading scheme have already had the effect of ramping up the price of carbon emissions, thereby further encouraging fuel switching from coal to gas. As a result, gas-fired generation in Europe escalated by almost 30% in 2017.

However, some of those plants still struggle to turn a profit as the growth of renewable generation reduces their load factors. Moreover, renewable energy and distributed energy resources, including batteries and demand-side technologies, are becoming reliable alternative sources of fundamental grid services (i.e. generation capacity and ancillary services), typically provided by thermal power plants. All this exacerbates the situation. Energy efficiency, especially in buildings, will also contribute to reduce gas consumption.

On the one hand, investments in gas-fired power plants are already at risk of becoming stranded assets. On the other, investments in gas infrastructures (network, LNG terminals and storage) face a different scenario due to the fact that in 2017 gas-fired generation represented 28% of total gas consumption in Europe (IEA 2018a). In other words, there is a larger share of gas demand, mainly represented by industry and buildings (i.e. gas used for heating) that will remain stable. All of this suggests that gas infrastructure will continue playing a fundamental role in order to serve these customers.

Another explanation for the continuing importance of gas infrastructure is that more LNG is being imported, especially from the US (IGU 2018). LNG volumes in the coming years are expected to grow for geopolitical reasons as well. According to King and Spalding (2018), Europe's regasification capacity, which is now sufficient to cover approximately 40% of its gas demand, will also ramp up quite significantly by 2021. This is the result of expansions that are under way or planned at some of Europe's existing LNG import terminals. All this LNG also needs to be transported through pipelines to final customers.

Moreover, the gas infrastructure may favor the integration of a greater share of renewables. Sector coupling between gas and electricity, which creates new links between energy carriers and the respective transport infrastructure, may facilitate the integration of renewables and help to achieve EU decarbonization goals (GIE 2018; OIES 2018; European Power to Gas 2017; FSR 2018). In particular, the transformation of renewable electricity into other energy carriers such as gas (e.g. synthetic gas, hydrogen) needs to be considered in order to pursue decarbonization goals (DNV GL 2017; E3G 2018; Wind Europe 2018d). For instance, in some sectors such as cement, fertilizers or refineries, power-to-gas is among the few cost-effective emissions abatement options available.

Finally, the gas infrastructure retains a strong role in ensuring security of supply, especially to satisfy seasonal peaks in heating demand that cannot be met cost-effectively by electricity (FSR 2018).

The gas infrastructure will remain a crucial security-of-supply asset for Europe, accommodating seasonal variations in both demand and supply, while alleviating the effects of extreme weather events.

2.6 The Impact of the R-Evolution on European Utilities

In order to fully understand the implications of the trends described in the previous sections for the energy sector, we now investigate the performance of European utilities. The aim of this analysis is to highlight how the transformations occurring in the energy sector are affecting the profitability of current market players. In particular, we start by exploring how European utilities generate their revenues (i.e. their revenue model) and then we look at their performance.

Based on the main source of revenues, we can distinguish between two categories of utilities, both of which we will analyze:

1. Network (or grid) companies;
2. Energy suppliers.

2.6.1 Utilities' Revenue Model

Regardless the energy vector (gas or electricity), network companies are responsible for the transmission/distribution of energy in their control area. As highlighted by Pérez-Arriaga (2013), due to the cost of establishing a transmission infrastructure, such as main power lines (or gas pipelines) and associated connection points, a network company is usually a natural monopoly. It makes no sense at all to develop parallel networks that would compete to provide the service in question. Due to the conditions that make networks a natural monopoly, and because of their key role as the meeting point of demand and supply, networks must be regulated. This regulation must guarantee suitable grid development and efficient market conditions (Pérez-Arriaga 2013). To be specific, according to the current European regulatory framework, the distribution of gas and electricity are activities carried out by companies that may also include other businesses (i.e. energy supply). However, regulation requires that transmission activities must be operated by a separated legal entity. As a result, the regulatory framework has a relevant impact on the business model (and the revenue model) of network companies and their organizations, especially TSOs (transmission system operators).

Looking more closely, we can distinguish the activities performed by grid companies as regulated and non-regulated.

Regulated activities consist in the development of new CAPEX in order to enable the transportation of energy and OPEX for the correct functioning of the system. These costs are covered by a tariff, set by the relative National Regulatory Authority (NRA) and the tariff is paid by final customers on their electricity bill. Moreover, the tariff is set in a transparent and non-discriminatory manner and should guarantee stability and long-term perspectives for network companies, their customers and investors. In general, the tariff amount covers the costs (both operating costs and capital costs) and ensures a return on capital invested. Specifically, the return on capital is the product of two terms, a base (RAB) and a rate of return (WACC), as illustrated by the following formula:

$$RAB * WACC = Return\ on\ capital$$

where:

- The Regulatory Asset Base (RAB) is basically the accounting value of owned assets;
- WACC (Weighted Average Cost of Capital) is determined by means of an evaluation model incorporating various parameters, such as the risk-free rate represented by government bonds, additional compensation for a risk-free rate requested by bond investors, return on equity in view of risk sensitivity.

Besides this main source of revenues (and costs), network companies can also run other activities outside the perimeter of the regulation. These so-called non-regulated activities are not covered by the tariff but respond to market forces and are conducted in a competitive regime. These activities include for example: O&M, EPC, TLC investments, private interconnectors (financed through third parties), consultancy.

Energy supply, instead, includes a set of activities carried out in a competitive regime, as listed here:

- Scheduled energy
- Generation capacity
- Ancillary services
- Market based instruments
- Retail activities

Starting from the first, scheduled energy, we have already discussed the fact that the introduction of renewables has compressed margins for most of the conventional energy suppliers, with coal-fired plants and traditional gas plants being squeezed. These two types of facilities, including efficient CCGT plants, are also facing more and more competition from renewables, distributed generation, and other demand-side response technologies for ancillary services and generation capacity auctions, (the second and the third activities listed above). This is proven by recent auctions in the UK, which highlight the non-economic unviability of coal-fired plants in favor of more competitive CGT plants and renewables (OFGEM 2017).

While revenues from scheduled energy on the market are decreasing due to the higher penetration of renewables, earnings from flexible frequency response are expected to rise. This is in part because these services will become increasingly vital for coping with the intermittency of renewables (AURORA 2018).

However, conventional generators including efficient CCGT plants are increasingly facing competition from renewables and distributed generation and other demand-side response technologies also for ancillary services.

Market-based instruments, such as energy attribute certificates, green certificates, etc. are another potential source of revenues for utilities.

Finally, retail activities include everything utilities do downstream, e.g. energy sales, home management services, energy management services, e-mobility, and so forth. Indeed, the evidence suggests that utilities are increasingly facing competition from new market players (i.e. ICT, automotive or the O&G sector).

2.6.2   Utilities' Financial Performance

In this part of our study we analyze utilities' market performance. In particular, we investigate whether there is any difference between network-only companies (i.e. TSOs) and other utilities (e.g. energy suppliers). The question arises from the fact that, over the past few years, profits from energy supply activities, especially merchant energy produced by conventional power plants, have significantly shrunk. We have already explained the reasons for such a trend in the previous sections (e.g. competition from renewables).

Meanwhile, the spread between financing costs and regulated returns of energy networks has widened, as the former have collapsed and the latter have been generally flat (IEA 2018b). As a consequence, we expect these two trends to be reflected in better performance of network-only companies (TSOs), whose main source of revenues are regulated activities held under a monopoly. This compared to the poorer performance of utilities, which may also have networks, but are more exposed to competition and market forces.

We start our analysis with the performance of the sectorial index, the Stoxx Europe 600 utilities (SX6P), which include almost 30 major listed utilities from all over Europe.

Over the period from October 2008 to October 2018, the European sectorial index for utilities underperformed the Euro Stoxx 50, including most of major European companies by market cap across all sectors, as shown in Fig. 2.6. This confirms that the trends described in the previous sections have been affecting utilities' performance.

As we can observe, utilities performed very poorly, on average compared to the Euro Stoxx 50.

In order to calculate the performance of TSOs, we first mapped both electricity and gas-network-only companies (TSOs) currently operating across Europe, analyzing:

Fig. 2.6 Performance comparison: SX6P Index vs Euro Stoxx 50 (Source: Authors' elaboration of data provided by Bloomberg 2018)

- their exposure to regulated business;
- the shareholder composition of these companies, distinguishing between financial and non-financial;
- the main shareholders (top 10 shareholders, distinguishing between financial and non-financial).

The following charts show the results for electricity transmission system operators of the major EU countries (Austria, Belgium, Denmark, France, Germany, Italy, Netherlands, Norway, Portugal, Spain, Sweden, Switzerland, UK). In detail, Fig. 2.7 illustrates the sources of revenues of European electricity TSOs. These data confirm the fact that regulated activities, which are covered by the tariff, represent the main sources of revenues for electricity TSOs (94% of the total, against 6% coming from non-regulated).

Figure 2.8 highlights that the majority of shareholders of electricity TSOs are non-financial companies, that is, 72% against only 28% represented by various financial actors.

Figure 2.9, instead, offers a graphic breakdown of financial and non-financial shareholders. As we can see, the main shareholder is the government (51% of the total), meaning that the majority of the electricity TSOs we analyzed are state-owned. The second-most represented category of shareholders is still a non-financial actor (i.e. corporation 16%), while the first category of financial shareholder is represented by investment advisors with a share of almost 16%.

In particular, among the most common financial shareholders, Lazard and Blackrock have the highest average share, i.e. 4.9% and 3.1% respectively.

Figure 2.10, Fig. 2.11, Fig. 2.12 show the corresponding figures for European Gas TSOs. As we can see, similar to electricity TSOs, gas TSOs also find their main source of revenue in regulated activities covered by the tariff (92% of total revenues against 8% coming from non-regulated).

Fig. 2.7 Electricity TSOs'
exposure to regulated business
(Source: Authors' elaboration
of data provided by
Bloomberg 2018)

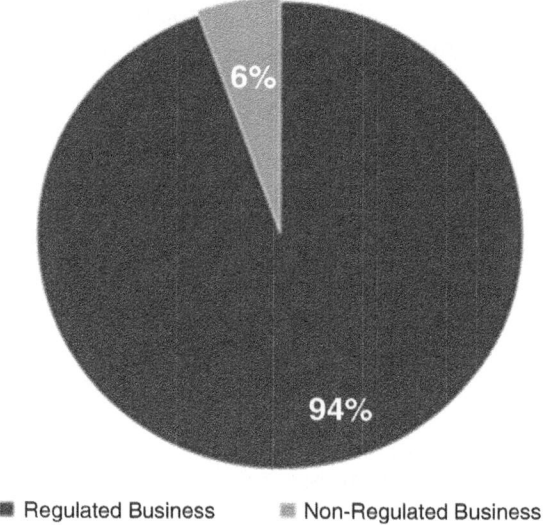

■ Regulated Business   ▒ Non-Regulated Business

Fig. 2.8 Electricity TSOs'
shareholder composition
(Source: Authors' elaboration
of data provided by
Bloomberg 2018)

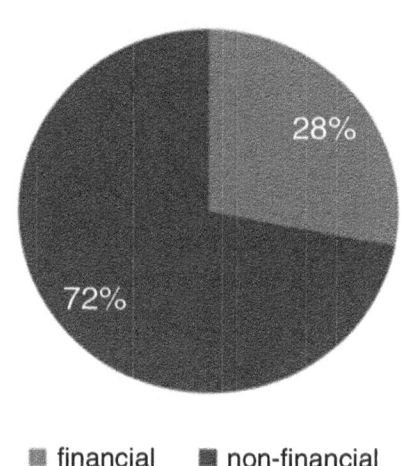

▒ financial   ■ non-financial

The main difference between electricity and gas TSOs is represented by the main category of shareholders: for the former, they are corporations, while for the latter they are investment advisors.

Among the most common gas TSOs financial shareholders, Blackrock and Lazard are the ones with the highest average share, i.e. 4.1% and 3.8% respectively.

Listed electricity transmission grid companies included in our analysis are: Terna (Italy), Elia System Operator (Belgium), Red Electrica de Espana (Spain), REN - Redes Energeticas Nacionais (Portugal), National Grid (UK). Listed gas transmission grid companies are: SNAM (Italy), Fluxys Belgium "D" (Belgium), REN -

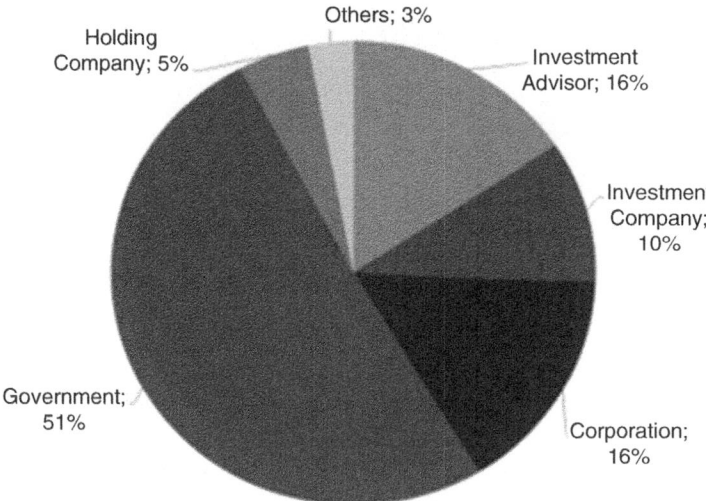

Fig. 2.9 Electricity TSOs' shareholder breakdown (Source: Authors' elaboration of data provided by Bloomberg 2018)

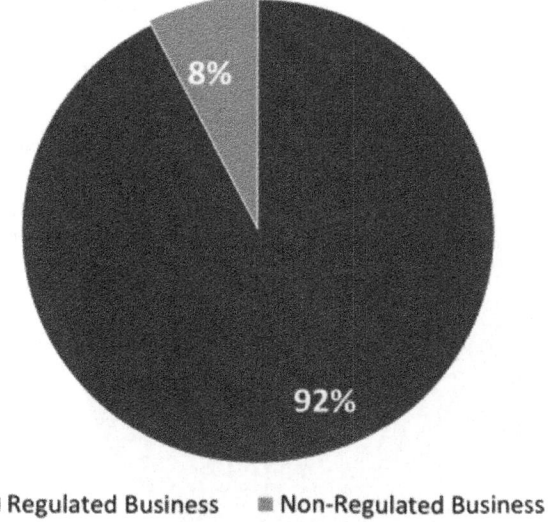

■ Regulated Business   ■ Non-Regulated Business

Fig. 2.10 Gas TSOs' exposure to regulated business (Source: Authors' elaboration of data provided by Bloomberg 2018)

Redes Energeticas Nacionais (Portugal), Enagas (Spain), National Grid (UK). Figure 2.13 and Fig. 2.14 show the performance of listed electricity and gas TSOs respectively, against the SX6P Index over the period from October 2008 to October 2018. As we can see, TSOs outperformed the SX6P Index.

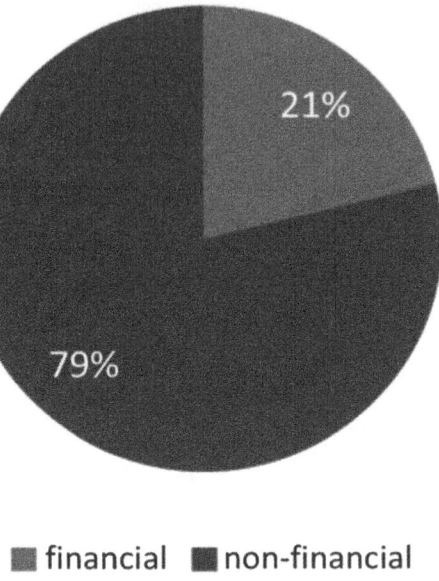

financial **non-financial**

Fig. 2.11 Gas TSOs' Shareholder composition (Source: Authors' elaboration of data provided by Bloomberg 2018)

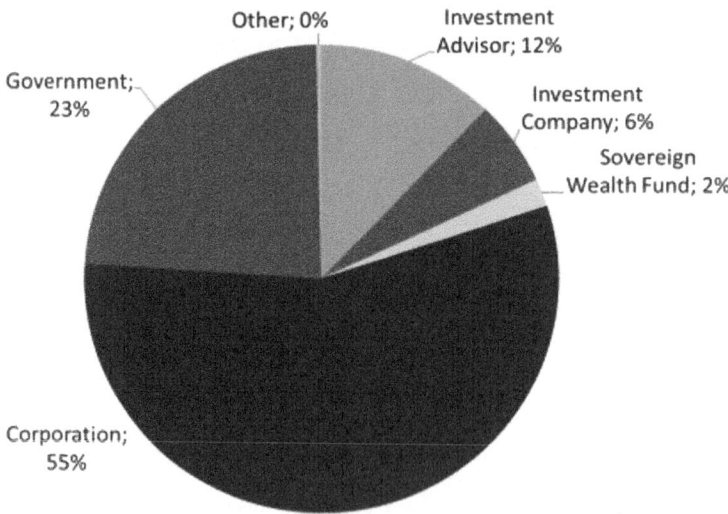

Fig. 2.12 Gas TSOs' Shareholder breakdown (Source: Authors' elaboration of data provided by Bloomberg 2018)

As confirmation of the poor performances of European utilities compared to TSOs, the earnings of the former have shrunk by a third since 2012 (Capgemini 2017). According to the IEA (2018b) this was due mainly to the reduced profitability

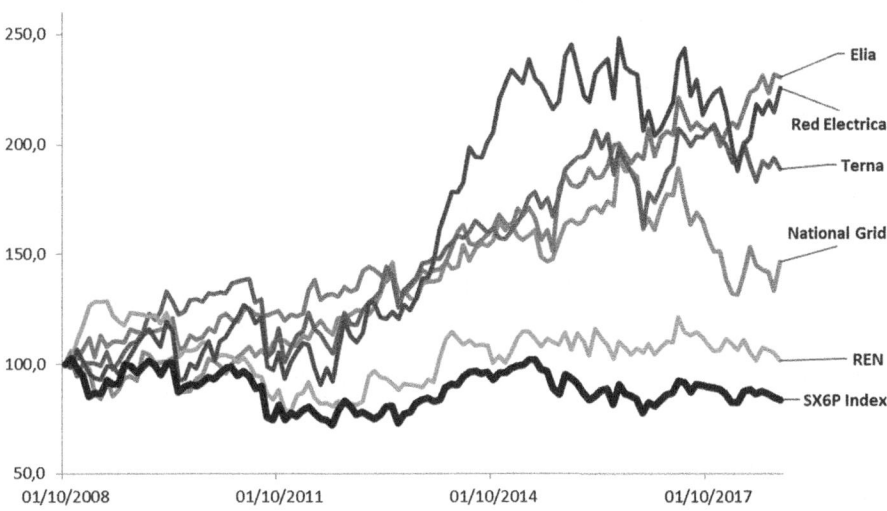

Fig. 2.13 Performance comparison: SX6P Index vs electricity transmission companies (Source: Authors' elaboration of data provided by Bloomberg 2018)

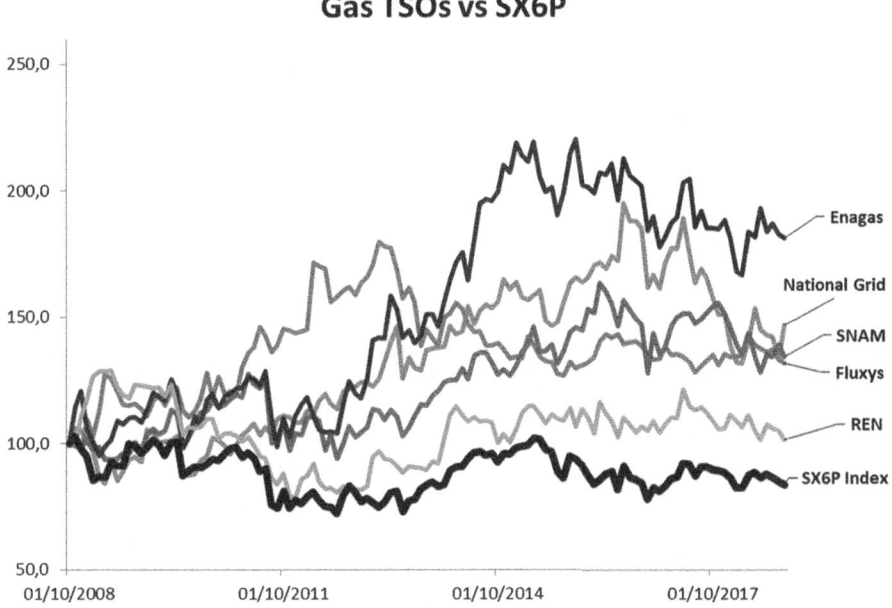

Fig. 2.14 Performance comparison: SX6P Index vs gas transmission companies (Source: Authors' elaboration of data provided by Bloomberg 2018)

of merchant-generating assets exposed to weak wholesale prices, as well as lower revenues" due to the retirements of such plants.

According to Capgemini (2017), utilities across Europe are reacting to the sector transformation by restructuring their asset portfolios to reduce exposure to risk and price volatility. As a result, utilities in mature electricity markets mothballed or even closed down some of their thermal power generation assets while seeking profitable opportunities in other areas, e.g. investments in regulated sectors.

This trend is confirmed by the fact that 80% of utility earnings in 2017 came from segments that offer more stable and predictable cash flows, like networks and renewables, compared with around 65% in 2012 (IEA 2018b). In other words, utilities are trying to improve their profitability shifting from merchant energy (energy sold on the market under competitive regimes), to regulated activities or renewable energy that can guarantee regular cash flows (e.g. through auction-based mechanisms).

In general, there is no single trend in terms of business model adaptations. Utilities are investing in different segments of the value chain, based on their view on the future.

For example, in 2016, RWE created "Innogy" to manage grids, renewables and the retail business, while E.ON formed "Uniper" (recently acquired by the Finnish utility Fortum) to separately manage fossil fuel assets (e.g. gas and coal generation).

Recently, E.ON and RWE agreed upon an asset swap based on which the former will buy the latter's subsidiary "Innogy"; while, at the same time, RWE will acquire E.ON's renewable assets as well as take back the same renewable assets which they had previously carved out with the creation of Innogy.

Some utilities are also increasing customer and service activities (e.g. integrating supply businesses with demand-side services, such as those related to electric vehicles). These companies are trying to achieve better financial discipline, including decreasing debt levels and reducing operational and structural costs (Capgemini 2017).

European utilities continued to review their investment strategies and to transform their business models also through mergers and acquisitions (M&A).

M&A activity increased in Europe by 30% in 2017, as utilities continued to sell-off non-core (mostly fossil fuel-based) assets to adapt their business models (an example here is the divestment of upstream oil and gas assets by Centrica and Ørsted) (EY 2018; ATKearney 2018; McKinsey and Company 2018).

The value of M&A transactions is expected to rise in 2018 and 2019 based on Fortum's acquisition of Uniper, and the asset swap between E.ON and RWE.

European utilities also acquired companies and assets related to digital technologies and distributed energy resources (Capgemini 2017). In the US for example, Enel acquired EnerNOC, a firm specialized in demand management, and behind-the-meter storage operator Demand Energy. In the UK, Centrica acquired REstore, specialized in management and aggregation of demand response capacity from industrial and commercial consumers (IEA 2018b).

There is also some M&A activity in "networks-only" utilities. The value of deals rose considerably in 2017 (BCG 2017). For instance, Macquarie acquired a minority stake in four gas distribution networks from UK National Grid for €5.4 billion. Caisse des Dépôts and Assurance acquired a 49.9% stake in RTE (the French electricity TSO) for €4.1 billion and investors led by J.P. Morgan acquired Spain's Naturgas for €2.6 billion.

2.7 Conclusions

The energy system is currently undergoing an unprecedented revolution. This paper aimed to provide a broad overview of the main transformations occurring in the sector and to develop an understanding of the potential implications for financial investors. In this regard, in our analysis we identified some trends that are set to put a large amount of existing and future assets at risk. In particular, investments related to fossil fuels appear to have the highest degree of risk and uncertainty, depending on the specific fuel, the technology adopted and the market under consideration.

With specific regard to the oil industry, in the coming years, on the one hand the demand for oil will progressively shrink because of the growing penetration of electric vehicles in the transport sector. On the other, oil consumption in industry, and, particularly in the petrochemical sector, will remain relatively stable. As such, subject to lower-than-expected progress in so-called green chemistry, investments in refineries and petrochemical facilities may appear more profitable than other investments in the industry.

The prospect for investments within the natural gas industry are more complicated to assess. In the long run there is a limited growth opportunity for natural gas if the world is to achieve the goal of maintaining the temperature increase to well below 2 °C. In the medium term, gas is considered as a "bridge fuel" during the transition to a decarbonized energy system. This is due to its lower carbon emissions compared to coal and other fossil fuels and the flexibility of gas-fuelled generators in balancing intermittent renewable energy. Also, it should be emphasized that while power generation usually represents the largest share of total gas consumption (32% in Europe in 2017), industry and buildings make up for the remaining part (IEA 2018a). Furthermore, the gas industry is currently trying to diversify its investments by expanding the use of gas in transport (e.g. LNG for shipping) as well as the production of renewable gas (e.g. biomethane and hydrogen). Moreover, the European market design is increasingly aimed at promoting stronger coupling between the gas and electricity sectors, further enhancing the use of gas infrastructure for the integration of renewable technologies (e.g. through biomethane or power-to-gas).

Indeed, because of its flexibility role in balancing renewables and its uses in sectors other than power generation (e.g. industry), natural gas cannot and should not be written off yet from any European scenario. In light of this, gas infrastructures (included LNG terminals, storage and pipelines) may still represent, under certain conditions an interesting investment opportunity, especially for the medium term (for instance in a market with widespread use of gas in the residential sector like Italy).

Focusing on the electricity industry, we mapped the revolution with a framework consisting of six key drivers: decarbonization, decentralization, electrification, digitalization, customer activation and convergence of industries. All of these drivers are completely reshaping the industry across its values chain, with massive implications in terms of economic fundamentals, investment opportunities and business strategies.

Clean energy portfolios, including less mature technologies like offshore wind, may offer valuable opportunities to different types of investors, including private equity firms. Likewise, similar opportunities may be associated with utility-scale solar assets, which have shown the largest cost decline in the last 10 years. Also the recent success story in the US suggests that the expected growth in corporate renewable procurement in Europe may further enhance such opportunities, combined with the more regulated approach, like auction-based mechanisms, which is still dominating.

Electrical energy storage is certainly gaining momentum but, due to regulatory and technologically uncertainty, it is still difficult to adequately estimate its economic value. This is especially true in markets with well-established gas networks. However, we consider that by any standard, energy storage will be the biggest game changer in the years to come, also because it is based on the same technology which is currently dominating in electric mobility, i.e. lithium-ion batteries.

As a result of these developments, conventional electricity generation, especially coal-fired and old gas-fired power plants are increasingly steadily losing profitability. In particular, investments in coal assets seem to be doomed, due to competition from renewables and the phase-out of these plants which is already planned in most European countries.

With regard to nuclear power instead, the fleet is ageing and the industry is facing a proliferation of problems of public acceptance, notably after the Fukushima nuclear power station accident. Without further lifetime extensions and new builds, we might expect a reduced role for the industry in the future. Moreover, nuclear power generation will face more intense competition from renewables coupled with storage, which may also put existing assets at risk in the coming years.

Nevertheless, assets that may be stranded in the long run can be attractive on shorter horizons. For instance, underinvestment in oil assets today could result in supply shortages and asset appreciation in the years ahead. Furthermore, some existing gas-fired power plants, granted by capacity payments, may represent a profitable investment for financial investors.

Recent figures provided by InfluenceMap (2018) indeed, demonstrate that major financial investors, including BlackRock, Vanguard and Axa, had multiplied their holdings in thermal coal by a fifth between 2016 and 2018 (Mooney et al. 2018), in spite of their publicly-announced decarbonization objectives.

We also analyzed the revenue models and performances of European utilities with the aim of understanding whether networks may represent a rather more secure investment for financial investors compared to utilities, that are more involved in energy supply activities. In this regard, we have seen that electricity networks have provided better financial returns, especially with regard to distribution. Indeed these networks still represent the key enablers of this R-evolution as well as the pillars of the European Energy Union.

Europe's largest utilities are responding with different business models to the challenges and opportunities provided by the six drivers. It is not clear yet which of these models if any will be better suited to compete against newcomers from within the sector as well as from "outside", especially oil & gas and ICT.

However, the usual disclaimer applies to our findings as well. In other words, the expected value of any investment in the energy sector will be significantly affected by changes in climate policy (e.g. carbon targets), market design (e.g. capacity mechanisms) and regulation (e.g. the cost of equity permitted by law).

References

Agora. (2018). *Energiewende and sandbag. The European power sector in 2017. State of affairs and review of current developments.*

Amelang, S., & Appunn, K. (2018). *The causes and effects of negative power prices.* Retrieved from https://www.cleanenergywire.org/factsheets/why-power-prices-turn-negative

ATKearney. (2018). *Mergers and acquisitionsin utilities 2017.*

AURORA. (2018). *GB balancing mechanism summary–October 2019.*

Baccelli, O. (2020). Future developments in the European transport infrastructure sector. In S. Gatti & C. Chiarella (Eds.), *Disruption in the infrastructure sector – challenges and opportunities for developers, investors and asset managers.* Heidelberg: Springer.

BCG. (2017). *Powering returns from energy network deals.*

Bloomberg. (2018). *The U.K. just went 55 hours without using coal for the first time in history.* Retrieved from https://www.bloomberg.com/news/articles/2018-04-19/u-k-goes-a-record-55-hours-without-coal-as-clean-power-expands

Bloomberg New Energy Finance. (2018a). *New energy outlook 2019.*

Bloomberg New Energy Finance. (2018b). *Electric vehicle outlook 2018.*

Boßmann, T. & Staffell, I. (2015). *The shape of future electricity demand: Exploring load curves in 2050s Germany and Britain.*

Boston Consulting Group. (2014). *Making big data work: Retail energy.*

Caldecott, B. (2018). *Introduction to special issue: Stranded assets and the environment.*

Capgemini. (2017). *World energy markets observatory–WEMO 2017.*

Carbon Tracker Initiative. (2018a). *Electric vehicles: The catalyst to further decarbonisation.*

Carbon Tracker Initiative. (2018b). *Powering down coal: Navigating the economic and financial risks in the last years of coal power.*

Chatham House. (2017). *The power of flexibility. The survival of utilities during the transformations of the power sector.*

Department of Energy–Energy Policy and Systems Analysis. (2016). *Maintaining reliability in the modern power system.*

Di Castelnuovo, M. & Vazquez, M. (2018). *Policy and regulation for energy storage systems.*

DNV GL. (2017). *The potential role of power-to-gas in the e-Highway 2050 study.*

E3G. (2017). *Infrastructure for a changing energy system. The next generation of policies for the European Union.*

E3G. (2018). *Renewable and decarbonised gas. Options for a zero-emission society.*

Ecofys. (2018). *Investment needs in trans-european energy infrastructure up to 2030 and beyond.*

Enel. (2017). *E-mobility revolution: Enel presents the charging infrastructure plan for Italy.* Retrieved from https://www.enel.com/media/press/d/2017/11/e-mobility-revolution-enel-presents-the-charging-infrastructure-plan-for-italy

Enel Green Power. (2018). *Deployment of renewable energy solutions: Challenges and opportunities [Lecture] Advanced Training Course 2018 at SDA Bocconi school of management, 21st November 2018.*

ENTSO-E. (2019). *ENTSO-E annual report 2018.*

Eurelectric. (2018). *Decarbonisation pathways. European economy.*

European Commission. (2017). *Report from the commission to the European parliament, the council, the European economic and social committee and the Regions.* Renewable Energy Progress Report.

European Energy Exchange. (2018). EEX EUA Spot. Retrieved from https://www.eex.com/en/market-data/environmental-markets/spot-market/european-emission-allowances

European Power to Gas. (2017). *Power-to-gas in a decarbonized European energy system based on renewable energy sources.* White Paper.

Eurostat. (2017). *Key figures on Europe.* Edition 2017.

Exxon Mobil. (2017). *2017 outlook for energy: A view to 2040.*

EY. (2018). *Power transaction and trends.*

Fell, H. & Kaffine, D. T. (2017). *The fall of coal: Joint impacts of fuel prices and renewables on generation and emissions.*

Florence School of Regulation. (2018). *Sector coupling 2.0: Power-to-gas in the EU decarbonisation strategy* [Workshop].

Friedrichsen, N., Klobasa, M. & Pudlik, M. (2015). *Distribution network tariffs. The effect of decentralized generation and auto-consumption.*

Gatti, S., & Chiarella, C. (2020). The future of infrastructure investing. In S. Gatti & C. Chiarella (Eds.), *Disruption in the infrastructure sector–Challenges and opportunities for developers, investors and asset managers.* Heidelberg: Springer.

Genoese F., & Egenhofer C. (2015). *The future of the European power market.*

GIE – Gas Infrastructure Europe. (2018). *Towards a sustainable future for gas transmission networks.*

GTM Research. (2016). *Utility AMI analytics at the grid edge. Strategies, markets and forecasts.*

GTM Research. (2017). *What is Tesla's vision for solar city?* Retrieved from https://www.greentechmedia.com/articles/read/what-is-teslas-vision-for-solarcity

GWEC. (2018). *Global wind report 2017.*

Hall, D. & Lutsey, N. (2017). *Literature review on power utility best practices regarding electric vehicles.*

Helm, D. (2017). *Burn out: The endgame for fossil fuels.*

Hook, L., Sheppard, D. & McCormick, M. (2018, October 31). New asian coal plants knock climate goals off course. *Financial Times.*

Husseini, T. (2018). *UK renewable energy overtakes fossil fuels, despite Brexit fears.*

InfluenceMap. (2018). Who own the World's fossil fuels. In: *A forensic look at operators and shareholders of listed fossil fuel companies.* Retrieved from https://influencemap.org/financemap

International Energy Agency. (2017). *Digitalization and energy.*

International Energy Agency. (2018a). *World energy outlook 2018.*

International Energy Agency. (2018b). *World energy investments 2018.*

International Energy Agency. (2018c). *Market report series: Energy efficiency 2018 analysis and outlooks to 2040.*

International Energy Agency. (2018d). *Global EV outlook 2018.*

International Energy Agency. (2018e). *Renewables 2018. Analysis and forecasts to 2023.*

International Gas Union. (2018). *2018 world LNG report.*

International Gas Union, Snam & Boston Consulting Group. (2018). *Global gas report 2018.*

IRENA. (2018). *Global energy transformation: A roadmap to 2050.* Abu Dhabi: International Renewable Energy Agency.

Karlsruhe Institute for Technology. (2013). *How to integrate electric vehicles in the future energy system?*

King & Spalding. (2018). *LNG in Europe 2018. An overview of LNG import terminals in Europe.*

Lazard. (2017). *Lazard's levelized cost of energy analysis–Version 11.0.*

Leger, S., Smeets, B., Swysen, T., Tryggestad, C., van Houten, J., & Wodarg, F. (2018). *What if the latest wind and solar auction results were the new reality of electricity prices?*

Levi, M. (2013). *Climate consequences of natural gas as a bridge fuel.*

McKinsey & Company. (2018). *How utilities can keepthe lights on.*

Mooney, A., Hook, L. & McCormick, M. (2018, December 9). BlackRock, Vanguard, Axa raise coal holdings despite climate fears. *Financial Times.*

Mountouri, D., Kienzle F., Poulios V., Dobeli C. & Luternauter, H. (2015). *Suitable network tariff design for the grid integration of decentralized generation and storage.* In: CIRED 23rd International Conference on Electricity Distribution, Lyon

National Grid. (2018). *Final auction results. T-4 Capacity market auction for 2021/22.*

Newell, R. G., & Prest, B. C. (2017). *How the shale boom has transformed the US oil and gas industry.*

OECD. (2017). *Investing in climate, investing in growth.*

OFGEM. (2017). *Annual report on the operation of the capacity market in 2016/2017.*

OIES – The Oxford Institute for energy studies. (2018). *Building new gas transportation infrastructure in the EU–What are the rules of the game?*

Pérez-Arriaga, I. J. (2013). *Regulation of the power sector.*

REN21. (2018). *Renewables 2918. Global status report.*

Rhodes, J.D., Webber, M. E., Deetjen, T., & Davidson, T. (2017). *Are solar and wind really killing coal, nuclear and grid reliability?* Retrieved from https://www.electrochem.org/ecs-blog/solar-wind-really-killing-coal-nuclear-grid-reliability/

Rocky Mountain Institute. (2014). *The economics of grid defection.*

Rocky Mountain Institute. (2015). *The economics of battery energy storage.*

Rocky Mountain Institute. (2017). *Your home or business can cut power plant emissions.* Retrieved from https://rmi.org/home-business-can-cut-power-plant-emissions/

Rocky Mountain Institute. (2018a). *The economics of clean energy portfolios.*

Rocky Mountain Institute. (2018b). *The consumer connection: A consumer-centric approach to delivering home energy services.*

Schmidt O., Hawkes A., Gambhir A., & Staffell I. (2017). *The future cost of electrical energy storage based on experience rates.*

Schwimmbeck, R. G. (2008). *Pipeline vs. LNG.*

Smil, V. (2017). *Energy and civilization: A history.*

Sorrell, S., Dimitropoulos, J. & Sommerville, M. (2009). *Empirical estimates of the direct rebound effect: A review.*

Staffell, I., Green, R., Gross, R., Green, T., Jansen M. & Clark, L. (2018). *Drax electric insights.* Quarterly – Q3 2018.

The Crown Estate. (2018). *Offshore wind operational report. January – December 2017.*

UNEP-Bloomberg New Energy Finance. (2018). *Global trends in renewable energy investment 2018.*

Venzin, M., & Konert, E. (2020). The disruption of the infrastructure industry: How investment decisions in the infrastructure industry are expected to change and how to prepare. In S. Gatti & C. Chiarella (Eds.), *Disruption in the infrastructure sector: Challenges and opportunities for developers, investors and asset managers.* Heidelberg: Springer.

WBCSD. (2017). *Corporate renewable. Power purchase agreements.*

WBCSD. (2018). *Innovation in power purchase agreement structures.*

Wind Europe. (2018a). *Financing and investment trends. The European wind industry in 2017.*

Wind Europe. (2018b). *Wind in power 2017. Annual combined onshore and offshore wind energy statistics.*

Wind Europe. (2018c). *Offshore wind in europe. Key trends and statistics 2017.*

Wind Europe. (2018d). *Breaking new ground. Wind energy and the electrification of europe's energy system.*

World Economic Forum. (2017a). *Game changers in the energy.* System emerging theme reshaping the energy landscape. In collaboration with McKinsey & Company. White Paper.

World Economic Forum. (2017b). *The future of electricity new technologies transforming the grid edge.* In collaboration with Bain & Company.

Zucker, A., Hinchliffe, T., & Spisto, A. (2013). *Assessing storage value in electricity markets.*

Future Developments in the Transport Infrastructure Sector

3

The Perspective of the European Context

Oliviero Baccelli

3.1 Introduction

The European transport infrastructure sectors will have to face probable evolutions due to macro-trends which, at different speeds, will influence the characteristics of freight and passenger demand and the suppliers of mobility services. The general political framework in the sectors is focused on offering safer, smarter and greener mobility services, but the economic and social costs of change are slowing the possible opportunities. In the coming decades, governments will rely more heavily on technology innovation to reach their policy objectives (e.g. decarbonization), within economic and social constraints, and to resolve any conflicting elements of said objectives. The push for strong, continuous GDP growth, for instance, is often at odds with the need to reduce consumption of resources and avoid major climate changes. Such contrasting challenges provide powerful incentives for the creation of innovative and balanced solutions in the transport infrastructure sectors.

The analysis carried out in this chapter deals with the probable rather than the possible and presents some specific cases as examples of the potential implications for long-term financial investors. This study of the macro-trends affecting the future of transport infrastructure investments is organized in four steps:

1. Demographic, economic and geopolitical macro-trends
2. The technological and organizational challenges to innovation
3. The role of the political and regulatory context at European level
4. Probable evolution of the transport infrastructure sectors and potential implications for long-term financial investors

O. Baccelli (✉)
GREEN – Center for Research on Geography, Resources, Environment, Energy & Networks,
Bocconi University, Milan, Italy
e-mail: oliviero.baccelli@unibocconi.it

© Springer Nature Switzerland AG 2020   53
S. Gatti, C. Chiarella (eds.), *Disruption in the Infrastructure Sector*, Future of
Business and Finance, https://doi.org/10.1007/978-3-030-44667-3_3

The first part of this research briefly describes the main aspects affecting mobility demand trends. These are related to demographic factors (e.g. population growth, ageing, urbanization, regional differentiations) passenger demand and trade patterns for freight demand (e.g. the slow-moving domestic demand, the unequal and uncertain pattern of the growth of international trade,[1] the movement of the earth's economic centre of gravity towards the East at European and international scale, the role of containerization for ports and the role of tourism in major destinations). These trends are affecting the evolution of the transport infrastructure investments and the decisions of long-term investors.

The second part of the analysis will be dedicated to understanding the technological and organizational trends affecting transport infrastructures and interdependencies between digital and physical infrastructure. For instance, e-mobility service providers and LNG suppliers are partnering with technology providers to power their businesses. Specific focus centers on EU tourism trends influencing transport nodes that handle international flows.

The third part of the research summarizes the main goals of the transport infrastructure policies at European level (e.g. Connecting Europe Facility program) and the main regulations requiring new investments (e.g. Alternative Fuel Initiatives, completion of the liberalization process at EU level, safety regulations affecting the advent of autonomous vehicles). One of the constraints in implementing public policies is the growing public debt that is affecting the capacity of governments to respond to all the challenges they face as discussed by Gatti and Chiarella in the Introduction.

Lastly, the final part of the paper addresses the implications for financial investors of the macro-trends analyzed in the previous chapters, with a summary of the probable impacts on airports, ports and railways infrastructures.

---

[1]The uncertain pattern in the growth of international trade, for instance, is due to medium-long term policies like Brexit or unexpected initiatives like the US president imposing import tariffs of 25% on steel and 10% on aluminum in June 2018. Anti-trade and anti-immigration policies also limit the international division of labor and are detrimental to productivity, which is the key driver of economic growth over time (Hofrichter 2017). Therefore, there is a risk that the world economy could see far greater dispersion of economic growth rates. An anticipator of this world trend could be considered the level of global foreign direct investment (FDI). According to the United Nation Conference on Trade and Development (UNCTAD) the World Investment Report 2018, FDI flows fell by 23% to $1.43 trillion in 2017 compared to 2016. This is in stark contrast to the accelerated growth in GDP and trade. The fall was caused in part by a 22% decrease in the value of cross-border mergers and acquisitions (M&As). But even discounting the large one-off deals and corporate restructurings that inflated FDI numbers in 2016, the 2017 decline remained significant. The value of announced greenfield investments (an indicator of future trends) also decreased by 14%. FDI flows to developing economies remained stable at $671 billion, seeing no recovery following the 10% drop in 2016. FDI inflows to the EU declined from $524 billion in 2016 to $304 in 2017.

3.2   The Demographic Megatrends Influencing Investments in Transport Infrastructures at EU Level

At European level, two of the most relevant global demographic megatrends do not prove particularly significant in terms of influencing the distribution of transport infrastructure investments. In fact, the general population growth[2] and the new urbanization[3] are the main characteristics of the demographic trends in Asia or Africa; however, these factors are not playing an important role in determining the amount and type of infrastructure needed in Europe. Table 3.1 shows the results of the United Nations probabilistic population projections for the major world areas.

According to Eurostat, the overall size of the population in EU27 is projected to be somewhat larger by 2040 than in 2016; after that it will drop slightly. The EU27 population is projected to increase only by about 1.8% between 2016 (445.3 million) and 2040 (at 453.3 million) when it will peak,[4] to then remain almost stable until 2050 and thereafter decline to 439.2 million in 2070. These almost stable general demographic trends in Europe are more articulated at national level. In fact, the global population dynamics are much more complex and differentiated among nations as detailed in the EU Institutional Paper 65/17 "The Ageing Report 2018".

While the total EU27 population will decrease by 1.4% over 2016–2070, there are wide differences in population trends across member states, with the population rising in half of the EU countries and falling in the other half. The total population change between 2016 and 2070 for the top five most populated EU countries is heterogeneous. Germany, Italy and Poland will observe a decline, respectively −3.9%, −9.7% and −18.7%, while France and Spain will have a population growth of 15.3% and 7.4%. In absolute terms, Poland will have the largest drop in population: −7.1 million inhabitants, while Italy will lose 5.9 and Germany 3.3 million. In the same period, France and Spain will see a rise of 10.2 and 3.5 million residents, respectively. In 2070, Germany will have 79.2 million inhabitants while France will have 77 million, with a difference of just 2.2 million; in 2016 the difference was 15.7 million.

---

[2] According to UN "World Population Prospects ", the world's population is projected to increase by slightly more than one billion people over the next 13 years, reaching 8.6 billion in 2030, and growing to 9.8 billion in 2050 and 11.2 billion by 2100 (United Nations 2018).

[3] At world level, the share of population living in urban areas is 545% in 2018; this is expected to reach 68% in 2040.

[4] For the same period in Asia the population growth rate estimate is 16.6%, while for Africa it is 75.8%, according to UN "World Population prospects (2017)".

Table 3.1 Probabilistic population projections: differences among European areas compared to other major world areas (in millions)

	Population in 2015	Population estimated in 2040	Population growth 2016–2040
World	7383	9210	+24.7%
Africa	1194	2100	+75.8%
Asia	4419	5154	+16.6%
Europe	740	728	−1.6%
Eastern Europe	293	269	−8.2%
Northern Europe	103	114	+10.7%
Southern Europe	152	145	−4.6%
Western Europe	192	200	+4.2%

Source: UN World Population Prospects (2017)

3.2.1 Demographic Determinants

Demographic determinants are:

1. The fertility rate
2. The mortality rate
3. The level of net migration

As far as fertility and mortality are concerned, it is assumed that these two factors tend to converge to that of the "forerunners". The fertility rate is projected to increase over the projection period in all member states except for France (the country with the highest total fertility rate (TFR) in 2016, namely 2.01). However, fertility rates in all countries are expected to remain below the natural replacement rate of 2.1 in the period to 2070. Table 3.2 reports the projection of total fertility rates between 2016

Table 3.2 Projection of total fertility rates 2016–2070

	2016	2030	2060	2070	Change 2016–2070
France	2.01	2.00	1.99	1.99	−0.02
Germany	1.49	1.53	1.64	1.68	0.19
Italy	1.33	1.42	1.60	1.66	0.33
Poland	1.37	1.56	.168	1.71	0.34
Spain	1.31	1.80	1.88	1.88	0.57
United Kingdom	1.80	1.81	1.86	1.87	0.07
Euro Area	1.56	1.67	1.76	1.79	0.23
EU28	1.58	1.69	1.78	1.81	0.23

Source: elaboration from EU Institutional Paper 65/17 "The Ageing Report 2018"

and 2070 for the major EU countries. The TFR is projected to rise from 1.58 in 2016 to 1.81 by 2070 for the EU as a whole. In the euro area, an increase of similar magnitude is projected, from 1.56 in 2016 to 1.79 in 2070.

The projections show higher life expectancy at birth being sustained during the projection period, albeit with considerable diversity across member states. In the EU, life expectancy at birth for males is expected to increase by 7.8 years over the projection period, from 78.3 in 2016 to 86.1 in 2070. Table 3.3 reports the projection of life expectancy at birth between 2016 and 2070 for the major EU countries. For females, life expectancy at birth is projected to be extended by 6.6 years, from 83.7 in 2016 to 90.3 in 2070, implying a convergence of life expectancy between males and females. The largest increases in life expectancies at birth, for both males and females, are projected to take place in the member states with the lowest life expectancies in 2016.

Assumptions on net migration typically are the most methodologically difficult, with high volatility over time and countries. Table 3.4 shows the projection of net migration as a percentage of population between 2016 and 2070 for the major EU countries. For the EU as a whole, annual net inflows are projected to decrease from about 1.5 million people in 2016 (0.3% of the EU population) to 805,000 people by 2070 (0.2% of the EU population). Cumulatively, net migration inflows during the period 2016–2070 are forecast to equal 11.3% of the total EU population and 12.8% of the total population of the euro area.

Table 3.3 Projection of life expectancy at birth 2016–2070

		2016	2030	2060	2070	Change 2016–2070
France	Male	79.5	83.1	85.5	86.6	7.1
	Female	85.6	88.4	90.3	90.3	5.5
Germany	Male	78.7	80.9	84.9	86.2	7.4
	Female	83.6	85.5	89.0	90.1	6.5
Italy	Male	80.7	82.5	85.9	86.9	6.2
	Female	85.3	86.9	90.0	90.9	5.6
Poland	Male	73.9	77.1	82.8	84.4	10.5
	Female	81.6	84.0	88.3	89.5	7.9
Spain	Male	80.5	82.3	85.9	86.9	6.4
	Female	86.0	87.4	90.3	91.2	5.2
United Kingdom	Male	79.6	81.6	85.4	86.5	6.9
	Female	83.3	85.3	89.0	90.1	6.8
Euro Area	Male	79.3	81.4	85.3	86.4	7.1
	Female	84.6	86.3	89.6	90.6	6.1
EU28	Male	78.3	80.7	84.9	86.1	7.8
	Female	83.7	85.6	89.2	90.3	6.6

Source: elaboration from EU Institutional Paper 65/17 "The Ageing Report 2018"

Table 3.4 Projection of net migration 2016–2070 (net migration as % of population)

	2016	2030	2060	2070	% of population
France	0.1	0.1	0.1	0.1	5.1
Germany	0.9	0.3	0.2	0.2	16.7
Italy	0.2	0.3	0.3	0.3	18.9
Poland	0.0	0.0	0.0	0.0	1.7
Spain	0.0	0.3	0.3	0.3	14.5
United Kingdom	0.4	0.3	0.2	0.1	11.8
Euro Area	0.3	0.3	0.2	0.2	12.8
EU 28	0.3	0.2	0.2	0.2	11.3

Source: elaboration from EU Institutional Paper 65/17 "The Ageing Report 2018"

Future transport infrastructure investment needs are closely linked to the rate at which populations grow (McKinsey 2017). As such, forecasts of economic and demographic variables are crucial in understanding how infrastructure demand will develop over the coming years. A country that faces major population increases over the next 25 years, for example France or Spain, is likely to need to invest more heavily to provide for that population upsurge, compared to one in which the population is expected to remain stable or decline in the coming years, like Germany or Italy. In fact, Italy has already lost 311,000 inhabitants in the period from 1 January 2015 to 31 December 2017 (Barbiellini et al. 2018; ISTAT 2018).

3.2.2 Urbanization

Globally, more people live in urban areas than in rural ones, as discussed by Gatti and Chiarella (2020) in Chap. 6, with 55% of the world's population residing in cities in 2018. In 1950, 30% of the world's population was urban, and by 2050 that figure is projected to rise to 68%. According to the World Bank World Development Indicators, the tendency of residents to gravitate towards urban areas to take advantage of the economic and social opportunities they offer has already been recorded in all the main European countries from 1960 to 2016. In 2016 in Europe the share of the population living in urban areas was close to 72% on average, with some differences among countries (Belgium 98%, Denmark 88%, France 80%, Germany 76%, Italy 69%, Poland 61%, Spain 80%). It is estimated that this percentage will reach 74% in 2040. Therefore, the role of new urbanization is limited in Europe 2040 scenarios for infrastructure investments. In fact, according to Eurostat data, metropolitan regions with at least one million inhabitants already provide homes to 39% of the EU population, employment to 41% of the EU's workforce and generate 47% of the continent's gross domestic product.

According to the 2018 ESPON project "European Territorial Reference Framework" (ESPON EGTC 2019), in aggregate terms, European spatial development patterns are not expected to change significantly in the coming decades. Land-taken will be reduced gradually, and towards 2050 most spatial development processes will involve regeneration. In fact, the general EU demographic trends do not favour a growth of urban population in most countries. However, regional disparities in adopting new technologies and the skill level of the work force will further advance regional and urban/rural differences. This trend will be reflected in disposable income data and mobility indicators.

3.2.3 Ageing

Ageing[5] is certainly one of the most relevant demographic trends to influence investment decisions in the transport infrastructure sectors at European level; this in light of the fact that the 15–64 population will decline, as discussed by Gatti and Chiarella (2020) in Chap. 6. In EU27, according to the European Commission document "The Ageing Report" (European Economy Institutional Paper 065/2017 and European Economy Institutional Paper 79/2018) the working age population will decrease from 290 million in 2016 to 262 million in 2040 (−9.6%). This will require a major increase in labour productivity and therefore more efficient mobility for commuters and business travellers.

The age breakdown of the EU27 population is projected to change significantly in the coming decades. Moreover, while in 2015 the largest cohort for both males and females is 45–49 years old, in 2070 it will be 70–74 for women and 50–54 for men. Overall, the median age will rise from 42.4 years old in 2015 to 46.7 in 2070. These projections are based on historical national parameters, fertility rates, life expectancy at birth and net migration. The structural changes related to the progressive rise in the segment of the population 65 years old and over are common to all the EU 27 countries. The percentage of the cohort of over-65 s will grow from 19.6 to 29.6 of the total EU27 population between 2016 and 2070 (in 2040 this figure will be 27.8%). This means in absolute terms the number will jump from 87 to 132 million (+45 million, +52%), but this percentage will be higher in countries like Portugal (34%), Italy and Poland (in both cases 33%) and lower in nations like Sweden and France (25% and 26% respectively).

As far as the implications of this ageing process for the EU and the euro area, the working age population (15–64 year olds) is projected to shrink during the period in question as a share of the total population, declining from 65.3% in 2016 to 55.9% in 2070.Total labour supply for people from age 20 to 64 in the EU is expected to fall by 9.6% from 2016 to 2070, of which 2% during 2016–2030 and a further 7.8% between 2030 and 2070. Because of these trends in Germany, Italy and Poland, the

---

[5]As fertility declines and life expectancy rises, the proportion of the population above a certain age rises as well. This phenomenon, known as population ageing, is occurring throughout the world. In 2017, there were an estimated 962 million people aged 60 or over in the world, comprising 13% of the global population. This global statistic is a very different number compared to the European one, which is 25%.

overall demand for mobility will generally drop and the number of car drivers and public transport users who are getting old or very old will multiply. On the contrary, in Sweden and France the role of demography on the overall passenger demand will be positive and will contribute to the need for new solutions for a rising and differentiating demand.

The impact of ageing on the transport infrastructure sectors will have different signs depending on the specific European context. In some major European countries (e.g. Germany, Italy and Poland), the combination of the two trends (a decline in the population and a proportional growth in the number of elderly people) will emerge as a constraint on public budgets. This in turn, due to higher social expenses, will lead to an accelerating contraction in remaining public funds for future infrastructure spending. Therefore, the proliferation of participation among long-term private investors in financing infrastructure assets seems to be of growing importance. The contract period of concession holdings or partnerships can be longer compared to the present 20–30 years, because more time is needed to amortize the investment in a context with limited macro-economic and demand growth (Roumboutsos et al. 2018).

In the medium-long term, in Germany, Italy and Poland public investments in transport will be more concentrated on maintenance, reducing traffic congestion and improving the safety and environmental sustainability of existing transport networks. New projects dedicated to responding to new flows in demand will take a back seat.[6] This is due to a diminishing population and the ageing factor. For instance, in Germany it was found that after accounting for retirement and reported mobility impairments, seniors still experience a steady decline in mobility as they age. In fact, on average, seniors travel about 100 fewer meters per day for each additional year of age over 65 (Institute for Mobility Research 2017). This decline stems from small gradual changes in lifestyle or incremental increases in health issues associated with ageing. In Italy, seniors over 65 have an Expressed Mobility Index (EMI) that is 31% lower than the average population (ISFORT 2017) while on average working people have an EMI that is 20.8% higher than the national mean. If the EMI for the different cohorts of the population does not change in the coming years, the Italian demographic trends (aging and shrinking of the working age population) will reduce the total mobility of the Italians by approximately 8.3% in the 2016–2040 period. This is a much higher rate compared to the population decline in the same period (−1.3%).

The growing public sensitivity to the needs of the ageing population will also have relevant effects on many other aspects of the mobility sector, especially with regard to technological innovations that can help offer new solutions to people with reduced mobility. Box 3.1 reports a synthesis of the consequences of ageing in terms of the technological aspects of mobility infrastructures.

---

[6]The role of international tourism will be a major driver in the growth of passenger demand, but in very specific nodes such as main airports and major tourism destinations as described in the following section.

Box 3.1 The Consequences of Ageing in Terms of the Technological Aspects of Mobility Infrastructures

For sensory, motory and cognitive reasons, mobility is becoming increasingly difficult with age. For the elderly, the possibility of maintaining or recovering mobility in satisfactory conditions of effectiveness, comfort and safety is a major challenge to sustain the social bond and meet the most elementary need for autonomy. To succeed, it is more and more necessary to take the needs and anatomical and functional characteristics of the elderly into account in designing infrastructure, equipment and services. This is a problematic issue in a physical and informational environment which is becoming increasingly complex (GOAL Consortium 2013).

The first response to these trends will probably be an expansion of "on demand" public services (like taxis, Uber, and Demand Responsive Transport Service). However, the development of new technologies in all fields may be an opportunity, if related innovations are suitably adapted and play a genuine palliative role with respect to age-related issues. For instance, advances in technology in recent years mean that it is becoming more common for new cars to be equipped with features such as rear-view cameras for reversing, blind-spot warning systems and even auto-parking technology. For older drivers with limited upper-body mobility, this can ensure their independence by giving them more driving years whilst keeping them and other road users safe. Moreover, the rapid advancement of technology means that driverless cars are now a real possibility; these vehicles are likely to be on the roads in a matter of years, rather than decades.

Most European governments are committed to the development of driverless car technology, recently authorizing testing on public roads[7] (UK Department for Transport 2015 and German Federal Government 2017). In the context of an ageing society, although in relatively early stages, this experimentation will potentially benefit the society as a whole, but older people will gain the major advantages of this evolution and will politically support it.

The role of new generation telecom technology infrastructures dedicated transport information transmission (5G networks, wireless, fibre optics, etc.) will increase in tandem with automated and connected driving, as discussed by Sacco (2020) in Chap. 4. These long-term trends will shape opportunities for financial investors who are interested in the telecom sector.

---

[7]With the Declaration of Amsterdam on connected and automated driving signed in 2016, EU member states, the European Commission and the private sector have agreed on joint goals and joint actions to facilitate the introduction of connected and automated driving on Europe's roads. This should prevent a patchwork of rules and regulations arising within the EU, which would be an obstacle to both manufacturers and motorists.

3.3   The Role of International Tourism in the Transport Infrastructure Sector

As emphasized in the previous paragraphs, the role of population growth and urbanization will be limited at EU level compared to what is happening in the world. But this does not mean that mobility demand will generally decline; in fact, non-systemic transport demand will probably grow in the main urban areas of the EU, as people visit friends and relatives and tourist visit different cities.

Over the past few decades, tourism has become a key driver of socio-economic progress through the generation of jobs, export income and infrastructure development for many destinations around the world. Since the end of World War II, international tourist arrivals (overnight visitors) have experienced continued growth worldwide, reaching 1323 million in 2017 (84 million more than in 2016, +6.7%). This is compared to 25 million arrivals in 1950, according to statistics from the United Nations World Tourism Organisation (UNWTO). By UNWTO region, Europe accounts for the largest share of international tourist arrivals, with 619 million recorded in 2016, or 50% of the world's total. This represents a 2% increase from 2015, with rather mixed results at the destination level.

Within Europe, the 28 countries of the European Union welcome the flow of international arrivals in Europe. The EU accounts for 40% of international tourist arrivals and 31% of international tourism receipts worldwide. The Schengen Area, which allows travellers to move freely across 22 EU countries and four extra-EU countries, greatly fosters intraregional tourism. The common currency shared by 19 of the 28-member states also facilitates tourism significantly. As in other world regions, inbound trends in EU destinations are driven to a large extent by outbound demand from EU source markets.

Air travel is the dominant mode of transport for EU destinations, with 55% of international tourists travelling by air in 2016 compared to 45% by land or water. In 1995 the market share of air travel was 38%. By group of countries, air travel is highest in EU destinations in Northern Europe (75% of arrivals), followed by those in Southern and Mediterranean Europe (67%), in Western Europe (44%) and in Central and Eastern Europe (28%).

In the EU, tourism is concentrated in coastal regions (principally, but not exclusively, in the Mediterranean), Alpine regions, and some of the EU's capital cities. The top 20 European NUTS 2 regions of destination account for 36% of all nights spent in European accommodation establishments. Of these NUTS 2 regions, 6 are in Italy, 5 in both Spain and France, 2 in Germany, 1 in Croatia and 1 in Austria. Within the EU-28, domestic tourists accounted for 54.6% of the total number of nights spent in tourist accommodation establishments in 2015, with the remaining 45.4% consisting of international tourists who may have travelled from other EU Member States or from outside of the EU (European Parliamentary Research Service 2015).

In order to understand the role of international transport, it is interesting to note that there are considerable regional disparities between the number of nights spent by domestic tourists and international tourists. Often in the 22 multi-regional EU member states we see a pattern of international tourists being particularly attracted to capital city regions. These developments may be driven by business travel as well as personal travel. In 14 of these 22 member states, the capital city region registered the highest proportion of overnight stays by international tourists in 2015.

The share of nights spent by domestic tourists in tourist accommodation establishments was relatively low for most capital city regions; this may be explained by the concentration of international tourists visiting capital cities, while domestic tourists may choose to explore other regions of their country which may be less well-known internationally. The clearest example of this trend was in the United Kingdom, where domestic tourists accounted for less than one in five (17.8%) of the total nights spent in London, while they made up almost two thirds (65.3%) of the total nights spent across the whole of the United Kingdom. In a similar vein, the shares of domestic tourists in the total number of overnight stays in Prague and Bucharest/Ilfov were approximately 40 percentage points lower than the shares of domestic tourists in the total number of nights spent across the whole of the Czech Republic and Romania.

Indeed, domestic tourists generally accounted for a much higher share of the total nights spent outside of capital city regions. They represented at least 50% of the overnight stays in every region outside of the capital city in Denmark, Germany, Ireland, France, Hungary, the Netherlands, Poland, Romania, Slovenia, Slovakia, Sweden and the United Kingdom. What is more, in four of these countries (Germany, Ireland, Poland and Sweden) domestic tourists made up a majority of the overnight stays in the capital city region too. By contrast, the total number of nights spent by international tourists outnumbered those of domestic tourists in both Croatian regions, as well as in five out of the six (relatively small) mono-regional EU Member States (Estonia, Cyprus, Latvia, Luxembourg and Malta) the exception being Lithuania.

There tended to be a relatively high concentration of international tourism within the most popular regions, whereas domestic tourism was often more dispersed across regions. This pattern was particularly apparent in some of the larger EU Member States and may be explained, at least in part, by a high share of international (first-time) visitors choosing to focus their trips on the most popular or well-known tourist sites. For example, in 2015 Île de France (the capital city region) hosted approximately one-third (33.1%) of the total nights spent by international tourists in the whole of France, whereas the southern region of Provence-Alpes-Côte d'Azur accounted for 12.8% of the total nights spent by domestic tourists. In a similar vein, Prague (the capital city region) counted 61.6% of the total nights spent by international tourists in the Czech Republic, while the most popular region for domestic tourists was Severovýchod (24.3% of the national total).

EU destinations reported 500 million international tourist arrivals in 2016. By region of origin according to UNWTO's classification (UNWTO et al. 2018), it is estimated that a total of 417 million arrivals (83%) came from Europe, of which 361 million (72%) from EU source markets and 56 million (11%) from European source markets outside the EU. The remaining 83 million arrivals originated from outside Europe (17%), of which 39 million from the Americas (8%) and 32 million from Asia and the Pacific (7%), while Africa and the Middle East accounted for respectively 6 million and 5 million of EU arrivals (1% each). Arrivals in the EU from source markets outside the Union, both extra-EU countries in Europe and markets outside Europe, totalled 139 million in 2016, up from 80 million in 2005. The 28 countries of the European Union recorded an extraordinary 8% increase in international tourist arrivals in 2017, following 5% growth in 2016. While arrivals from intra-EU source markets rose by 2% a year on average between 2005 and 2016, arrivals from outside markets ticked up at a rate of 5% a year. Growth has been strongest for arrivals from the Middle East at almost 10% a year on average, but from a comparatively small base volume. Arrivals from Asia and the Pacific and from Africa were both up by 7% a year on average, while arrivals from the Americas increased by 4% a year (UNWTO 2018).

According to the UNWTO scenario (UNWTO et al. 2018) advanced economy destinations in the EU are projected to see arrivals grow by 7 million a year on average, to reach 487 million in 2030. A total of 443 million arrivals were recorded in this group of destinations in 2016. Emerging economies are expected to see an increase of 2 million a year, hitting 75 million in 2030. Arrivals in EU destinations from European source markets are expected to rise by 1.9% a year on average through 2030, of which from markets within the EU by 1.6% a year and from extra-EU by 3.5% a year. Interregional arrivals are projected to increment by 2.4% a year, with the fastest growth expected to come from Africa (4.3% a year) though from a low base, followed by Asia and the Pacific (3.1% a year) and the Middle East (2.6% a year). The slowest growth is expected to come from the Americas (1.6% a year). As result of the relative acceleration of arrivals from outside the EU, the share of arrivals in EU destinations from EU source markets is expected to decrease slightly to 70% by 2030, while the share of extra-EU source markets in Europe will have increased to 13% and those from interregional source markets to 15%.

International arrivals have exceeded the expectations of the projection in the period from 2010 to 2016, particularly in the EU (European Parliamentary Research Service 2018). This trend is fuelled by stronger-than-expected intraregional demand and a robust economic recovery. Enhanced air and rail connectivity, more affordable travel and the rise of new tourism and information services through digital platforms have contributed to this remarkable upsurge. Weaker growth in North Africa and the Middle East has also partly redirected tourism flows to Europe, much of which to Southern and Mediterranean Europe.

The cruise sector is a specific niche of the tourism market which is particularly relevant for Italy and Spain (+18.1% passenger movements in Mediterranean ports from 2008 to 2017, passing from 21.8 to 25.9 million). According to a survey by the Cruise Lines International Association (CLIA), in 2017 the ocean cruise market in Europe expanded to count more than 6.9 million passengers, a 2.5% increase compared with 2016. European cruising has been steadily on the rise for the past 10 years led by the German, UK and Irish markets.

Tourism trends will have a relevant role in shaping new infrastructures at EU level primarily because the total number of arrivals is growing. However, another reason for this is that the tourism phenomenon is characterized by the more relevant role extra-UE tourists play. In fact, these arrivals will be concentrated for the most part in the major capitals and international and intercontinental airport and air-rail infrastructures. The uptick in the cruise market also calls for new terminals in port areas, especially in the main destinations in the Mediterranean. As in the airport market, in the cruise terminal sector the most relevant infrastructure investments are based on public-private partnerships or concessions contracts (Satta et al. 2020).

3.4 The Organizational, Technological and Regulatory Innovation Challenges in Main Transport Sectors

The long-term social trends related to tourism, the ageing EU population and middle-class growth at worldwide level described in the previous sections will have a general impact on transport infrastructure sectors, but mainly in the major metropolitan areas and more specifically in the international nodes. In order to better understand the specific drivers of potential growth in each transport infrastructure sector (airport, port, railways), it is relevant to analyze the specific peculiarities relating to organizational, technological and political aspects that characterize each sector.

3.4.1 Airports

The story of aviation in Europe has been one of continuous growth and expansion since the inception of the modern civil aviation industry, with airports across the continent collectively breaking through the 1.5 billion passenger mark in 2008 and 2 billion in 2016. The market suffered when Europe's economies were embroiled in the global financial crisis in 2008/2009, but since then, buoyed by low fuel prices and a recovering world economy, European air passenger traffic has grown at a CAGR of 5.6% per year between 2010 and 2016. During 2017 the reported growth in traffic was the fastest in the last decade (+8.5%), with commercial airlines carrying 5.3% more passenger traffic than in 2016 and the largest low-cost carriers (LCC) in Europe reporting a rise in short-haul passenger traffic of 13.2%. These strong upward traffic trends came in the face of GDP growth in Europe of only 2.8%, suggesting that European aviation is not entirely dependent on GDP to generate traffic growth. During the first 6 months of 2018, European airports posted 6.7% more passengers, confirming the positive trend.

The vast majority of capacity growth over the past decade can be attributed to new types of carriers that have been able to diversify the service supply and reach new passenger targets.[8] Therefore at present a different classification applies to

---

[8]According to ACI-Europe data, 84% of passenger growth at the top twenty European airports between 2007 and 2017 was generated by low cost carriers that were able to generate 148.2 million passengers while traditional full-service carriers only counted 28.5 million.

airlines in Europe compared to a decade ago: Full Service Carrier, Regional/Commuter; Charter/Leisure, Low Cost Carrier, Ultra Low Cost and, Low Cost Carrier with Long-Haul. The three low cost segments, which are the product of the evolution generated by the liberalization process completed at EU level in 1997, are responsible for the rapid and substantial growth in European air passenger traffic and are forecasted to expand unabated in the future. Box 3.2 proposes the new airline classification.

Box 3.2 The New Airline Classification, the Result of the Combination of New Technologies and New Business Models

Full-service carriers, like Lufthansa or Air France, are operating a wide national and international route network (based on the hub-and-spoke principle). The main elements of this long-standing concept are the home airports—the so-called "hubs". Airports with a hub accommodate flights from other national and intercontinental airports (spokes); these flights are then bundled and subsequently redistributed to intercontinental connecting flights. The focus on a central air traffic intersection (hub) enables a wide flight network to operate. During the flight, full-service airlines also offer additional services (mostly free of charge), such as on-board catering, an entertainment system, seat reservations, and so forth. This business model also offers cargo and freight transport, in addition to passengers.

Regional airlines, like CityJet or Adria Airlines, operate with geographically limited coverage. This means that although in some cases these airlines offer excellent on-board service, they do not fly to the same number of destinations or offer the same service categories as the full-service airlines. Regional airlines serve a variety of functions at the local level and on many thinner routes, e.g. smaller short-haul markets that feed into larger carriers. These companies may be seen as complementary to the full-service airlines they are often linked to.

As for charter/leisure carriers, which in the literature is often synonymous with non-scheduled flight service, there is no single definition. Fundamental characteristics of traditional charter flights are related to partial or complete sales of seat capacity to organizations like tour operators, companies who sell the transportation service either on its own or as part of a package to end customers (passengers). Compared to scheduled flights, charter traffic normally offers less cabin comfort as well as less flexibility (fewer flights, less convenient flight schedules and less favorable booking and rebooking conditions). Furthermore, the price level of the charter airlines is often below that of the scheduled airlines. In addition, charter airlines like Neos or Blue Panorama are not allowed to transport air freight in the hold on passenger flights. This means that they are not able to realize economies of scope. Nevertheless, charter airlines have a cost advantage compared to scheduled

(continued)

Box 3.2 (continued)

air traffic airlines, as their expenses on computer booking systems, administration, sales and marketing are relatively low because they charter or sell the entire flight to tour operators. Perhaps the biggest game-changer in aviation is the huge impact of low-cost carriers (LCCs) on European aviation. This is the outcome of the liberalization process completed in 1997 and the standardization and simplification of all aspects of commercial aviation related to the web technologies and digitalization processes. The LCC segment is responsible for the rapid and substantial rise in European air passenger traffic and is forecasted to grow unabated in the future. This is due in part to the adoption of more sophisticated and differentiated business models that will be briefly described in the following paragraphs.

The traditional low-cost carriers (LCCs) offer flights on selected routes at low fares due to essential savings in sales and service costs. LCCs like EasyJet or Vueling do not operate on the hub-and-spoke principle which entails high coordination and costs. Instead LCCs offer point–to–point connections, which are direct, short to medium distance flights. Low-cost carriers often avoid major airports (and prefer regional airports instead); this allows them to have a very flexible and cost-efficient network planning and flight routes, and lower operating costs. Mainly due to a higher capacity utilization of the aircrafts, a unique fleet of aircrafts, strong cost management and focus on air transportation alone ("no frills"), LCCs can offer lower fares to customers. Passengers often have to pay for service on board (food and drink), stowed luggage and seat reservations, all of which cuts costs and at the same time opens up new sources of income.

Ultra-Low-Cost Carriers (ULCCs), like Ryanair or Wizz Air, achieve significantly lower costs than LCCs or other commercial carriers, and aggressively collect ancillary revenue for unbundled services. As a result of lower base fares, these companies realize lower unit revenues than other carriers, even when ancillary revenues are taken into account.

The fundamental characteristics of Low-Cost Carriers with Long-Haul (LCCLHs), like Norwegian, are their cost advantages on long haul flights due to a higher utilization and seating density; they also avoid the use of large hub airports. New aircraft technology like the Boeing 787, Airbus 350, and larger single-aisle aircraft, as well as evolving passenger preferences and stable fuel prices are encouraging LCCs (and restructured full service airlines) to consider new growth opportunities on long, thin routes. What were previously niche city pairs are becoming increasingly mainstream as more LCCLHs come online and disrupt entrenched business models. This makes long thin markets viable, routes that were not feasible before 2012 when new long-haul aircraft entered into the market. This is positive for secondary airports seeking to expand their long-haul networks with airlines which are operating, or have on order, new technology aircraft.

The European passenger market is the most advanced and fragmented at global level and therefore the most resilient to possible crises.

Airbus' Global Market Forecast (GMF) for 2018–2037 offers a forward-looking view of the air transport sector's evolution. This forecast takes into account factors such as demographic and economic growth, tourism trends, oil prices, and the development of new and existing routes. Ultimately this report highlights demand for aircraft covering the full spectrum of sizes from 100 seats to the very largest aircraft over 500 seats. For the 20-year period in question, the compound average growth rate for passenger traffic in the European market is projected at 3.3%. All three major flows connecting Western Europe are expected to develop: Western-Europe–USA; Intra-Western Europe, expected to grow 1.7 times (corresponding to a CAGR of 2.8%) and Western-Europe–Middle East, 2.6 times respectively[9] (CAGR of 5%).

According to the best available information, the long-term growth will not slow down in the coming decades. Therefore, airport capacity constraints are becoming more widespread and evident. The lack of airport capacity, in fact, is the number one challenge for European aviation, according to the European Commission and Eurocontrol. The 2018 "Challenges of growth" by Eurocontrol (2018) in the most likely scenarios underscores that traffic in Europe is expected to grow to just over 16 million flights in 2040 with a total increase of 53% compared to 2017. That is an average increment of 1.9% per year. Eurocontrol emphasized that 111 of the most important European airports are planning a 16% increase in capacity between them, which equates to 4 million more runaway movements. This upward trend is focused on the top 20 airports, which are planning for growth of 28%, or 2.4 million runaway movements, nearly two-thirds of the expansion in total capacity. These 20 airports saw 53% of all flights as arrivals or departures in 2017, although they account for only 35% of the available capacity.

The airport expansion at European level is more concentrated in major airports, despite it being more difficult to create additional capacity at these sites, because many of the easier initiatives have already been taken. These new investments include the additional runaway at Heathrow, with a completion date set for 2026, and the opening of the Berlin Brandeburg Airport (end 2020). It is not surprising that all the major infrastructure funds have recently been involved in specific investments in this sector.[10]

---

[9]Boeing "Commercial market outlook 2018–2037" indicates similar average growth rates: 3.6% for the traffic within Europe, 3% to North America, 4.8 to Middle East, 5.6% to China and 4.6% to Africa (Boeing 2018).

[10]For instance, in 2017 Macquarie's European Infrastructure Fund 3 sold the majority of Copenhagen Airports shares to Danish Labour Market Supplementary Pension; Deutsche AM and Infravia acquired a 60.7% interest in SAVE, which owns four airports in Italy, including Venice, and one in Belgium; Ontario Teachers' Pension Plan sold 14.4% of its interest in the UK's Birmingham Airport and 30% of Bristol Airport to two Australian pension funds (T-Corp from New South Wales and Sunsuper Superannuation Fund).

Yet despite planned European airport capacity expansions, they are not considered sufficient. Eurocontrol underscores that by 2040 there will be demand for 1.5 million more flights than can be accommodated, 8% in the most likely scenario. That is 160 million passengers unable to fly. The gap is spread across 17 countries, and even with their ambitious capacity expansion plans, both Turkey and the United Kingdom are still forecast to have additional capacity gaps. Even with 8% of flights lost (that could double to 16% in the higher scenario, with a gap of 3.7 million flights), in 2040 in Europe there will be 16 airports that are as congested as Heathrow is now.

The new growth drivers are related to technological, organizational and social aspects:

- New aircraft types, new carriers and "de-constructed fares" enhance variety and reduce the cost of long-haul travel, boosting demand.
- Growing economies continue to drive both European and in-bound tourism.
- There is a higher propensity to fly among a more mobile millennial generation that expects to travel more often.
- Middle-class growth creates a larger population with more disposable income.

Among the driving forces in the sector, there is also the technology evolution, which will reduce costs both for airlines and airports and therefore push up demand.

In particular, the new aircraft technologies proposed by Boeing and Airbus such as the B787, A350, B737 MAX, A330 and A320 Neos have been developed for extended range and fuel efficiency. Boeing claims that state the B787 is 20% more fuel efficient than the B777 (Boeing 2018). This makes long thin markets viable, routes that previously were not. In addition, this could be positive for secondary airports (i.e. not the top 20) seeking to expand their long-haul network with airlines who are operating or have on order the new technology aircraft (for instance Norwegian or Air Italy). Moreover, it is clear from the current order books and forecasts that there are thousands of aircraft required to fulfill traffic growth over the coming years. For instance, in 2018 the two biggest European low-cost carriers had record orders (Easyjet: 140 A320s and A321s, and Ryanair: 135 firm orders and 75 options on B737–200 max). The technology evolution of long-range planes (like B787 or A350 or A321LR) will contribute to the fragmentation of the long-haul passenger market which is currently very concentrated with more than 90% in only 65 cities in the world. Therefore, new airports (secondary hubs or new generation hubs) will also benefit from this evolution. The emergence of the business model of Low-Cost Carriers with Long-Haul (LCCLH) is driving an upsurge in traffic and a fragmentation of non-stop city pairs on Europe–North America routes. The LCCLH share of North Atlantic departures grew from 1.1% in summer 2012 to 6.3% in summer 2017. The number of unique city pairs served non-stop by LCCLH similarly escalated from ten in summer 2012 to 64 in summer 2017.

Getting the most out of existing airport infrastructures will require a search for new sources of revenues that could come from extending the role of transport nodes, with valued added services to the passenger. These services could relate to enlarging the catchment area through new types of intermodal links or technologies and organizational innovations. Box 3.3 reports a case of a new type of air-rail intermodal link.

Box 3.3 How to Extend the Airport Catchment Area: The Case of the Marconi Express in Bologna

An interesting example of the potential role of a PPP transport infrastructure that could augment revenues for airport operators is the Marconi Express, a monorail shuttle that will link Bologna Central Station to Marconi Airport (5 km) in 7 min 20 s running mainly in a viaduct. From March 2020 there will be a Central Station/Airport integrated platform. A multi-modal platform of this kind represents an important competitive factor because it improves the accessibility of the metropolitan area thanks to an automated people mover that will link one of the most important high-speed railway network nodes at national level with an airport that sees more than 8 million passengers. Design, construction and management of the service are delegated to the Marconi Express project company, constituted by the CCC (Consorzio Cooperative di Costruzione) for a 75% share, and by TPER (public company for Emilia-Romagna Transport) for the remaining 25%. The construction company owning the majority of the special purpose vehicle will probably sell its shares in a few years after the completion of the works, offering opportunities for long term financial investors.

At world level, more than 80 airports have rail or people-mover links under construction or in the advanced planning stage.

Among airport technologies, self-check-in and baggage drop-off enable passengers to spend significantly less time at the airport before boarding their flight. At home or at work, passengers can check-in for the flight, check their luggage, pay for additional services and at the airport simply print their boarding passes and drop off their suitcases at the baggage self-check counter. It only takes a minute. Then they can proceed through security. The implementation of these new bag-drop technologies is part of investment programs in many airports which aim to support automated and paperless service technologies. More and more airports are installing eGates that allow passengers to independently pass through security controls at the entrance to the departure zone, or to board the aircraft by scanning their mobile or paper boarding pass.

Automated and paperless service technologies (eGates and self-check-in) and new baggage services (home bag drop or self-drop off for commercial baggage) will change the layout of airports. This will allow for more space for commercial activities and require less time for boarding/security procedures. As a result, passengers will have more free time at the airport, which could have potential positive consequences on commercial revenues. Well-designed strategic rethinking of airport areas could generate revenue growth and cost optimization, offering new opportunities for long-term financial investors. Box 3.4 presents a specific case of new value-added services at Gatwick Airport.

Box 3.4 New Value-added Services at Airport: The Gatwick Case
Gatwick Airport is considered a pilot case for the new relationship between airlines and airports that will impact infrastructure lay out and passenger experience, and therefore influence infrastructure and commercial investments. In summer 2018 EasyJet, Europe's leading airline, launched a partnership with home bag-drop service AirPortr, giving passengers travelling from London Gatwick the option to check their luggage in online and then have it collected from their doorstep by professional drivers and taken directly to the airport. The new service was implemented because research shows that over three quarters of travelers would prefer to be luggage free on the day of their flight, which is why EasyJet and AirPortr partnered to provide this service allowing travelers to start their trips at home. AirPortr will pick up luggage from the passenger's doorstep, and safely deliver it to easyJet's bag drop before it is flown to one of the airline's 110 destinations from Gatwick. Customers can then collect their baggage at their destination's baggage reclaim. Approximately 1000 ground staff and baggage handlers working for EasyJet at Gatwick Airport, who are directly employed by the logistics organization DHL, will take care of the passengers' baggage. AirPortr launched the world's first fully integrated home bag check-in service with British Airways in 2016 and in 2018 Finnair, Cathay Pacific and American Airlines joined the AirPortr digital platform in London.

3.4.2 Ports

Two policy considerations are worth mentioning as a premise for the analysis of the investment opportunities in the port sector and implication for investors. The first is related to potential demand: the uncertainty arising from wide-ranging geopolitical, economic, and trade policy risks, as well as some structural shifts, have a negative impact on maritime trade. Of immediate concern are inward-looking policies and rising protectionist sentiment that could undermine global economic growth, restrict trade flows and shift trade patterns. The second is related to the geopolitical dimension of port development. This dimension strengthens the case for public funding, as the absence of related mechanisms would accelerate foreign participation in the development of critical port infrastructure. Given the emergence of China's Belt and Road Initiative (BRI), a platform with mechanisms to provide financial support for port development, and certain Russian investments (for instance in pipelines), Europe may consider offering instruments for port financing, both for member states' ports and for current and prospective trading partners, especially in

North Africa, as initiatives to secure the geopolitical interests of the EU (European Council on Foreign Relations 2018[11]).

In line with projected economic growth and based on the income elasticity of seaborne trade estimated for the 2000–2017 period, UNCTAD Review of Maritime Transport (UNCTAD 2018a, b) expects world seaborne trade volumes to expand in coming years. According to UNCTAD projections, this expansion will occur at a compound annual growth rate of 3.8% from 2018 to 2023, based on calculated elasticities and the latest figures of GDP growth forecast by the International Monetary Fund for the same period. It is expected that containerized and dry bulk commodities trade will record the fastest growth. Tanker trade volumes should see an uptick, although at a slightly slower pace than other cargo types. Dry bulk commodities are projected to experience a compound annual growth rate of 4.9% between 2018 and 2023, while containerized shipments are expected to rise by 6%, supported by positive economic trends, imports of metal ores to China and steady growth on the non-main-lane trade routes. Further, crude oil trade is forecast to grow by 1.7% from 2018 to 2023, and combined petroleum products and gas volumes by 2.6%.

UNCTAD scenarios are in line with forecasts produced by Lloyd's List Intelligence, Clarksons Research Services, and Drewry Maritime Research. The growth of maritime flows at a global scale will also require new investments in European ports. The September 2017 European Commission "Delivering TEN-T, Facts & Figures" study reveals that European seaports (EU-27) currently face substantial investment needs of around €48 billion (€5 billion annually) for the period from 2018 to 2027. As these are mostly driven by dynamic and continuous trends, such as the rapid development of the logistics industry, port-related industry and evolving environmental requirements, port investments will remain crucial in the future.

According to the 2018 European Seaport Organization (ESPO) study, "The infrastructure investment needs and financing challenge of European ports" (ESPO 2018), investments in basic infrastructure, maritime access infrastructure, and transport-related infrastructure (transport connections to rail, road, and inland waterways) make up 65% of all port projects submitted by port authorities. Box 3.5 presents the case of a 2018 PPP transport infrastructure project which will improve the efficiency of the intermodal connections to the port of Rotterdam.

Box 3.5 The Blankenburg Port Connection PPP Project

Some maritime access infrastructure investments have been able to attract the interest of specialized infrastructure funds. One of the most recent financial closes is the €1 billion Blankenburg Connection PPP project in the

(continued)

---

[11] The report underscores that the Maritime Silk Road already affects Europe in five main areas: maritime trade, shipbuilding, emerging growth niches in the blue economy, the global presence of the Chinese navy, and the competition for international influence.

Box 3.5 (continued)
Netherlands. This is a design, build, finance and maintain (DBFM) project which will improve road links between Rotterdam and its port, and is the largest PPP project awarded in the Netherlands to date. The A24 Blankenburg Connection consists in fitting a three-lane highway in between two existing highways. This large and complex project involves the DBFM of a new highway connection of approximately 4 km (linking the A15 and the A20 roads to the west of Rotterdam) including a land tunnel around 500 m long (the Holland Tunnel), an immersed tunnel of nearly 900 m (the Maasdelta Tunnel), two major flyovers and widening of the existing A20. Following a construction period of 5.5 years, the consortium will then maintain the new road connection for 20 years. The BAAK consortium—Macquarie Capital (70% of SPC), Ballast Nedam (15% of SPC) and DEME (15%of SPC)—reached financial close on 17 October 2018. The European Investment Bank provided 50% of the term loan, totaling around €330 million, backed by the European Fund for Strategic Investments (EFSI).

Port investment projects most often concern container and Ro-Ro traffic, which are both expected to grow according to forecasts commissioned by the European Union.

According to a 2018 joint research project between TT Club and McKinsey & Company (TT Club and McKinsey & Company 2018), there were some points of broad consensus on the next 25 years in the container sector. This is considered the most relevant port segment for infrastructure needs in the coming years since containers today transport 23% of dry seaborne trade tons (and close to 100% of everyday goods like televisions, toys, and clothing). According to the study, the physical aspects of the industry (containers, terminals, ships) are unlikely to change; trade flows will become more balanced between and across regions; automation will be broadly adopted; digital, data, and analytics will fundamentally shift the sources of value creation; and the industry's leading players in 2043 may well look very different from today's leading companies (though they may be the same or similar). Industry players can work now to ensure flexibility in the future, including paying more attention to the dynamics around the end-consumer (as e-commerce disrupts retail and last-mile logistics), building organizational discipline around monitoring the "trigger points" behind different futures, and radically digitizing and automating. Autonomous technologies available today and in the not-too-distant future are extremely promising for the industry. There remains an exceptional learning curve in terms of adopting these technologies and maximizing their value.

European ports are facing several challenges that have a major impact on the requirements for infrastructure investments:

- New trends in the maritime industry (in the container market vessel sizes are augmenting, increasing market power through alliances);

- Digitalization and automation;
- The decarbonization agenda, building resilience to climate change and the overall greening of vessels.

The consequences of these macro-trends are complex and consequently there are many more requirements for developing new and adapting existing port infrastructure than simply expanding capacity.

The liner shipping industry witnessed further consolidation through mergers and acquisitions and global alliance restructuring. Three global liner shipping alliances dominate the capacity deployed on the three major east–west container routes, collectively accounting for 93% of all deployed capacity. Alliance members continue to compete on price while operational efficiency and capacity utilization gains are helping to maintain low freight rate levels. By joining forces and forming alliances, carriers have strengthened their bargaining power vis-à-vis seaports when negotiating port calls and terminal operations. Alliance restructuring and larger vessel deployment are also redefining the organization of the market: selection of ports of call, the configuration of liner shipping networks, the distribution of costs and benefits between container shipping and ports, and approaches to container terminal concessions. In particular, within ports, the buying power of the alliance carriers can create destructive competition between terminal operators and other port service providers, such as towage companies. This can lower the rates of return on investment for the port industry, resulting in the decline of minor container ports and the disappearance of smaller independent terminal operators.

ICT and digital infrastructures account for 4% of the projects submitted by port authorities, according to a 2018 ESPO study (ESPO 2018). Digital infrastructures, mainly Port Community Systems (PCS), enable smooth data exchange. A PCS makes intelligent and secure exchange of information possible between public and private stakeholders by allowing a single submission of data which becomes available for (selected) third parties to optimize, manage and automate port and logistics processes (e.g. documentation for exports, imports, hazardous cargo, ship manifest information, port health formalities and maritime statistic reporting). Thus, digital infrastructure is aimed at eliminating unnecessary paperwork (which can cause delays in cargo handling), improved security, cutting costs and greater environmental sustainability, thanks to the reduction of emissions due to better utilization of assets (e.g. less empty trucking). An example is NxtPort, a data-sharing platform in the Port of Antwerp. NxtPort collects and shares data across a number of actors (including shippers, forwarders, ship's agents, carriers, terminals, insurance brokers, among many others) in order to increase participants' operational efficiency, safety, and revenue. Another example is TradeLens, a new company owned 51% by Maersk and 49% by IBM. The digital joint venture was created at the beginning of 2018 with the aim of providing a platform connecting a large number of stakeholders in the industry, thereby covering each stage of the transportation process from shippers to ports and terminals to national authorities.

Of the various technology trends expected to contribute to operational efficiency in port areas in the long term, autonomous driving is unique. In fact, the ability of autonomous driving to have a significant impact on total cost of ownership (TCO) makes this technology a game-changer that has the potential to spur industry consolidation in some specific context (container and Ro-Ro terminals). Container terminals have been a laboratory for automation since 2000, when Rotterdam inaugurated the first terminal with a fully autonomous distribution system from shore to stock areas. But the greatest savings can be obtained if the role of autonomous equipment could be extended outside of terminal area as well. The trajectory toward full autonomy in the port sector is long—more than 20 years before trucks are expected to drive on the road to and from ports fully autonomously. However, first use cases are expected to hit the market within the next few years on some selected routes where autonomous driving and platooning (with driver on leading truck) will contribute to concrete operational efficiency. Still, there are many open questions (e.g., the legal framework, technological redundancy). On top of that, the autonomous driving playing field will be far from even. Smaller terminal operators will find it more difficult to obtain the necessary resources, and the potential entrance of new, technology-driven market players will intensify competition.

Stricter requirements on environmental performance and the uptake of alternative fuels (e.g. LNG and eventually hydrogen) could offer new opportunities in order to enlarge the spectrum of services offered by port terminals operators. The Directive on the deployment of alternative fuels infrastructure requires all maritime ports of the TEN-T Core network to be equipped with LNG refuelling points by 2025. Under the same Directive, Onshore Power Supply should be installed as a priority in these ports, and in other ports by 2025, unless there is no demand and the costs are disproportionate to the benefits. Some of the investment needs of ports are driven by international (IMO), EU and national environmental regulations; the need to invest in adequate waste reception facilities being one example. According to the 2018 Fraunhofer Institute study entitled "Digitalization of Seaports," (Fraunhofer et al. 2018) despite today's reluctance to deploy LNG more often in shipping, use of this alternative fuel will become more common, and require specific port investments. The main explanation for this is related to environmental regulations, but there are also technical reasons due to the high degree of reliability and the low maintenance needs of LNG engines. A comprehensive LNG bunkering network is established in the North and the Baltic Seas. Barge shuttle LNG between the LNG import terminals and the berths within the ports where the vessels are bunkered. There will also be installations in ports, supplying the vessels with electric energy. Depending on the specifics in the country and the costs of electric energy, this may also involve LNG PowerPacs and barges as electric energy suppliers. Feeder ships as well as some tugboats will use batteries or diesel-electric engines.

3.4.3 Railways

After having completed the liberalization process in the long-distance bus sector,[12] the passenger rail market is the only major EU transport sector where the process is still incomplete (UNECE 2018). Therefore, the expectations to see new entrants in the market and the necessity of new infrastructure investments are high.

A number of recent developments in EU policies, such as liberalization programs and environmental regulations, will enhance the role of railways in the transport sector. These initiatives are already leading to an upgrade in the quality and choice of services available, more responsiveness to customer needs, and greater economies of scale. Moreover, these trends are boosting the competitiveness of the railway sector by significantly reducing costs and lightening the administrative burden on railway stakeholders.

Between 2001 and 2016, four legislative packages were adopted with the aim of gradually opening up rail transport service markets for competition, making national railway systems inter-operable and defining appropriate framework conditions for the development of a single European railway area. These include charging and capacity allocation rules, common provisions on the licensing of railway undertakings and train driver certification, safety requirements, the creation of the European Agency for railways and rail regulatory bodies in each member state, as well as rail passenger rights.

The Fourth Railway Package is a set of six legislative texts designed to complete the single market for rail services (Single European Railway Area). Its overarching goal is to revitalize the rail sector and make it more competitive vis-à-vis other modes of transport. It comprises two 'pillars' which have been negotiated largely in parallel: the technical pillar and the market pillar. The first was adopted by the European Parliament and Council in April 2016, while the market pillar was adopted in December 2016. The market pillar is considered the most important one for the growth of the railway market because it will complete the process of gradually opening the market, a process which started with the First Railway Package. This pillar establishes the general right for railway undertakings established in one member state to operate all types of passenger services everywhere in the EU, and lays down rules aimed at improving impartiality in the governance of railway infrastructure and preventing discrimination; this pillar also introduces the principle of mandatory tendering for public service contracts in rail. Competition in rail passenger service markets will encourage railway operators to become more responsive to customer needs, improve the quality of their services and their cost-effectiveness. Competitive tendering of public service contracts will enable savings of public money for operations that could be used for investments. The market pillar

---

[12]Regulation (EC) No 1073/2009 on common rules for access to the international market for coach and bus services.

is expected to deliver more choice and better quality of rail services for European citizens, these being the overriding objectives.

The market pillar regulations and directives deal with common rules for rail operator accounts (REG 2016/2337/EU), competitive tendering for public service rail contracts (REG 2016/2338/EU), and full opening of the domestic passenger market (DIR 2016/2370/EU). EU member states have until December 2018 to transpose the Directives into national legislation.

The opening of the rail passenger market has been pursued by several EU countries in advance of the legal deadlines imposed by EU law, to different degrees and with varying results. New commercial (open access) services have been introduced in the Czech Republic, Germany, Italy, Austria, Sweden and the United Kingdom. While the reasons for success or failure in operating a new rail business are diverse, a common trait is that, in the absence of safeguards against unfair practices, new entrants face serious obstacles.

In 2018, the sector was still heavily concentrated, and characterized by a low number of newcomers and the persistence of large market shares of incumbent operators. But in the coming years the completion of relevant infrastructure projects and the progress of liberalization programs at EU level will contribute to a proliferation of new services. For instance, in 2017 both Italian high-speed railways operators (Trenitalia and Italo—Nuovo Trasporto Viaggiatori) obtained from the UK Department for Transport the "UK Rail Franchising PQQ Passport." The Passport allows the company to participate to tenders regarding rail transport throughout the UK.

Trenitalia Industrial Plan 2017–2026 emphasizes the perspective role of strengthening existing cross-border relationships (for example the Thello services to France, the Venice–Ljubljana–Belgrade service or new traffic with Switzerland following the opening of the Gotthard and Ceneri base tunnels). Also key is the introduction of new services on the most potentially lucrative European routes: Paris–Brussels, Paris–Bordeaux, Hamburg–Cologne, Milan–Zurich–Frankfurt (a link that started at the end of 2017 crossing three countries), Athens–Salonica (thanks to the purchase of Trainose) and London–Edinburgh. All of this is thanks to the liberalization of European railways, which will start in 2020 with the Fourth Railway Package.

In this new context, some national operators have already adopted low-cost strategies in order to be able to compete against new potential rivals and increase the market volume: French SNCF Ouigo and Spanish Renfe's EVA are two examples. Also, private operators such as German Locomore, now owned by Flixbus, tried to find a place in the high-speed rail market following a low-cost strategy.

Box 3.6 The Italian Experience in the High-speed Railway Service Competition

The potential of modern long-distance railway services has been underscored by the Italian market, where traffic on the high-speed line between Torino and Salerno surged from approximately 15 million of passengers per year in 2009 up to 41 million in 2017 after the completion of the high-speed line and the entrance of the new railway operator Italo—NuovoTrasportoViaggiatori. This private Italian rail company competed directly with the incumbent, and has drastically reduced its operational costs, turning into a lighter cost structure. Italo has achieved a cost per available seat kilometer (CASK) of four-euro cents, lower than the main European low-cost airlines.[13]

Thanks to higher load factors due to demand growth and a more efficient commercial business model, between 2009 and 2017, national rail ticket prices have dropped by almost 40%. Travelers can find price competitive rail tickets. This is exactly what happened in the airline industry: a competitive market can drive down prices, cut journey times and improve the rail customer experience.

Thanks to EU railways liberalization the market will assist to new organizational models and new technologies implemented by railways operators and these trends will generate new demand of long-distance journeys that will partially change the target of the main central station of the major metropolitan area at EU level and increase the value of the commercial areas in and around central stations. Moreover, new high-tech depots will be necessary to repair and maintain the new high-speed trains. This type of infrastructure (stations and depots) could be an interesting infrastructure asset for concession holding companies or for public-private partnership contracts, as was the case in the airport sector. Madrid Chamartin, London St. Pancreas and Roma Termini are among the most interesting examples of new generation railways stations, where private investors were able to increase commercial and advertising revenues and generate efficiency through economies of scales and specialization in order to create value for shareholders and for transport users. An interesting example of this type of long-term investment is the one carried out by Antin Infrastructure Partners in Grandi Stazioni Retail. This company operates the long-term leasehold providing exclusive rights to the commercial leasing and advertising spaces of the 14 largest Italian railway stations. Other examples are investments by Ceetrus, prior to June 2018 known as Immochan, for Gare du Nord in Paris and for Vigo Viala in Spain.

---

[13]The revenue for available seat-kilometer (RASK) in 2017 was six-euro cents; therefore, Italo generated a high margin thanks to low costs. The Global Infrastructure Partners Fund (GIP) completed the acquisition of Italo in April 2018. The CASK for Easyjet in 2016 was 6.44 euro cents, according to Easyjet Annual Report.

3.5 The Role of the Political Context at European Level

Transport investment priorities at EU level are strictly related to general EU strategies and sectoral policies. In fact, transport is considered a cornerstone of European integration and is firmly linked to the establishment of the single market. As one of the first common policy areas of today's European Union (EU), transport was seen as vital for fulfilling three of the four freedoms of a common market as established in the Treaty of Rome in 1957: the free movement of individuals, services and goods. Without smooth transport connections and networks, there would be no such movement. This is why EU transport policy has always focused on overcoming obstacles between member states and creating a single European transport area with fair competition conditions for and between the different forms of transport: road, rail, air and water. The main challenges for the transport sector in the EU include creating a modern, multi-modal and safe transport infrastructure network, and transitioning towards low-emission mobility, which also involves reducing other negative externalities of transport.

The following sub-sections will be dedicated to a summary of the main goals of the EU infrastructure and decarbonization policies. Also discussed is the role of the European Investment Bank (EIB) as the enabler to reach these goals and to increase public–private partnerships in the EU transport infrastructure sector (Regele 2018).

3.5.1 The EU Infrastructure Policy

The European Union has a tradition spanning more than 20 years (starting with the entry into force of the Maastricht Treaty in November 1993) of transport infrastructure policy with the goal of connecting the continent from East to West, North to South. The specific aims are to close the gaps between member states' transport networks, remove bottlenecks that still hamper the smooth functioning of the internal market and overcome technical barriers such as incompatible standards for railway traffic. EU policy promotes and strengthens seamless transport chains for passenger and freight, while keeping up with the latest technological trends such as European Rail Traffic Management System (ERMTS) in the railway sectors and the use of the Galileo satellite system.

In the 2014–2020 period, the budget for the Connecting Europe Facilities (CEF) program dedicated to transport was €23 billion. This, in combination with funds from other EU sources and the European Investment Bank, should stimulate investments and ensure the successful implementation of the new infrastructure policy. The focus on environmentally friendly transport will improve the sustainability of transport systems in Europe. Selected projects are mostly concentrated on the strategic sections of Europe's transport network (the "core network") to ensure the highest EU added-value and impact. The largest portion of the funding has been already devoted to developing the European rail network (for projects like the Brenner or Lyon-Turin transalpine basis tunnels), decarbonizing and upgrading road transport, developing Intelligent Transport Systems and deploying Air Traffic Management (ATM) systems.

The European Commission proposal for the 2021–2027 budget for CEF Transport is €30.6 billion, including a general envelope of €12.8 billion, and a Cohesion Fund (CF) allocation of €11.3 billion. In addition, the Commission proposed that the Union enhance its strategic transport infrastructures to make them fit for military mobility. A dedicated budget of €6.5 billion has been established through the Connecting Europe Facility, therefore the proposed total budget for core and comprehensive European networks will be €37.1 billion, €14.1 billion more than the previous program (+61%). In the member states whose gross national income (GNI) per inhabitant is less than 90% of the EU average, the CEF general funds can be integrated with the Cohesion Fund (CF). The CF focuses on transport and environment infrastructure. With regard to transport, it can support the Trans-European transport networks (TEN-T) or other priority projects of European interest, as identified by the EU (such as development of rail transport or reinforcement of public transport).

3.5.2 The Role of the Decarbonization Program

The European Commission Transport White Paper (European Commission 2011) set a target of 60% lower greenhouses gases GHG emissions by 2050 compared to 1990 (or −70% compared to 2008) with the aim to be "firmly on the path towards zero." Also, the EU's recent general policies confirmed Europe's path to low carbon economy and the ambition of becoming the world leader in renewable energy, growing the markets for EU-produced goods and services, for instance in the field of energy efficiency.[14] According to this general principle, in the transport sector the EU proposed a strategy for low-emission mobility[15] that should make an important contribution to modernizing the EU economy, helping to reduce emissions from the transport sector and meeting the EU's commitments under the Paris Agreement. EU investment instruments are geared towards supporting higher efficiency of the transport system in a technology neutral way, low-emission alternative energy for transport and low- and zero-emissions vehicles.

The investments dedicated to decarbonization will become more and more relevant, especially after April 2018 when the United Nations International Maritime Organization (IMO) adopted an initial strategy for reducing greenhouse gas

---

[14]The EU became the first major economy to present its climate plan (i.e. Intended Nationally Determined Contribution or "INDC") on 6 March 2015, reflecting the 2030 climate and energy policy framework set by the October 2014 European Council and the European Commission's blueprint for tackling global climate change beyond 2020 (The Paris Protocol – A blueprint for tackling global climate change beyond 2020, COM (2015) 81 final).

[15]A European Strategy for Low-Emission Mobility, COM (2016) 501 and "Delivering on low-emission mobility: A European Union that protects the planet, empowers its consumers and defends its industry and workers" COM/2017/0675.

emissions from ships, setting out a vision to reduce GHG emissions from international shipping. More than one hundred nations agreed to peak GHG emissions from international shipping as soon as possible and to reduce the total annual GHG emissions by at least 50% by 2050 compared to 2008. At the same time, these countries committed to pursuing efforts towards phasing them out as called for in the vision as a milestone on a pathway of CO_2 emissions reduction consistent with the Paris Agreement temperature goals. As an example, in this context the establishment of LNG refueling points across the TEN-T corridors and at maritime ports is one of the public-private partnership investments strongly supported by EU general policies, CEF program and European Investment Bank (EIB) instruments.

The Cleaner Transport Facility (CTF) is a new initiative launched in December 2016 by the EIB and European Commission (EC) to assist investments, by both public and private entities, in cleaner transport projects through existing EIB products and new financial instruments. The objective of the CTF is to support the accelerated deployment of cleaner transport vehicles and help meet their associated infrastructure needs. The CTF is an umbrella that deploys the EIB's technical and financial capacity to adapt to specific market needs in order to explore viable business models and boost opportunities to finance cleaner transport with EIB loans covering up to 50% of the project costs. Public and private entities can be borrowers e.g. public transport authorities/operators, leasing companies, vehicle manufacturers, or infrastructure operators/managers.

3.5.3   The Role of the European Investment Bank as an Early Mover in More Innovative Sectors

The European Investment Bank (EIB) provides financing on favorable terms and with maturities sometimes exceeding 30 years, helping confidence-building and encouraging other private and public investment, through the risk mitigation and more visibility of the project in question. Transport is by far the largest sector in which the EIB has been active since its foundation. The role of the EIB in the transport sector also encompasses addressing a number of market failures, related in particular to the non-internalization of positive externalities of the underlying projects by private financiers. In concrete terms, these failures manifest themselves in a relative scarcity of financing, in particular equity funding, for innovative projects for the decarbonization and digitalization of transport, for instance. The EIB's role is also to be an early mover in more innovative segments; this may help to reduce the risk perception of these market segments and unlock interest from other investors as well. In sum, the EIB acts as an important anchor investor to attract other financiers in order to reach a higher multiplier effect of the investment.

The EIB mix of financial instruments for supporting the EU transport policy include also the European Fund for Strategic Investments (EFSI), which is a jointly launched initiative by the EIB Group and the European Commission to help overcome the current investment gap in the EU. EFSI operations aim to mobilize private investment in projects which are strategically important for the EU. For instance, backed by the European Fund for Strategic Investments (EFSI), the EIB is supporting the Dutch Blankenburg Connection PPP project for the completion of the port access in Rotterdam.[16]

The Loan Guarantee Instrument for Trans-European Transport Network Projects (LGTT) is another innovative financial instrument set up and developed jointly by the European Commission and the European Investment Bank (EIB) which aims at facilitating greater participation of the private sector involvement in the financing of Trans-European Transport Network infrastructure ("TEN-T"). The LGTT has been signed by a limited number of motorway projects, maritime projects, high speed rail PPP projects. The Advisory Services Department of the European Investment Bank serves 41 European PPP Expertise Centre (EPEC) member organizations. These organizations are typically national or regional PPP units, and other public entities in charge of PPPs, as well as the European Commission. Therefore, the EIB has a leading role in supporting and favoring private investments in transport infrastructure sector at European level.

Among the most recent EFSI operations in the transport sector is an investment in a European Infrastructure Fund and in the private investment plans for Portuguese ports, both completed in March 2018. The latter is presented in Box 3.7.

Box 3.7 An Example of EFSI Operation: The Private Investment Plan for Portuguese Ports 2017–2019

The EIB supports a project for upgrading and expanding two port terminals in Portugal. This project contributes to the EU and EFSI policy objective to develop strategic transport projects including on the TEN-T, as the investments are located in the ports of Leixoes and Lisbon, which are part of the core TEN-T port network and nodes in the Atlantic TEN-T Core Network Corridor. This operation will have positive impacts on the environment by supporting maritime transport, in particular short sea shipping, as an alternative to other less sustainable transport modes, promoting intermodal transport and in particular improving rail accesses to the ports. Additionally, the port of Leixoes is located in a less-developed region of Portugal and as such the projects contribute to economic, social and territorial cohesion by creating temporary jobs during construction, direct jobs for the port operations and indirect employment by enhancing the competitiveness of the Portuguese industry supply chain. The project responds to a market failure by reducing the negative externalities of transport and addresses a sub-optimal investment situation. In fact, the counterparty for this operation, Yilport Iberia S.A., new to the EIB, is constrained by the limited sources of financing available from commercial banks for long-term asset financing in Portugal. The EIB's financing of this project would also constitute a strong signal of the bank's

(continued)

---

[16]The innovative DBFM innovative project is described in Box 3.5.

> **Box 3.7** (continued)
>
> support of the port sector in Portugal, in the context of the "Port Competitiveness Strategy 2026" presented by the Portuguese Ministry of the Sea, which anticipates investments in excess of €2.1 billion until 2026. EIB support is considered crucial to address the persistent under-investment in the sector, which has led to capacity bottlenecks.

3.6   The Potential Implications for Long-term Financial Investors

Transport infrastructure investments are often large, capital-intensive projects that have significant up-front costs, but the benefits or returns accrue over very long periods of time, often many decades. This longevity (and the associated difficulty of ascertaining adequate returns over such a long horizon) can pose a challenge to private financing and provision. Strong focus on reducing potential inefficiencies in the investment process, such as poor project selection, implementation, and monitoring, is therefore crucial in order to avoid nonproductive infrastructure, to limit the long-term output gains, and to prevent an unclear balance between private and public expenditures. This chapter focused on the future developments in the transport infrastructure sector in the perspective of the European context. The aim is to contribute to a better understanding of some of the major megatrends affecting the sector that could have potential implications for long-term private financial investors.

The main growth drivers in transport infrastructure sector are related to social, technological, organizational and political aspects and can be summarized as follow:

- Long-term demographic trends are differentiated among EU countries (and among regions in the main countries); therefore, the impact on mobility growth will be differentiated as well. This calls for context-specific analysis.
- Regional disparities in the adoption of new technologies and the skill level of the workforce will further deepen regional and urban/rural differences. This trend will be reflected in disposable income and mobility indicators, favoring mobility trends in major metropolitan areas.
- Intra-EU and Extra-EU mobility (both passengers and freight) is growing at higher rates compared to national and regional movement, shaping new infrastructure demand on international gates: airports, terminals at main ports (for containers, dry bulk goods and cruise ships), and intermodal links to the main nodes.
- Opportunities coming from new technologies (automation, PCS, Egates, etc) and alternative fuels (electricity and LNG) will require specific investments in order to

facilitate the innovations required by competitive dynamics and new EU and international laws.

- New source of revenues could come from extending the role of transport nodes with value added services (new types of intermodal links that will extend the catchment area like people movers or intermodal junctions, or home bag-drop services).

Emphasis should also be given to potential synergies between the energy, transport and telecom sectors as discussed by Venzin and Konert (2020) in Chap. 5, in particular as regards the deployment of alternative fuels in the first two fields. To mention a few examples here, new grids needed for e-charging, 5G deployment for future automation of transport, new storage in fuel cells and hydrogen for security of supply and storage of alternative energy. All these can be made available to transport. Besides investments in hard infrastructure, attention also needs to be given to the various questions of digitialization, vertical and horizontal commercial organization and implementation of value-added services, through harmonization of operational rules and close cooperation between operators.

Other trends with a major impact on revenues and profits of the entire industry in the coming years will be the trajectory of oil prices, the implementation of fuel efficiency requirements (CO2), and new emission regulations regarding NOx and particulates, especially at local level (in major urban areas). Additional investment costs for emission compliance and fuel efficiency programs could raise the operational costs of transport operators and reduce potential demand, especially in lower price segments. These factors could also amplify regional and urban-rural differences, and could also be reflected in mobility indicators.

As a summary of the implications for the industry and its ecosystem of the game changers analyzed in this chapter, long-term transport infrastructure investors have two sources of value creation:

- to increase operational efficiency at both node and link level, and
- to succeed in capturing new opportunities in order to enlarge the spectrum of services offered by infrastructure operators.

While cost programs have been a core element of the transport industry for many years, new technologies (e.g., from digitization, automation and artificial intelligence) continue to provide potential for cost optimization along the full value chain, especially in ports and airports. Besides simply raising profitability, a focus on operational efficiency is also vital to finance required investments into new opportunities that may, for instance, come from a new regulatory framework, like the liberalization process at EU level in the railways sector or decarbonization programs throughout the entire industry.

References

Airbus. (2018). *Global market forecast (GMF) for 2018–2037*. Toulouse: Airbus.

Barbiellini, A. F., Gomellini, M., & Piselli, P. (2018). *Il contributo della demografia alla crescita economica: Duecento anni di storia italiana*. Occasional Papers, Banca d'Italia, Rome.

Boeing. (2018). *Commercial market outlook 2018–2037*. Seattle: Boeing.

ESPON EGTC. (2019) *A territorial reference framework for Europe* (Final Report). Brussels.

Eurocontrol. (2018). *Challenges of growth: European aviation in 2040*. Brussels: Eurocontrol.

European Commission. (2011). *Roadmap to a Single European Transport Area – Towards a competitive and resource efficient transport system* (White Paper, COM/2011/0144 final). Brussels.

European Commission Economic and Financial Affairs. (2017). *The 2018 ageing report. Underlying assumptions & Projection methodologies* (Institutional Papers 065). Brussels.

European Commission Economic and Financial Affairs. (2018). *The 2018 ageing report. Economic & budgetary projections for the 28 EU Member States (2016–2070)* (Institutional Papers 79). Brussels.

European Council on Foreign Relations. (2018). *Blue China: Navigating the maritime silk road to Europe*. Brussels: European Council on Foreign Relations.

European Parliamentary Research Service. (2015). *Tourism and the European Union: Recent trends and policy developments*. Brussels: European Parliamentary Research Service.

European Parliamentary Research Service. (2018). *Global trends to 2035 – Economy and society*. Brussels: European Parliamentary Research Service.

ESPO – European Seaport Organization. (2018). *The infrastructure investment needs and financing challenge of European ports*. Brussels: ESPO.

Fraunhofer Center for Maritime Logistics and Services and Hamburg Port Authority. (2018). *Digitalisation of seaports*. Hamburg.

Gatti, S., & Chiarella, C. (2020). The future of infrastructure investing – Challenges and opportunities for investors and asset managers. In S. Gatti & C. Chiarella (Eds.), *Disruption in the infrastructure sector: Challenges and opportunities for developers, investors and asset managers*. Heidelberg: Springer.

German Federal Government. (2017). *Strategy for automated and connected driving*. Berlin: German Federal Government.

GOAL Consortium. (2013). *Growing older, staying mobile: Transport needs for an ageing society. EU Funded Collaborative Project*. Brussels.

Hofrichter, S. (2017). *The economics of populism: Why populism matters to growth and markets*. Update – Allianz Global Investors, Number 3, Munich.

Institute for Mobility Research. (2017). *The emerging travel patterns of older adults*. Munich: Institute for Mobility Research.

ISFORT. (2017). *Audiomob survey 2017*. Roma: ISFORT.

ISTAT. (2018). *Bilancio demografico nazionale*. Roma: ISTAT.

McKinsey. (2017). *Improving infrastructure outcomes through better capital allocation: Capital projects & infrastructure*. London: McKinsey.

Regele, F. (2018). *Infrastructure investments*. London: Springer.

Roumboutsos, A., Voordijk, H., & Pantelias, A. (2018). *Funding and financing transport infrastructure. Business models to enhance and enable financing of infrastructure in transport*. London: Routledge.

Sacco, F. (2020). The evolution of the telecom infrastructure business. In S. Gatti & C. Chiarella (Eds.), *Disruption in the infrastructure sector: Challenges and opportunities for developers, investors and asset managers*. Heidelberg: Springer.

Satta, G., Parola, F., Musso, E., & Vitellaro, F. (2020). Financial operators in port infrastructures: Typologies, objectives and global strategies. In M. Wilmsmeier (Ed.), *Geographies of maritime transport*. Cheltenham: Edward Elgar Publishing.

TT Club & McKinsey & Company. (2018). *Brave new world. Container transport in 2043.* London.

UK Department for Transport. (2015). *The pathway to driverless cars: Summary report and action plan.* London.

UN- United Nations. (2017). *World population prospects.* New York: UN- United Nations.

UN- United Nations. (2018). *World urbanization prospects.* New York: UN- United Nations.

UNCTAD – United Nation Conference on Trade and Development. (2018a). *World investment report.* Geneva: UNCTAD.

UNCTAD – United Nation Conference on Trade and Development. (2018b). *Review of maritime transport.* Geneva: UNCTAD.

UNECE – United Nations Economic Commission for Europe. (2018). *Railway reform in the ECE region.* Geneva: UNECE.

UNWTO – United Nation World Tourism Organisation. (2018). *Annual report, 2017.* Madrid: UNWTO.

UNWTO – United Nation World Tourism Organisation and the Directorate-General for Internal Market, Industry, Entrepreneurship and SMEs (DG GROW) of the European Commission. (2018). *European union tourism trends.* Brussels.

Venzin, M., & Konert, E. (2020). The disruption of the infrastructure industry: Coming changes in investment decisions and how to prepare for them. In S. Gatti & C. Chiarella (Eds.), *Disruption in the infrastructure sector: Challenges and opportunities for developers, investors and asset managers.* Heidelberg: Springer.

The Evolution of the Telecom Infrastructure Business

4

Unchartered Waters Ahead of Great Opportunities

Francesco M. Sacco

4.1　The Converging Evolution of Telecommunications

If it is true that "you could not step twice into the same river" (Heraclitus[1]), by supporting the evolution of the Internet, telecom infrastructure is transforming itself, to ultimately become part of the river, resembling the very nature of the Internet. But what actually is the nature of the Internet?

The Internet is at the dawn of the digitization era, where everything and everyone will be connected everywhere. Most of our daily tasks will be automated, our lives will be simplified and our decision making improved. It will be challenging to stay disconnected and live a normal life. This will not be the final stage of Internet evolution but, as argued by Steve Case (2016), the beginning of the third Internet era.

The first Internet era was defined by the building of the Internet infrastructure (1985–2000), a very creative period of pioneers who laid the foundations for everything that followed, linking content online with a URL and making it discoverable. During the second wave (2000–2015), mostly consumer centric, the focus turned from connecting people to creating new ways for them to access information, leveraging the smartphone revolution, a seamless integration of hardware, software and services which unleashed the app economy. Companies like Google and Facebook were able to develop on top of the Internet infrastructure to create search and social networking capabilities, while apps like WhatsApp and Snapchat became the most successful smartphone companions. The third era, or wave, is on the way. It will be characterized by a period in which the Internet is integrated into every aspect of everyday life, in increasingly ubiquitous ways. This

---

[1]As quoted by Plato in Cratylus, 402a.

F. M. Sacco (✉)
Insubria University, Varese, Italy

SDA Bocconi, Milano, Italy
e-mail: francesco@francescosacco.com

© Springer Nature Switzerland AG 2020　　　　　　　　　　　　　　　87
S. Gatti, C. Chiarella (eds.), *Disruption in the Infrastructure Sector*, Future of
Business and Finance, https://doi.org/10.1007/978-3-030-44667-3_4

will vastly transform most of the major "real world" sectors like entertainment, health, education, transportation, energy, financial services, food and other industries representing the largest part of the world economy.

However, the Internet is the most unintended telecommunication success. Its achievements represent a revolution that happened despite the efforts of telecom companies to harness it, only to end up being ruled and transformed by it.

During the first Internet wave, the telecom infrastructure was the critical and exclusive gateway enabling slow, painful access to a world of marvels online under the standard telecom paradigm of circuit switching. In circuit switching, two telephones (or two computers) establish a communication channel (circuit) through the network before they can communicate. The circuit works as if the telephones were physically connected. This direct "like" connection guarantees that the full bandwidth of the channel is dedicated only to the call, and remains connected for the duration of the communication session. Circuit switching is relatively inefficient since the communication channel is reserved whether or not the connection is used. But it has the advantage of ensuring the best possible quality to the communication, given the available resources. Accordingly, during the first Internet wave a dial-up Internet connection allowed users to navigate or to talk over the phone, but not to do both unless they had a second and very expensive dedicated data line.

In the second wave, the "always on" imperative forced telecom providers to change the underpinning communication technology from circuit switching to packet switching. In packet switching every communication is split into small pieces, called packets, transmitted through the network independently. Each packet is labelled with its destination address and a sequence number for ordering it in relation to other packets. At the destination, the original message is reassembled based on the packet number to reproduce the original message. In this way, every packet can be routed via a different path and the network bandwidth is shared by packets from multiple competing communication sessions, resulting in a more efficient use of the network but also a potential loss of quality compared to the service guaranteed by circuit switching. But the risk was worth the savings, because network capacity was becoming a scarce resource.

Packet switching saw its first large scale adoption on mobile phones, permitting people to talk on the phone and navigate at the same time, but then spread to the Internet, with application like Skype and to more traditional fixed lines. The technology behind voice over the phone changed, adopting Internet communication standards, splitting the conversation flow into thousands of data packets sent best effort, without any guarantee of any quality of service, over a normal data line using Voice-over-Internet-Protocol (VoIP) technology. This transformation unveiled big opportunities to telco operators along with new services to the final users. But this was also the beginning of the "internetization" of telecom technologies, the inner transformation of the telecom infrastructure, which was adopting more and more solutions and technologies developed or refined by Internet players. From then on, the transformation soon became irreversible.

However, during the upcoming third wave, this evolution of telecom infrastructure will go even further down this path. Telephone exchanges will be converted into data s, telecom equipment will be virtualized on commoditized computer hardware, and traditional network architectures will turn into software-defined networks.

It will be more of a revolution than anything that has ever occurred in the past of telecommunications. As we will illustrate in this section, these developments are needed to serve the rising demand for services that will have a growing number of connected devices, all transmitting more data and requiring higher network quality. Because the importance of telecommunications networks has never been so critical.

4.1.1   A Growing Number of Connected People

If the health of an industry were to be judged only by the demand for its products or services, the outlook for the telecommunications sector could not be better.

First, the potential market for telecommunications—the entire world population—continues to grow, and to no small degree. An average growth rate of 1.2% per year may not look like much, but in 18 years (from 2000 to 2018) it equates to an increase of 1.5 billion people, a total growth of 25% in world population.

Second, in telecommunications, everything else grows even faster. In the same period the number of Internet users rose by 3.8 billion (14% CAGR) and mobile subscriptions by 7.8 billion (15% CAGR), adding more than 4.9 billion mobile-unique users to the telecommunication market (a 13% CAGR). Only fixed-telephone subscriptions have decreased, albeit just by 52 million (–0.7% CAGR, Fig. 4.1).

However, this scenario is destined to last long. Between 2018 and 2022, the world population increase will be 318 million, which means the growth rate will slow to 1% CAGR (a –17% change). Instead, only 621 million Internet users will be added (3.6% CAGR, a 75% drop) and just 605 million mobile subscriptions (1.7% CAGR, an 88% decrease), with 290 million new unique mobile users (1.3% CAGR, –90%). Fixed-telephone subscriptions will continue to decline but at a quicker pace, losing 87 million lines (–2.5% CAGR, decreasing eight times faster).

However, this evolution will not be the same in every country, a fact which will impact the kind of telecom infrastructures that will serve these new potential users. The main reason for this is that there are more people and population grows faster in the poorest countries. While in developed countries, that represent just 17% of the world population, the average growth rate is only 0.4%, in developing countries (83% of world population) it is more than triple (1.4%) and less developed countries, a subset of developing countries that stands for 13% of the world population, see more than six times the growth rate (2.6%). This means that of the total population growth since 2005 (1.1 billion people), about 94% (more than a billion) were not born in the wealthiest and most developed countries. For those populations, being the largest share and occupying the greater part of our planet, the cost of telecommunications infrastructure will be a real issue because fixed broadband networks are far more expensive to implement and have many more constraints than mobile networks.

As a consequence, even if it is true that "the world is going mobile", the imperative "mobile first" means different things in different areas of the world,

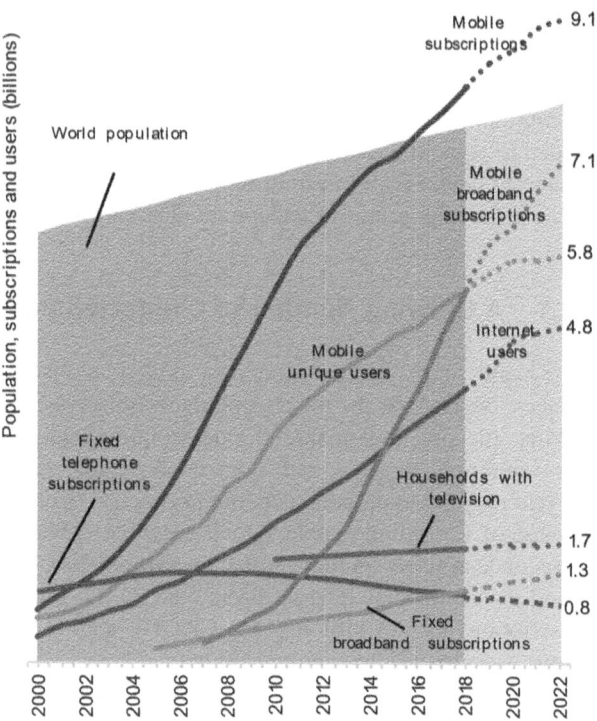

Fig. 4.1 The evolution of the global population, subscriptions and users in telecommunication services (source: World Bank, ITU, GSMA and author's estimations, 2018)

and this will continue to be the case. If at a global level the ratio between mobile broadband users and fixed broadband users in 2018 was 4.9 to 1, this ratio is undoubtedly destined to grow all over the world to create an ever-expanding distance between developing countries and developed countries (Fig. 4.2). In the more prosperous nations of the world, this ratio will be 3.4 mobile users for each user on the fixed network, while developing countries will range from 5.9 to 1, up to 21 to 1 in less developed countries.

These differences are significant not so much for the relative distances that appear among different areas of the world, but for the differences in absolute terms that create incentives for the development of the telecommunication networks of the future. About 17% of the world's population lives in developed countries, where population growth is low, but telecom operators can afford to take on investments in fixed broadband networks even if people are increasingly abandoning fixed telephony. The rest of the world, whose population is still growing at varying rates, will not go through the same model of development in telecommunications as the most developed countries. On the contrary, less developed regions are focusing most of their efforts on developing mobile telecommunications networks or something similar but with a low cost for coverage, such as satellites provide. These fundamental differences are reflected not only in the development plans of telecommunications operators but also in those of telecom equipment producers. Both must decide which

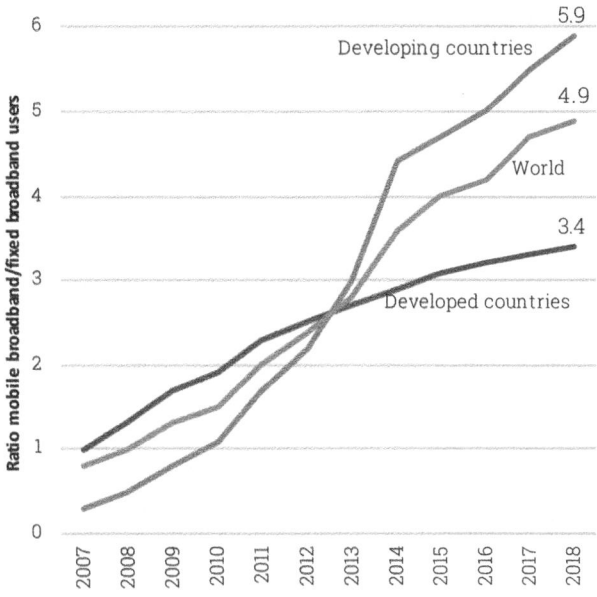

Fig. 4.2 Ratio evolution between mobile broadband and fixed broadband users in developing and developed countries (source: ITU, Global and Regional ICT statistics 2018, https://www.itu.int/en/ITU-D/Statistics/Pages/stat/default.aspx)

direction to push development efforts for new technologies in mobile and that decision will impact on everybody else is interested in the future of Internet services.

4.1.2 A Growing Number of Connected Devices

Telecommunication operators have seen their customer base grow over the last 20 years by more than eight billion subscribers. But, the most significant growth factor for the future will no longer be the number of users, but the number of connected devices owned by each user.

Between 2018 and 2022, more than 22 billion new Internet of Things (IoT) devices will be connected, with an average growth rate of 34% per year. Sensors, cameras, smart speakers, smart lockers and hundreds of other types of devices will accumulate investments of more than 4.6 trillion dollars. Another 10 trillion dollars will be added to this figure between 2023 and 2026, to install more than 31 billion connected devices, reaching an installed base of more than 64 billion devices and an average annual expenditure of 3.3 trillion dollars in 2026 (Fig. 4.3).

This enormous number of devices, once connected, is destined to change many sectors, and indeed our entire world. While the number of annual installations (Fig. 4.4) is expected to skyrocket from the current 1.5 billion in 2018 to 8.3 billion in 2023, the average cost of an installation, which could involve many devices, will decline from 2019 until 2022 thanks to economies of scale. Then, it will rise again due to an expansion in the average size of the installation. This proliferation of IoT devices everywhere and in every aspect of our future life has already begun, but only just. Soon, with a Cambrian explosion creating thousands of new IoT typologies and

Fig. 4.3 IoT installed base
and yearly spending
2016–2026 (source: Business
Insider Intelligence, The
Internet of Things Report
2019)

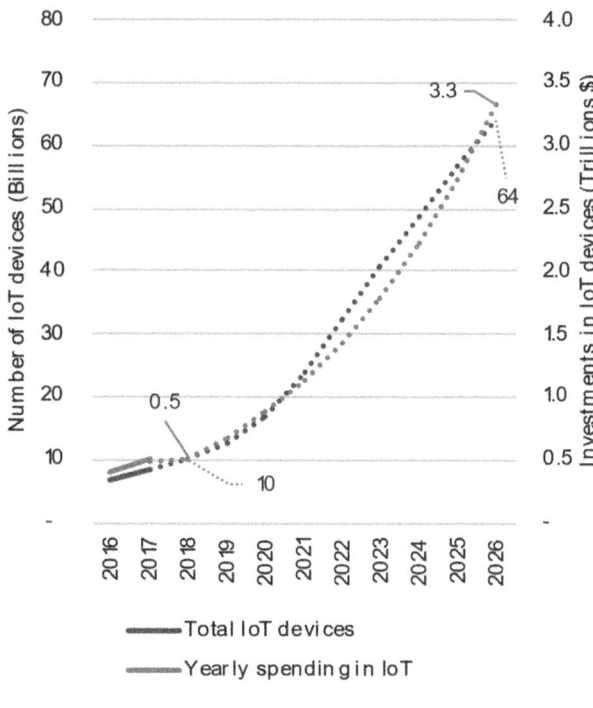

Fig. 4.4 IoT annual
installations and average
yearly spending per
installation 2016–2026
(source: Business Insider
Intelligence, The Internet of
Things Report 2019)

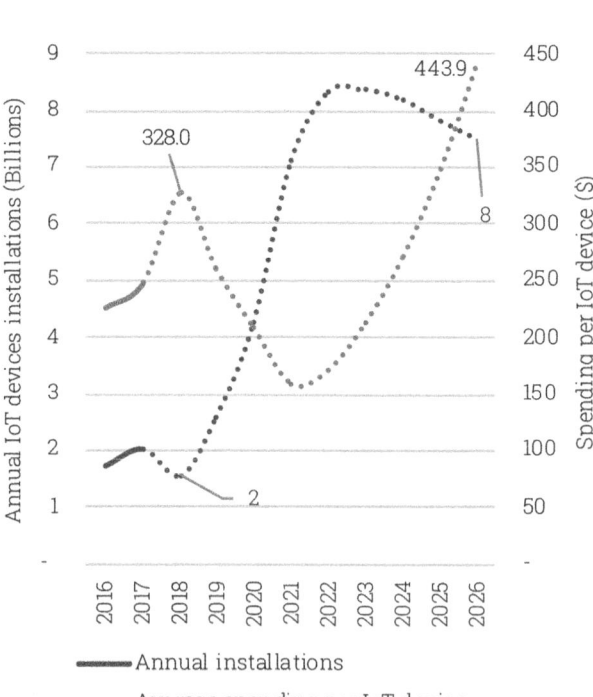

use cases, a long journey will begin that will make these objects more and more intelligent, useful and reliable, thanks to the use of artificial intelligence, new communication technologies and better planning.

IoT devices already power much of the developing data-based economy, and are transforming the relationship between the physical and digital worlds for enterprises, consumers, and governments. Companies are using devices to automate and optimize workflows and decrease labor costs. The most-used types of IoT solutions are remote monitoring devices, asset tracking systems, smart facility management and wearables.

The consumer and business IoT markets differ significantly. The former is made up of the portions of the IoT that serve end users in their homes or personal lives, like smart speakers, smart home devices, smart thermostats or smart lockers, but not only devices. Companies like Samsung and Whirlpool are integrating smart appliances with ecommerce applications, and beginning to build services out of smart home devices.

Governments are investing in creating smart cities using a range of technologies aimed at reducing crime, saving money, facilitating small business and improving environmental conditions. Smart cities leverage IoT devices like connected sensors, lights and meters to gather data to analyze. These data provide insights on infrastructure, population and public services, and enable cities to create efficiencies that affect the lives of their residents, as discussed by Gatti and Chiarella in Chap. 6.

No matter how you look at it, the IoT market is destined to bring great changes, becoming a natural complement of our daily life, just as smartphones are today. On average, on a global scale, we will go from 1.1 IoT devices per capita to 7 in just 8 years. But in many advanced economies, such as the US, growth will be much stronger, going from 2.5 to 26 IoT devices per capita.

This will represent a major challenge for telecommunication infrastructure, especially because this trend is coupled with a skyrocketing number of users, subscribers and devices. As we will see later in this chapter, telecommunication infrastructure should deeply evolve its technology and architecture to acquire the ability to connect and serve these users. But, even if the technical answer to this challenge is very complex, the main result will be simple: a huge growth in data traffic.

4.1.3 A Growing Flow of Data

Overall, Internet traffic will triple from 2017 to 2022, from 122 exabytes[2] (EB) per month to 396 EB by 2022 (Cisco 2018), which represents a CAGR of 26% (Fig. 4.5).

---

[2]An exabyte (EB) is 10^{18} bytes. All words ever spoken by human beings until 2002 (Klinkenborg 2003) could be stored in approximately 5 exabytes of data. An exabyte is formed by one thousand petabyte (PB) and one thousand exabytes (1000 EB) is equal to one zettabyte (ZB).

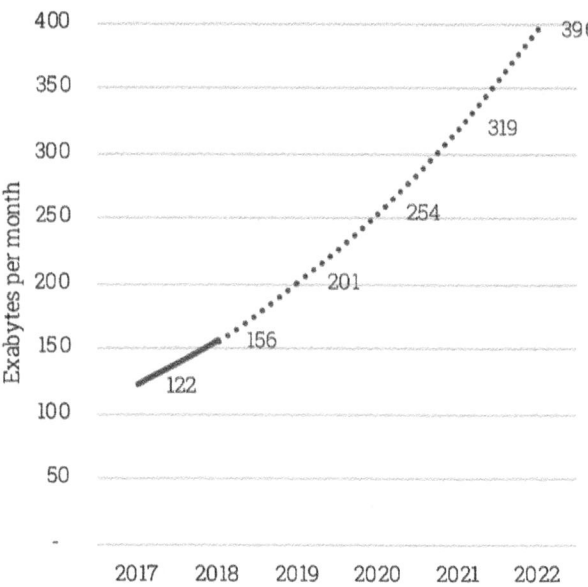

Fig. 4.5 Forecast of Internet traffic per month by 2022 (source: Cisco VNI Global IP Traffic Forecast, 2017–2022, November 2018)

Globally, the per capita increase in Internet traffic has followed a similarly steep growth curve over the past few years. In 2000, per capita Internet traffic was 10 megabytes (MB) per month; in 2007 it was well under 1 gigabytes (GB) per month to reach 16 GB per capita in 2017. This number will top 50 GB per capita by 2022.

Internet traffic continues to proliferate, exceeding all expectations. Indeed, this forecast represents a slight rise over past predictions, which projected a CAGR of 24% from 2016 to 2021 (Cisco 2017), mainly caused by an increase in the share of mobile traffic as a percentage of the total IP traffic.

All this traffic will not be distributed evenly between fixed and mobile networks in different countries; instead there are a variety of models of network usage and device adoption. However, these models are more complex than the simple distinction between developing and developed countries. For example, there is a rising number of nations who have seen a rise in fixed traffic which rivals that of their mobile traffic. The United States is the outlier in this trend, with an upturn in fixed Internet traffic of 26% in 2017 and in mobile of 23% over the same time period. Japan, Korea, Canada, Germany and Sweden, all have fixed growth that is only slightly lower than mobile, but most countries have significantly higher rates for mobile than for fixed connections (Fig. 4.6).

The relationship between fixed and mobile networks is more complex than that of two alternative worlds. When more mobile data is transmitted, this does not necessarily mean more traffic on mobile networks. In fact, just the opposite is true: a continuously increasing part of data traffic, e.g. from smartphones, is offloaded to wifi networks which are connected to wired networks (Fig. 4.7). For this reason, streaming movies or music on mobile devices usually transits on fixed networks, not mobile ones. This offloading role of wifi networks, which became dominant in 2015

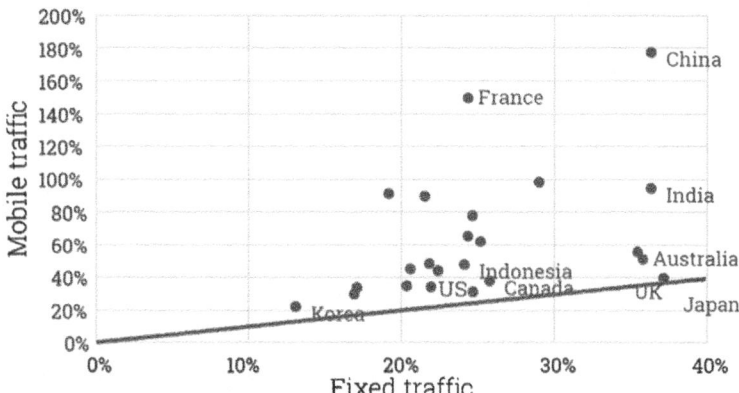

Fig. 4.6 Fixed and mobile Internet traffic growth rates (source: Cisco VNI Global IP Traffic Forecast, 2017–2022, November 2018)

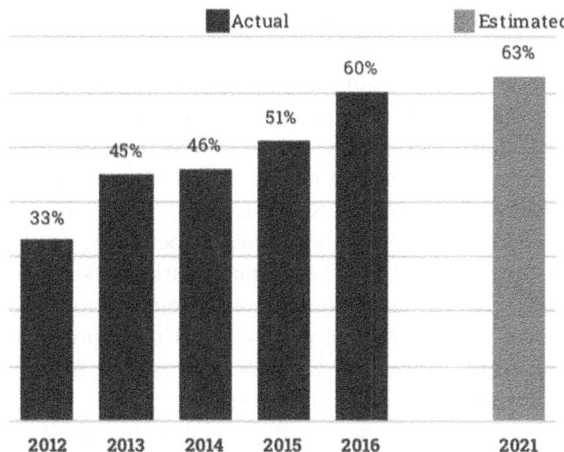

Fig. 4.7 Offloading of mobile traffic to wifi, % of global mobile traffic (source: Cisco VNI Global IP Traffic Forecast, 2017–2022, November 2018 and Venkateshwar et al. 2019a)

and never stopped growing, will top 63% of the global mobile traffic in 2021. In fact, mobile networks could not handle all the data traffic generated by all the mobile devices if it were not for wifi networks, at least not with the current network architecture.

Public wifi networks keep multiplying (Fig. 4.8). Globally, total wifi hotspots (including homespots[3] and public hotspots) will quadruple from 124 million in 2017

---

[3] A homespot is a wifi located at home that can offer connectivity to the public, being part of a network managed by an operator.

Fig. 4.8 Global public wifi hotspots: 2015–2022 (source: Cisco VNI Global IP Traffic Forecast, 2017–2022, November 2018 and Venkateshwar et al. 2019a)

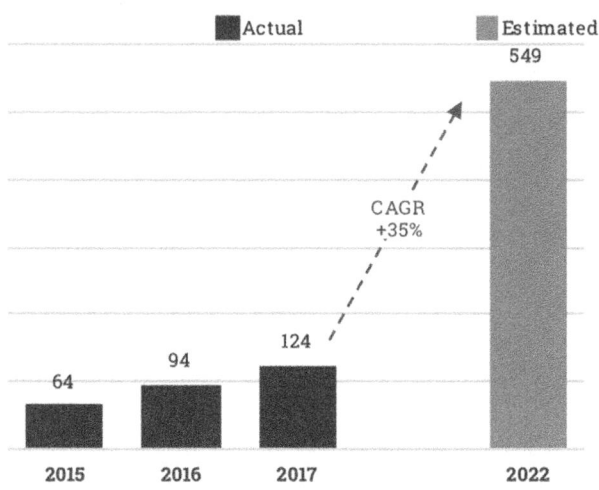

to 549 million by 2022. Hotels, cafes and restaurants will have the highest number of hotspots by then globally, but the fastest growth is in healthcare facilities such as hospitals. This continuous expansion is the reason for the emergence of associations like the Wireless Broadband Alliance (WBA), founded by AT&T, BT, Cisco Systems, Comcast, Intel, KT Corporation, Liberty Global, NTT Docomo and Orange, among others. Together they manage more than 30 million hotspots globally like a consortium. Their goal is to create opportunities for service providers, enterprises and cities to improve customer experience on wifi and similar technologies, but also to eventually serve new markets like IoT. Flexibility and low cost make wifi networks an important cornerstone for mobile users. Although intrinsically unsecure and insufficiently effective at managing interferences, in an environment increasingly dense with wireless devices, wifi networks behave naturally like an infrastructure without really being one.

Globally, the rise in Internet traffic will be higher on mobile networks than on fixed networks (Table 4.1). So, it is not surprising that the percentage of total data transmitted on the move will increase as well. However, fixed network traffic will remain dominant by far, even if its share will decrease slightly, from 85 to 78% of the total. In contrast, consumers, who represent the largest traffic segment, generating 83%, will create even more traffic in the future (27% CAGR between 2017 and 2022) compared to businesses (23% CAGR).

From a geographical point of view, despite becoming the second-fastest growing IP traffic area (surpassed by Latin America) Asia Pacific is—and is destined to remain—the region with the highest share of total Internet traffic in the world, which will go from 38% in 2018 up to 44% in 2022. North America is in second place, with Europe a distant third, where it will stay until 2022. Instead, thanks to its very high growth in Internet traffic, Latin America will replace the Middle East and Africa in the penultimate position.

Table 4.1 Global Internet traffic growth 2017–2022

By type (EB per month)	2018	2022	2018 (%)	2022 (%)	CAGR (2017–2022) (%)
Fixed Internet	107	273	85	78	26
Mobile data	19	77	15	22	46
By Segment (EB per Month)					
Consumer	129	333	83	84	27
Business	27	63	17	16	23
By Geography (EB per Month)					
Asia Pacific	59	173	38	44	32
North America	52	108	33	27	21
Western Europe	22	50	14	13	22
Central and Eastern Europe	10	25	6	6	26
Middle East and Africa	9	19	6	5	21
Latin America	5	21	3	5	41
Total traffic	156	396	100	100	26

Source: Cisco VNI Global IP Traffic Forecast, 2017–2022, November 2018

However, the growth rates of Internet traffic inside these main continental areas reflect only the evolution of their final users' activity. Everyone on the Internet is connected to everyone else, but not all of them are equally important for all the others. At a global level, the volumes of international Internet traffic between geographic areas, no matter the direction, naturally give rise to a ranking of importance depending on the concentration. As shown in Fig. 4.9, it is no surprise that the U.S. and Canada are still the center of the global Internet. In fact, they attract and concentrate the largest share of traffic, measured in terabits per second (Tbps).[4] Although less so than in the past, their central position is still indisputable. These countries are followed by Europe, which is a hub for the Middle East and Africa, with Asia in third place but rapidly rising.

4.1.4 The Evolution of the Consumer Market

This top-down scenario of demand evolution in the telecommunications market would not be complete without adding some apparently marginal details about the ongoing transformation of the telecom infrastructure and its structural components.

The first, and most important, concerns the characteristics of consumer traffic, by far the most important component of the demand for communication services. Not only is consumer demand growing faster than business, this growth applies to both

---

[4]A terabit (Tb) is 10^{12} bit. A terabit is formed by one thousand gigabits (Gb); one thousand terabits (1000 Tb) is equal to one petabit (1 Pb). Usually, download speed is measured in bits and multiples of bits per second (like terabit per second or Tbps), while data storage is measured in bytes and its multiples (like terabyte or TB); a byte is made up of 8 bits.

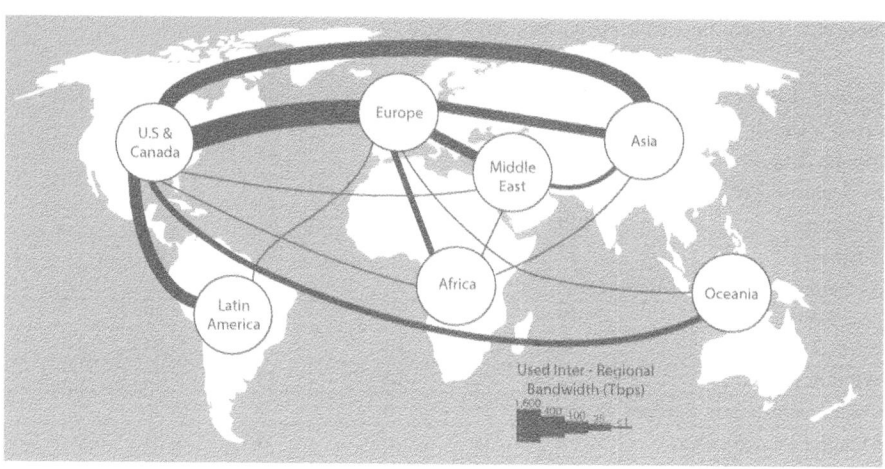

Fig. 4.9 Global inter-regional traffic: Tbps (source: TeleGeography 2019)

Table 4.2 Global consumer Internet traffic growth: 2017–2022

By type (EB per Month)	2018	2022	2018 (%)	2022 (%)	CAGR (2017–2022) (%)
Fixed Internet	86	225	84	77	27
Mobile data	16	68	16	23	47
By Subsegment (EB per Month)					
Internet video	77	240	75	82	34
Web, email, and data	15	31	15	11	22
Online gaming	3	15	3	5	59
File sharing	7	7	7	2	−3
Consumer Internet traffic	102	293	100	100	31

Source: Cisco VNI Global IP Traffic Forecast, 2017–2022, November 2018

fixed and mobile traffic, with the latter rising at almost twice the fixed rate (Table 4.2).

The main source of traffic is—not surprisingly—video, which in 2018 represented about 75% of total traffic. With an average growth rate of 34% (CAGR), in 2022 video will account for 82% of the total, the equivalent of ten billion DVDs per month. In part, this leap will be boosted by the increase in transmission quality. In Ultra-High Definition (UHD or 4K), the bit rate for video streaming runs at about 15–18 Mbps, more than double the HD rate and nine times more than Standard Definition (SD). Given that by 2022 about 62% of the installed flat-panel TV sets will be UHD, up from 23% in 2017 (Cisco 2018), this proliferation of video usage should come as no surprise.

Furthermore, 4K video is not the final step in the evolution of video quality. BS8K, the first broadcast channel in 8K technology (also known as Full UHD or FUHD, requiring double the bit rate of 4K) was launched by the Japanese company NHK on December 1, 2018. This move aimed to begin experimenting in view of the 2020 Summer Olympics in Tokyo, which will be broadcast entirely in 8K. Raising the bar on the average video quality, video traffic is likely to intensify even further.

Apart from video traffic and web browsing, online gaming will be the most important traffic generator, growing ninefold between 2017 and 2022. Gaming on demand (or cloud gaming) and streaming platforms for gamers have been in development for several years, and now they appear to be sufficiently mature from a technological standpoint. In traditional on-console gaming, such as with a PlayStation or Xbox, graphical processing is performed locally on the gamer's console or computer, without creating Internet traffic. With streaming platforms for gamers, instead, the graphics of the game are produced on a remote server and transmitted over the network to the gamer, just like a Netflix video streamed from the cloud to the user. As cloud gaming becomes more and more popular, gaming could turn into one of the largest Internet traffic generators. This would bring with it an important advantage: a powerful ally in the fight against counterfeiting and piracy. This was a winning move in the music industry, and it is succeeding in the movie business too. Case in point is the fact that file sharing is no longer increasing in absolute numbers and in proportion is actually seeing a downturn, from 7 to 2% of the total traffic (−3% CAGR).

Virtual Reality (VR) and Augmented Reality (AR) applications today are still too insignificant to be included in a ranking like the one in Table 4.2, but in the future they could be the biggest potential traffic generators. Indeed, VR and AR are poised to grow 12-fold over the next 5 years (65% CAGR), a promising development that stems mainly from downloads of large virtual reality content files and applications. But this will prove to be a very conservative prediction if virtual reality streaming wins the popularity it deserves.

Another major trend is the fact that busy-hour traffic (defined as traffic in the busiest 60-min period of the day) continues to grow faster than average Internet traffic (calculated as the simple "average" of the Internet traffic during a day), which is quickly losing relevance (Cisco 2018). This phenomenon is noteworthy because service providers plan network capacity according to peak rates rather than average rates, and those two measures are diverging (Fig. 4.10). Between 2017 and 2022, global busy-hour Internet use will grow at a CAGR of 37%, compared with 30% for average Internet traffic, a gap destined to widen more and more.

Again, video is the main underlying reason for accelerated busy-hour traffic growth. Video has a "prime time," unlike other forms of traffic, which are spread almost evenly throughout the day (such as web browsing and file sharing). Because of this video consumption pattern, the Internet now has a much busier busy hour, and Internet traffic at this time will grow faster than average traffic. More specifically, this happens because video, which is gaining traffic share, has a higher peak-to-

Fig. 4.10 Average Internet traffic and busy-hour traffic (source: Cisco VNI Global IP Traffic Forecast, 2017–2022, November 2018)

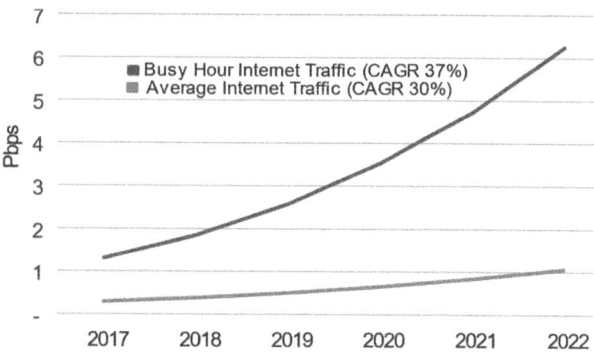

average ratio than data or file sharing. In addition, the composition of Internet video is changing, with more live video, ambient video and video calling; all these uses have a peak-to-average ratio even higher than on-demand video. For telecom operators, this trend will create more demand for faster and more reliable connections. But it also represents a source of pressure for augmenting investments to add network capacity, which is already scarce.

Speed is always a critical factor in Internet traffic, but sometimes for counterintuitive reasons. The Jevons paradox, or the Jevons effect, is well-known in environmental economics: increased efficiency in the use of a resource leads to increased consumption of that resource (e.g. a higher number of fuel-efficient cars leads to more car usage and then greater fuel consumption). This paradox contradicts governments and environmentalists, that generally assume efficiency gains will lower resource consumption, ignoring rebound effects from improved efficiency. But this paradox applies to telecommunication usage as well as to fuel-efficient cars. And in fact, service providers have discovered that users with greater bandwidth generate more traffic. When speed accelerates, users stream and download greater volumes of content. By 2022, around the globe, households with high-speed fiber connectivity will generate 31% more traffic than households connected by xDSL or cable broadband (Cisco 2018). The average fiber-to-the-home (FTTH) household generated 86 GB of traffic per month in 2017, and will produce 264 GB per month by 2022.

From the point of view of telecommunication infrastructures, this means that telco operators must also calculate the rebound effects of their investments, increasing their access to infrastructure more than proportionally compared to past trends after network performance upgrades. On top of this, these operators should also invest more than proportionally to improve the bandwidth of the backhaul connection[5] every time they invest in upgrading the access technology of their networks, migrating for example from ADSL to FTTH. If such upgrades are not monetized at all, or partially monetized, as has happened several times in the past, then the net

---

[5]In a network, the backhaul connection is the portion that includes the intermediate links between the core network, or backbone network, and the access networks (fixed or wireless).

effect for a company investing in improving its network performances will be a decline in profitability. This will be accompanied by reduced network quality (unless additional investments are made to cover the corresponding rebound effects) and, again, lower profitability.

4.2   The Evolution of the Telecom Network as a Consequence of Demand Evolution

It is rare that a product can revolutionize an entire industry. But the iPhone launch in 2007 set in motion a chain of changes that, like a tectonic event, radically transformed the mobile telecommunications landscape. This device converted the "raw material" offered by the industry from voice communication with some messaging and little data, to a data service. Voice and messaging are still offered and promoted separately. However from a technological point of view, they are both a data service wrapped in a different package, although not yet billed as the main service, which is still voice at 52% (Fig. 4.11).

In this industry in which the raw material has completely changed, the network can no longer be taken for granted by its users. In the past the most difficult test for any telephone network was the ability to handle the explosion of calls on Mother's Day. In this new scenario, the busiest day for a network can happen any day. For example, when a new season of a popular series is released and could be watched in streaming, or when a smartphone OS upgrade is made available, or every time there is a new popular event, or a combination of these circumstances. A network today needs to be always ready for reaching a new higher peak (Donovan and Prabhu 2017).

Fig. 4.11 Breakdown of global wireless revenues (source: Bloomberg, Ovum, Company Reports, Barclays Research, 2019). Note: Messaging and data revenues estimated at percentage of total wireless data service revenue

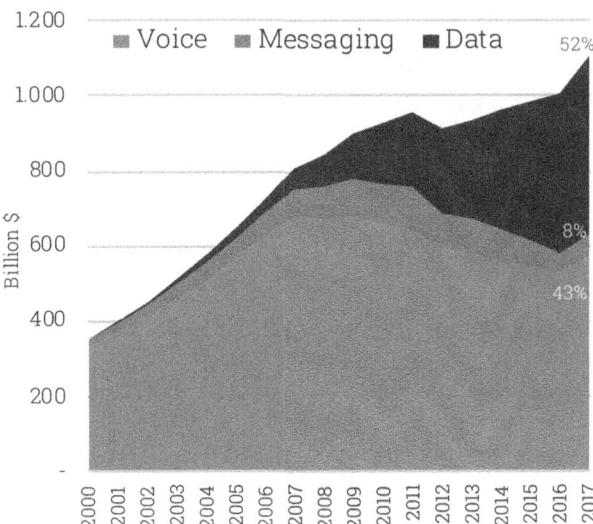

Moreover, as we have seen in Sect. 4.2, there are more and more people all over the world with more connected devices transmitting more data creating higher peaks of network utilization for uses that are increasingly critical, this will create a problem for telecom infrastructure difficult and expensive to be solved using traditional equipment. If network loads cannot be forecasted and continue to grow at such a rapid pace, the rigidity and the cost of traditional equipment make it very expensive to respond in an effective way. Capacity should be gauged on peaks, remaining unused for the rest of the time; but overcapacity should also be factored in to create a safety margin for the continuous growth of traffic.

If only the ability to quickly scale up capacity and scale out geographically could ensure high-quality, sustainable user experience during the rapid expansion of network traffic, then a network should behave like cloud computing. What this means is the network should be able to expand its capacity automatically, following predefined rules, when there is a peak in demand—and all this without active intervention by the telecom provider. Then, when the peak is over, the network should reduce the capacity allocated to manage the peak and reallocate it to deal with another peak in another area. Or this surplus capacity could be put on stand-by, waiting for another surge in traffic demand somewhere else. But there are two practical constraints to consider here: to create savings, telecom operators should use a commodity hardware and centralize resources to make it possible to reallocate them as needed.

Managing the network like cloud computing, without specialized, dedicated hardware but using standard commodity servers, is possible only if operators radically switch away from traditional network equipment and use software defined networks (SDN) and network function virtualization (NFV) instead.

SDNs call for a completely different approach, abstracting physical networking resources (e.g. switches, routers) and replacing them with software. SDN is a solution developed by telecom operators years ago but widely and successfully adopted in data centers. A SDN centralizes network intelligence and decision making while the forwarding components which implement central ruling remain distributed. An internal study by Bell Labs shows that SDNs reduce operational costs by more than 50% compared to legacy technologies, and improve optimal traffic by as much as 150% of capacity utilization (Weldon 2016). In addition, SDNs make it possible to separate non-mission-critical workloads, transferring compute and store processes to low-cost data center facilities and services, such as those offered by public cloud providers.

Complementing SDN with NFV has an even stronger impact on savings and flexibility in network management. NFV can replace on software (virtualize) any network devices (load balancers, firewalls, intrusion detection devices, for example) and run them on commodity hardware. The network and almost all its components can be reconfigured and provisioned to quickly meet fluctuating needs and demands via software.

For a network, changing 'quickly' does not mean change instantaneously. However, in the new paradigm of virtual network infrastructure even milliseconds could mean something because latency[6] and bandwidth[7] are the most critical requirements that networks need to manage, even more so in the future, and they are strictly interconnected.

4.2.1 The Problem of Bandwidth and Latency in Telecommunication Networks

Often Internet service providers advertise their connection using bandwidth as the main metric for speed. They claim that their connection is as fast as 100 Mbps or that their speeds is 20% faster than their competitors. But these claims are misleading. Bandwidth is the amount of data a user can receive every second; it is not a measure of speed. If the Internet connection were a pipe, bandwidth would measure how wide, or narrow, the pipe was, and latency would be how fast a drop of the liquid it carries moves from one end to the next.

Distance is the primary cause of latency. The optic impulse, moving approximately at the speed of light, induces 4.5 ms of latency for every 1000 km, and therefore requires a proximity of about 100 km or less to support a response time of 1 ms.

The other cause of network latency are the delays induced by network hops.[8] Every hop adds some delay to a transmission, because data packets must be routed and/or queued for delivery over an interface that may have lower capacity than the sum of the input flows. This queuing delay is less than a millisecond on average, but in times of severe congestion this can add up to tens of milliseconds. If traffic congestion cannot be managed or avoided, the performance of latency-sensitive services will be unpredictable.

In order to offer low-latency service guarantees, providers must minimize the number of network hops and maximize the available bandwidth. These dual requirements essentially mandate the creation of edge computing nodes[9] and ultra-

---

[6]Latency in a network is the amount of time it takes to send information from one point to another. Latency is usually measured in milliseconds (ms). It could be measured one-way (the time from the source sending a packet to the destination receiving it) or round-trip (the one-way latency from source to destination plus the one-way latency from the destination back to the source). Round-trip latency is more often quoted because it can be measured from a single point.

[7]Bandwidth is the maximum transmission capacity of a network channel. Usually bandwidth is measured in bits per second (bps), kilobits per second (Kbps), megabits per second (Mbps) or gigabits per second (Gbps).

[8]When communicating over the Internet, data passes through several intermediate devices (like routers) rather than flowing directly over a single wire. Each such device is a network "hop" because it causes data to hop between network connections, creating delays. A hop count is considered a measure of distance in networks.

[9]An edge computing node is a solution for bringing storage and computing power closer to the location where it is needed. Edge nodes reduce the volume of data that must be moved, the consequent traffic, and the distance data must travel. That provides lower latency. reduce the

high-capacity networks in fiber optics to provide the required connectivity to these nodes.

Low latency is critical requisite for ensuring that SDN and NFV work in an effective way. But this characteristic is also important when considering interactions with humans. A nerve impulse travels at a maximum speed of approximately 100 meters per second (m/s) in the human body. Therefore, the time required to propagate a signal from the hand to the brain, excluding the time required for the brain to process the signal, is approximately 10 ms. As network latency approaches this same level, it is possible to enable interactions with a distant object with no perceived difference compared to interactions with a local object (Weldon 2016).

In autonomous cars, at 120 km/h, 3 m distance corresponds to 100 ms of delay. With about 90% of this time allocated to the processing required for the driving application to make the decision and the vehicle to act on the resulting instructions, only 10 ms can be allocated to network latency, with little tolerance for variance and extremely high availability required. Similarly, a low-latency and high-bandwidth network is key in enabling a new wave of innovative VR and AR applications, with content and processing power in the cloud. Physiologically, the vestibulo-ocular reflex (VOR) in humans coordinates eye and head movements to stabilize images on the retina. Studies have shown the VOR to require approximately 7 ms. Therefore, to avoid user disorientation, including occasional nausea, a similar level of latencies must be guaranteed to VR and AR applications by the network to achieve mass market adoption (Weldon 2016).

4.2.2   The Telecom Network and Its Evolution

Telecom networks are changed at every level, global and national. If reducing latency and increasing bandwidth to serve a growing demand is the main driver of this evolution, at the top level, where there are the international cables and cloud data centers, controlling connections is the main issue.

The structure of global telecom networks can be mapped in a simplified way as in Fig. 4.12. The big international cables that encircle the globe connect to nation-al and local networks in facilities called international telephone gateways (for voice calls) or Internet Exchange Points (for Internet connections). Here the big carriers exchange their traffic or interconnect their networks.

International telephone gateways have maintained almost the same hierarchical structure of the past, with international carriers at the top, receiving and routing international traffic from national and local operators. Internet Exchange points, in contrast, are developing a quite different structure as compared to previous years. First, there were as many as 488 in 2018, including exchanges in marginal locations for traffic routing. This increase in number has diluted the traffic of large

---

number of network hops, and transmission costs too. An edge computing node can be used for SDN, NFV, IoT or any computational need that is requested from or through the network.

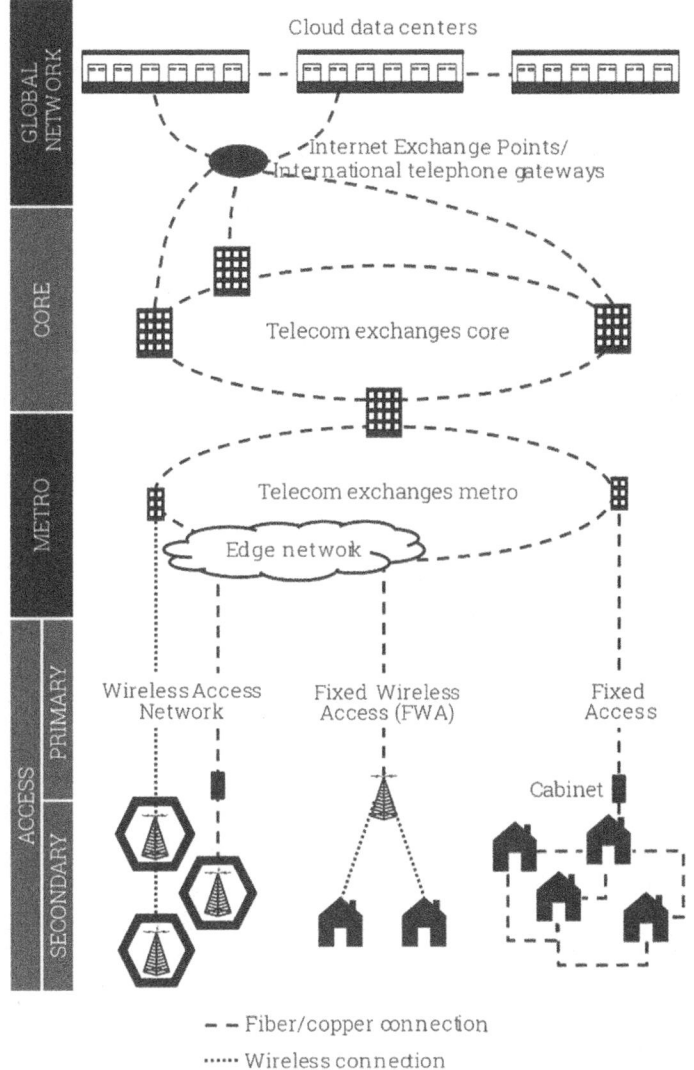

Fig. 4.12 A simplified map of a telecom network

interconnection hubs, at the same time reducing the risk of traffic congestion while shortening the average distance of communications and average latency.

Second, but more importantly, since 2010 big content providers, including Google, Facebook, Microsoft and Amazon, have started buying international cables to route traffic generated by their own companies and their clients on their own infrastructures. In 2006, the percentage of traffic controlled by Internet backbone providers was 80%. In 2018, for the first time, they were surpassed by content

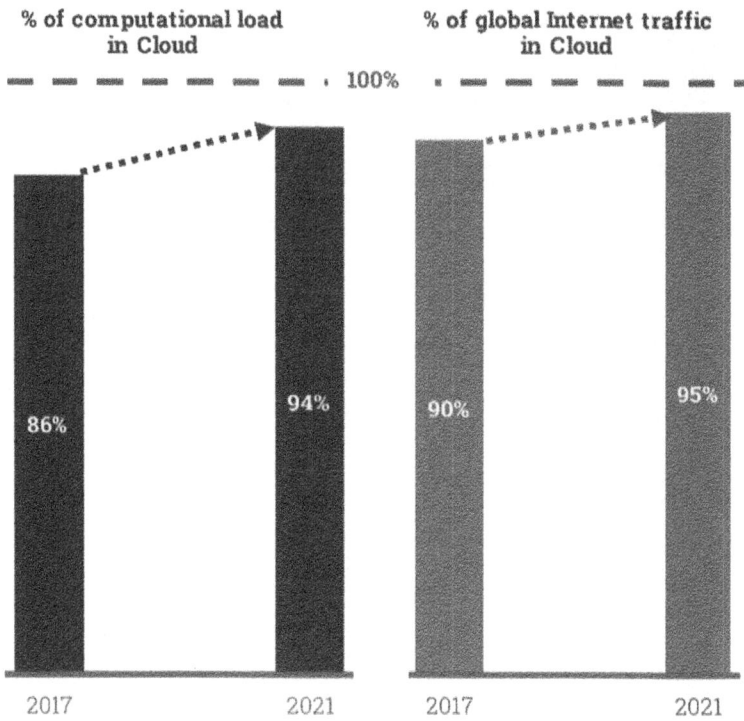

Fig. 4.13 Cloud computing—global computational load and traffic (source: Cisco Global Cloud Index: Forecast and Methodology: 2016–2021, 2018)

providers, who routed 54% of the global international traffic on their international cables (TeleGeography 2019).

Finally, the main providers of cloud computing services, who are these same content providers, have moved their cloud data centers up in the Internet hierarchy, connecting them in many cases directly to the exchange points. This choice is justified by the fact that 86% of the global computational load is already performed in the cloud (a figure that will reach 94% in 2021, Fig. 4.13). This is an enormous share. More importantly it should be noted that 90% of the total Internet traffic goes through the cloud (hitting 95% in 2021).

At a lower level, under the international gateways or the Internet exchanges, there are national networks with their telecom exchanges at core and metro level. National telecom networks are organized hierarchically to cover the entire territory of a given country and interconnected to each other through a redundant backbone. Between the network at the metro level and the access level lies the edge network, which will be tremendously important for the future of telecommunications. At a lower level, there is the access network, connecting urban telecom exchanges to end users. This is divided into a primary network, which goes from the telecom exchanges to the distribution cabinet, and a secondary network, from the cabinet to the final user.

Mobile networks and fixed wireless access (FWA) networks can interconnect to one other and with the central office using radio links, without laying cables. This type of connection is cheaper but also lower quality compared to cable. For this reason, especially in mobile networks, radio links have been gradually set aside and left as residual solutions, with preference going to fiber optic connections.

From the map in Fig. 4.13, it is easy to see that there is a single network that connects all its components and users, even if controlled by different players using different technologies. But from the point of view of the final user it may seem different, because access to the network could be either fixed, mobile or FWA.

The Future That Comes from the Cloud

Cloud computing is a very successful business model. In 2020 its global turnover will surpass that of more traditional IT (IDC 2017). The market leader Amazon Web Services (AWS) had revenues of $25.7 billion in 2018 but was able to maintain 47% growth year-on-year. Microsoft, its closest contender, garnered revenues of $23.2 billion, up 56% from 2017.

The market is highly concentrated in the hands of a few companies: AWS, Microsoft, IBM, Google and Alibaba together hold 75% of the total market (Gartner 2019).

However, cloud computing could be considered a successful technology model too:

- SDN and NFV implement solutions that have been the norm in cloud computing for years.
- Edge computing has already been tested by cloud providers that today are offering specialized solutions.
- IoT will be a potential market for telecom operators but it is an actual market for cloud providers.
- Cloud data centers are far more energy efficient than telecom central offices.
- The first successful implementation of augmented reality on a global scale was Pokemon Go in 2016 on Google's edge network.

4.2.3 The Evolution of Fixed Networks

Before the deregulation of the telecommunication industry in the early 1990s, telecom operators offered a limited portfolio of content and services, built on proprietary platforms and limited to the walled garden of their network realm. Fiber to the home (FTTH) was seen as the ultimate solution for broadband access; PayTV video services were considered to be the killer application that would fund the cost of deploying a new optical access infrastructure. Just after the start of the deregulation process, the advent of the Internet and of the World Wide Web opened a new perspective, providing a platform for sharing content efficiently.

However, after the initial excitement, the realization emerged that the cost associated with deploying new wired infrastructure in fiber to every home was enormous. It would take decades to roll out the new networks, and video services offered limited additional revenue potential. Combined, these factors meant the estimated returns on the investments would come in more than a decade, a period that was deemed unacceptable by investors and shareholders.

Consequently, access network providers started looking for alternative technologies to reuse their existing infrastructure to enable faster deployment of broadband services with an acceptable return on investment. In 1997, incumbent telecom operators started using new digital subscriber line (DSL) technology over their twisted pair copper wires. At the same time, cable operators introduced cable modem technology over their coaxial cable, using the so-called hybrid fiber-coaxial (HFC) technology. Both DSL and cable modems were relatively economical to deploy and offered acceptable bandwidth. The result was that FTTH was nearly shelved everywhere and restricted to greenfield deployments where the relative economics were comparable to those of copper-based technologies (Weldon 2016).

However, there were two noteworthy exceptions: Japan and Korea. In both cases, fiber deployments in metropolitan areas were considered by the government a long-term strategic priority and the relative density of houses made the economics more affordable. Later, China joined these two countries, due to a lack of existing copper infrastructure in large parts of the country and a desire to create a future-proof solution.

Access capacity for DSL services improved exponentially. Asymmetric digital subscriber line (ADSL), followed by its improved version (ADSL 2), was well suited for early web browsing on the Internet, while very-high-bit-rate DSL (VDSL) was ideal for the delivery of video. Then the introduction of vectoring gave new impetus to investments. VDSL was able to support up to 100 Mbps and if multiple pairs of copper were available, it was also possible to combine their capacity through bonding across pairs, further enhancing performances. The latest DSL standards, Vplus and Gfast, are about to be deployed.

As with DSL, the same happened for cable networks using the data-over-cable service interface specification (DOCSIS) standard. In 1997, with DOCSIS 1.0, it was created the first specification for a non-proprietary, high-speed data service infrastructure capable of providing Internet web browsing services. DOCSIS 1.1 offered the ability to differentiate traffic flows to upgrade the service quality, while DOCSIS 2.0 expanded the upstream bandwidth allowing VOIP telephony. DOCSIS 3.0 significantly boosted capacity by bonding channels which, combined with the new-and-improved DOCSIS 3.1, reached 10 Gbps downstream and 1 Gbps upstream. This thanks to the use of a wider spectrum and better modulation.

Similarly, the evolution of the optical network has improved its already high performances, reducing its costs as well. Passive optical network (PON) has emerged as the most economical choice because it enables multiple subscribers (typically 32) to share a downstream laser passively split to each home with individual drop fibers, based on a tree-like structure. The first generation of PON was the Gigabit PON (GPON) standard, which allowed 2.5 Gbps downstream and 1.25 Gbps upstream. In light of the international success of the GPON, 2010 saw the release of a second generation called XG-PON (or 10-GPON), with transmission capacity amplified significantly compared to the previous generation, (with shared speed of 10 Gbps downstream and 2.5 Gbps upstream respectively). This standard, although already available for some years, has not been widely adopted due to its higher cost compared to the much more common GPON system. Starting in 2012, a new standard, called NG-PON2 (Next-Generation Passive Optical Network 2) was launched, with two possible options: TWDM PON (Time and Wavelength Division Multiplexing—PON) and PtPWDM PON (Point-to-Point Wavelength Division Multiplexing—PON). The TWDM PON consists of the overlapping of several systems (up to 8) XG-PON operating at different wavelengths, thus creating a multi-channel optical transmission system. This new system is capable of offering on the single optical shaft up to eight times the transmission capacity of a single XG-PON system to reach 80 Gbps downstream and 20 Gbps in upstream or, optionally, even 80 Gbps symmetrically. The PtPWDM PON option refers to a system in which each optical channel is dedicated to the individual user, using software to create a point-to-point system on a point-to-multipoint physical network. In 2016, the standard of an additional PON, halfway between XG-PON and NG-PON2, was introduced; this new standard was called XGS-PON. It is a "symmetrical" version of the XG-PON system (10 Gbps symmetrically) but it is simpler than the NG-PON2 systems (as it is not multichannel). XGS-PON has already reached technological maturity and garnered commercial interest thanks to the abundant availability of upstream bandwidth, which makes it more suitable for future applications (Weldon 2016). A key feature of the different PON generations is that, using a different allocation of wavelengths, they can coexist on the same infrastructure. Therefore, the new generation can be incrementally introduced into the network, even where the consolidated GPON technology has already been adopted, to gradually offer the higher speed service only where the need arises.

As a final remark on the evolution of fixed networks, we can say that DSL and DOCSIS standards have evolved, improving their performances and the quality of their electronics. At the same time, however, their cost has increased, while the optimal length required for the piece of copper cable has decreased, requiring instead a fiber connection that comes closer and closer to the user. It is legitimate to ask whether it is no longer rational to keep investing in copper, given its high maintenance costs and the lack of a long-term outlook for the old copper networks. In contrast, PON technologies have continuously shored up their performance and minimized their limitations, coming closer and closer to performance of an active connection (one fiber straight from the central office to the user). But while the perceived value of a good Internet connection is increasing, overcoming the problem of its cost, PON standards cannot yet offer anything more than a fast, cheap connection, without added services on top that can differentiate it from competition or create additional value.

4.2.4 The Evolution of Mobile Networks

Retrospectively, the evolution of mobile telecommunications seems simple: a new generation every 10 years. The first generation of mobile phones (1G) appeared on the scene in the 1980s, exploiting analog technology supporting voice only calls with poor battery life and voice quality, little security and a tendency to drop calls.

Then, in 1990s the cell phones received their first major upgrade when technology went from 1G to 2G on GSM networks. This was a radical transformation. The switch from analog to digital communications brought in call and text encryption along with data services such as SMSs, picture messages and MMSs. Voice calls were free from background noise due to digital modulation. Only with 2.5G, also known as GPRS, packet switching came into picture with data transmits at 64–144 kbps, making voice calls possible during data transmission. With the GSM Evolution (EDGE or 2.75G), the speed hit 1 Mbps to satisfy increasingly data-hungry users.

Data transmission was also the key to the evolution to 3G, introduced commercially in 2001. The goals set out for this third generation of mobile communication were to facilitate data transmission and to support a wider range of applications at a lower cost. The 3G standard was based on a new technology called UMTS (Universal Mobile Telecommunications System) and a new core network architecture able to support more active calls and/or data transmits at the same time. The maximum speed for 3G was around 2 Mbps for non-moving devices and 384 Kbps in moving vehicles, giving rise to the term "mobile broadband," which first applied to 3G cellular technology. As with the previous generation, 3G evolved into the much faster 3.5G and 3.75G, as more features were introduced to prepare for the advent of the following generation.

Conceived in 2000 but only deployed in 2010, 4G or LTE (Long Term Evolution) was first released in 2008. It is still the dominant mobile technology, and also the first to be globally adopted. Very different from its previous iteration, 4G was essentially made possible only thanks to advancements in electronics. 4G can provide high speed, high quality and high capacity to users while improving security and lowering the cost of voice and data services, multimedia and Internet over IP. Potential and current applications included mobile web access, IP telephony, gaming services, high-definition mobile TV, video conferencing, 3D television and cloud computing services. The top speed shot up to 1 Gbps for a stationary or walking user and 100 Mbps when the device was moving.

In all these generations there were two constants. First, every new generations added more frequencies to the previous. Second, newer generations of phones were designed to be only backward-compatible, so a 4G phone can communicate through a 3G or even 2G network but not the other way around. The same will be true for the fifth mobile generation (5G), which will gradually be rolled out beginning in 2019.

5G networks are not an evolution of 4G networks, because their architecture is completely revolutionized with respect to the previous generation. This has several consequences for businesses that we will analyze in Sect. 4.5.2. To make a comparison, what the markets wanted from the evolution of 4G networks is the equivalent in the automotive industry of demanding a car that is 100 times lighter and 100 times more resistant: the only way this is possible is by completely upending the paradigm. More specifically, the new network will upgrade existing 4G networks in several ways:

- 5G networks can be 100 times faster than their 4G antecedent, up to 10 Gbps.
- Latency will potentially decrease up to 1 ms, which is 30–50 times better than before.
- It will be possible to have up to one million connections per km^2, 100 times more than 4G, which would be useful to support IoT.
- Mobility will be improved, enabling connectivity on high speed trains moving up to 500 km/h, which is about 1.5 times better than 4G.
- 5G will support NFV, SDN and network slicing,[10] while 4G networks were inflexible.
- The radio interface will be 90% more energy efficient than 4G.

Mobile phone standards up to 4G were defined to serve the needs of a mass market. On the contrary, 5G was designed to serve a sum of vertical markets with very different and somewhat conflicting needs. What Some of these verticals have the constraint of low latency and great bandwidth, no matter the conditions, as with virtual reality applications; others have only the constraint of low power consumption, no matter the latency or the available bandwidth, as some IoT devices.

With 5G there will be no discernible differences between wired and wireless connections, opening a range of possibilities that can take advantage of near-instantaneous response and high data speeds. 5G will offer companies blazing-fast connections and the ability to use the cloud seamlessly for computation-intensive tasks with real-time decision-making, or for retrieving all the data needed for local decision-making.

However, big opportunities do not come at a small price. The challenge is how to meet government-mandated coverage goals even where business justification is lacking. It has been estimated that the rollout cost for 5G across Europe would be significantly higher than for 4G, running between 300 and 500 billion € (GSMA 2019b), an enormous commitment for European telecom operators.

In parallel with the evolution of mobile telephony standards, there have also been some developments in the use of the radio spectrum for mobile communication. The

---

[10]Network slicing is a form of virtual network architecture using SDN and NFV. A single network connection is sliced into multiple virtual networks that can support different radio access networks, or different service types on the same radio access. Each virtual network (network slice) comprises an independent set of network functions created by software suitable for the requirements of the particular use case. Each will be optimized to provide the resources and network topology for the specific service and traffic that will use the slice. For example, a doctor can simultaneously perform an ultrasound, which requires low and constant latency with an average throughput, while downloading the patient's medical records, a task needing a high throughput but which is insensitive to high and varying latency.

portion of the spectrum used for any radio communication is very important. To prevent interference between various users, every use of radio waves is strictly regulated by national laws and coordinated by an international body, the ITU. Different parts of the radio spectrum are allocated for different technologies and applications. Mobile telecom operators and broadcast television stations have well defined limits. In some cases, parts of the radio spectrum are sold or licensed to operators of transmission services. But being a fixed and scarce resource contended by an increasing number of users, the radio spectrum has become more and more congested and precious.

A part of the spectrum is "unlicensed" or "license-free", having predefined rules to mitigate interferences. Basically, anyone can use these bands and if they obey these rules, they have the right to transmit within given power limits. But they have no right to receive. In other words, no one has any guarantee that there will not be interference from other similar systems, as would be the case with 2G, 3G or 4G bands. Nevertheless, if the transmission is local and covers only small distances, this problem is usually negligible. Indeed wifi, that has the lion's share of data transmission (see Sect. 4.1.3), works only in the unlicensed spectrum.

While other wireless technologies like LoRa[11] or Multefire[12] only use the unlicensed spectrum, standards like WiMax[13] use both the licensed and unlicensed spectrum. But technologies such as LTE, which is the base for 4G, typically work on licensed spectrum, although they can be implemented using unlicensed bands in private implementations covering a plant, an office, or a stadium, for example. The global opportunity for "private LTE" (and in the future possibly "private 5G") in industrial and business critical environments is significant. The global revenues for the private LTE addressable market will skyrocket from $22.1 billion in 2017 to $118.5 billion in 2023 at a 32.3% CAGR. The relative device shipment volumes will jump from 170.7 million in 2017 to 765.1 million in 2023 at a 28.4% CAGR (Harbor Research 2018).

In the U.S., the unlicensed spectrum is even more appealing given the presence of the Citizens Broadband Radio Service (CBRS). This is a relatively large part of the spectrum of 150 MHz in the 3550–3700 MHz range, almost all included in the 5G range. What is unique about this band is the fact that it is one of the few in the US that

---

[11]LoRa (Long Range) is a patented wireless data communication technology used in IoT applications. Operating in the unlicensed spectrum, LoRa is able to achieve an extremely long-range connectivity, more than 10 km using extremely low power. This technology competes with other low-power wide-area network (LPWAN) technologies like narrowband IoT (NB IoT), LTE Cat M1 and, in the future, 5G LPWA (Low-Power Wide-Area).

[12]MulteFire is a wireless technology that operates standalone in unlicensed and shared spectrum, based on LTE technology. MulteFire is designed to co-exist with wifi and other technologies operating in the same spectrum. It targets vertical markets including industrial IoT, enterprises, and various other vertical markets.

[13]WiMAX (Worldwide Interoperability for Microwave Access) is a family of wireless broadband communication standards based on the IEEE 802.16 set of standards, providing wireless communications on the licensed and unlicensed spectrum. It was initially designed to provide from 30 to 40 Mbps but with its latest updates can offer up to 1 Gbps for fixed stations.

is authorized for multiple use cases, rather than being licensed to one operator or available for unlicensed use only. The Federal Communications Commission (FCC), the American regulator, has authorized three categories of users under its CBRS rules but left the use of the entire band to unlicensed users, albeit with the lowest priority. The importance of the CBRS lies in being a credible potential base for cable operators to offer a wireless service with a small investment, and powerful leverage for unconventional operators to disrupt the telecom business.

There are different ways to create disruptions in the infrastructure sector, as explained by Venzin and Konert (2020), but the CBRS could change a significant part of the telecommunication ecosystem, especially in rural areas. Google, Amdocs, CommScope, Federated Wireless, Key Bridge, and Sony have already applied to become administrators of the CBRS band and ensure real-time allocation of bandwidth between various users, based on the kind of license. Amazon also is undertaking significant testing involving the CBRS band, not just for a wireless network but also to backhaul infrastructure. As example is the use of AWS to support private LTE networks running on the CBRS spectrum. The growing interest in the CBRS spectrum of big players such as Google and Amazon highlights other potential paths of evolution for technology. For instance, if this spectrum does allow more localized networks, each with their own network cores (similar to local cable companies), companies such as Google and Amazon are well positioned to serve as neutral host networks that manage traffic across private networks through a centralized hub (Venkateshwar et al. 2019b).

4.3 The Value of the Networks for OTTs and the Consequences for Traditional Telecom Operators

There is an interesting AT&T video from 1993 that describes the future of telecommunications as they imagined it then,[14] just before the Internet era began. There would be e-mail, mobile telecommunications, smartphones, e-commerce, search engines, and cloud computing. Everything that was imagined back then came true. But telecommunications companies such as AT&T and many others which had accurately envisioned the future were not the protagonists who were able to bring that future about. Telecommunication companies have invested in many of these services, such as search engines, e-mail, messaging apps, digital content and more. But in the end, they were unable to capitalize on their efforts and were forced to stand on the sidelines watching while others reaped the fruits of the Internet.

The real beneficiaries of the Internet revolution were a bunch of start-ups that became Internet giants. The telecom operators call them the over-the-top players (OTT) because they provide their services directly to their users, bypassing the

---

[14]The title of this short video is "What Is The Cloud—By AT&T" and is available at https://www. youtube.com/watch?v=_a7hK6kWttE (last retrieved March 13, 2019).

companies traditionally acted as controllers or distributors of any service provided through telecommunications networks. But telecommunications operators, after losing control of the access to the network, now risk losing the battle to manage the value created around the network too. And that could have a big impact on the future of telecommunication infrastructures.

The main threat comes from telecom companies losing economic relevance. In 2018 there were 17 telecommunication companies in the list of the Fortune Global 500 with cumulated revenues of $1.22 trillion. On the same list the technology companies were 46, with revenues of $2.66 trillion. Among the ten largest companies by capitalization in the world at the end of 2018, seven belonged to the technological sector with an accrued value of $4.1 trillion, 78% of the total. None was in the telecom business (Financial Times Global 500 rankings). The same ranking in 1997, before the dot.com bubble burst, showed a cumulated 1.5 trillion dollars of value, of which 20% was represented by two tech companies. Just one telecom company was included in the list and was valued 10% of the total capitalization. In between, there was a process of value erosion for telecom operators that today manage a business that is much more important for its users than themselves.

Together, the American GAFAM (Google, Apple, Facebook, Amazon, Microsoft) and the Asian BAT (Baidu, Alibaba, Tencent) form the OTT group. This is a *de facto* oligopoly dominating most segments (search, social media, communication, e-commerce, video) with very few real competitors. The companies that do compete typically operate in a single segment (e.g. Netflix, Uber, Airbnb, JD. Com, Expedia), or in a local market (e.g. Yandex and Mail.ru in Russia, Naver and Daum in South Korea, Rakuten in Japan) (iDate 2019). The two groups have significant differences in their financial performance: the GAFAM quintet out-earns the BAT trio by a ratio of several dozen to one. But the Asian OTT have an extraordinary growth trajectory: +30% on average per annum for the past several years. Plus OTTs EBITDA-to-revenue ratio exceeds 30% in most cases, the only exception being Amazon, but it is for a good reason.

To keep revenues growing, Amazon is continuously cross-financing its ventures scarifying its margins, to end up once again joying profits well above those of other OTT companies. In both GAFAM and BAT, capex is relatively low. Most invest less than 10% of their revenue in infrastructure (compared to 18% for telcos) with the exception of Google and Facebook, which are heavily investing in data centers and submarine cables (iDate 2019). Because of their low capex, OTTs players have an enormous amount of free cash flows to invest. This huge influx of liquidity allows the Internet giants to make dozens of small but strategic acquisitions a year without Antitrust intervention (The Economist 2019) to protect their core business and further fortify their positions. Investing in start-ups but sometime also in veteran players alike enables them to move rapidly into new sectors, including non-digital ones (iDate 2019). For example, Amazon spent $13.7 billion to acquire Whole Foods.

Nonetheless, the OTTs rely mainly on telecom networks for their business and their evolution. They all offer or use cloud computing or cloud-based services as a core activity. Consequently, the telecom network is a key conditioning factor for

Table 4.3 A summary of OTT activity in telecommunication infrastructures and adjacent markets

		Google	Facebook	Microsoft	Amazon	
App & Services		Search Engine, Maps, App Stores, YouTube, Google Music, GSuite	Social network, instant messaging, immersive reality	Search Engine, office app, Windows, gaming	Ecommerce, AWS, Prime Video, Alexa, Music	
OTT Comm. App		Meet, Duo	Messenger, WA, Instagram, Oculus Rift	Skype, Skype Business, Teams	Chime	
Int. Cables		Proprietary	Proprietary	Proprietary	Proprietary	
Data centers	SW	SW	Proprietary	Open	Proprietary/ Open	Proprietary
	HW	HW	Control	Open	Proprietary/ Open	Proprietary
Satellite Networks	SW	SW				Iridium Cloud Connect
	HW	HW				Blue Sky, Iridium
Wireless networks	SW	SW	CBRS Alliance, SAS, ESC, Google Fi, Loon	Terragraph, TIP, Open Cellular		CBRS
	HW	HW	CBRS Alliance, Loon	Terragraph, TIP, Open Cellular		CBRS
Wired networks	SW	SW	Proprietary	Terragraph, TIP/open	Proprietary/ open	Proprietary
	HW	HW	Google Fiber	Terragraph, TIP		

them. In fact, many have invested in research into telecom infrastructures to keep up the pressure on telco companies to upgrade networks and improve connectivity in underserved areas or in underdeveloped countries, to expand their markets.

Below we will provide a short analysis of the main initiatives undertaken by OTTs. Our aim is to evaluate their impact on the evolution of the telecom business but, mostly, on the evolution of telecom infrastructures, as summarized in Table 4.3.

4.3.1 Google Alphabet

The foremost telecom investment from the OTTs is Google Fiber. Launched by Google in 2010, Google Fiber was later moved under the Access division after Alphabet Inc. became Google's parent company in 2015. Google Fiber was substantially reorganized in 2016, when Alphabet started slashing capital expenditures for its Other Bets segment, where the fiber company was the biggest source of cash drain. "Capex for that segment totalled $181 million in 2018, down significantly from $493 million the year before and $1.37 billion in 2016. Google at the time credited the bulk of that sum to deploying its fiber network" (Gallagher 2019).

Whether intentionally or not, Google Fiber has certainly had something to do with the pace at which 1 Gbps broadband was deployed by telecom operators, such as AT&T, Verizon and the US cable industry. According to the Internet & Television American Association, speeds of up to 1 Gbps are available today across 80% of the US via cable networks, a upward leap from just 5% in 2016. It's hard to say how much credit for that pace should be given to the spectre of Google Fiber, but some are convinced that its role was decisive, even as cable providers are planning to push toward symmetrical 10 Gbps speeds (Baumgartner 2019).

Because Google's mission is "to make sure that information serves everyone, not just a few," other Alphabet companies are also pursuing initiatives with similar goals. An example is Project Loon, started in October 2017 within X (formerly Google X) and spun out into a separate company, named Loon LLC, in July 2018. The company uses high-altitude balloons placed in the stratosphere between 18 and 25 km using the LTE standard to create an aerial wireless network. At the beginning Loon used the unlicensed spectrum, but then the company started cooperating with local telecommunication operators using the cellular spectrum to deliver basic Internet connectivity to more than 100,000 people in Puerto Rico and to some of Kenya's most inaccessible regions in 2019. A huge impact with a modest investment.

4.3.2 Facebook

Similar to Google, Facebook's mission is "to bring affordable access to selected Internet services to less developed countries by increasing efficiency and facilitating the development of new business models around the provision of Internet access." In keeping with this mission, Facebook launched Internet.org in 2013.

Based on a partnership with Samsung, Ericsson, MediaTek, Opera Software, Nokia and Qualcomm, as of December 2018, more than 100 million people are using an Internet connection based on Internet.org and its app, Free Basics, which delivers its services. In March 2014, as part of the Internet.org initiative, Facebook announced a connectivity lab with the goal of bringing the Internet to everybody and acquired Ascenta, a maker of solar-powered drones. Then the company expanded this lab activity to low-Earth orbit and geosynchronous satellites for establishing Internet connectivity in other areas. For all three projects Facebook looks like relies on free space optical (FSO)[15] or laser communication (Harris 2019).

In 2016, for a similar purpose but with a different nature, Facebook launched at Mobile World Congress in Barcelona the Telecom Infra Project (TIP). Born as a collaborative effort with an engineering focus, TIP and its annual meeting (TIP Summit), have become the most prominent reference point for all those who seek to generate disruption in the telecommunications infrastructure sector. Funded at its start by Facebook, TIP is jointly steered by its group of founding tech and telecom companies. The project has more than 500 participating member organizations, including all the main telecom operators, suppliers, developers, integrators, start-ups and other entities. TIP is organized in three strategic networks areas that collectively make up an end-to-end network: Access (including Radio Access Network, or RAN solutions), Backhaul, and Core and Management. In 2019 at Mobile World Congress TIP was able to showcase the interoperability of its technologies in its first end-to-end telecom network demonstration.

4.3.3 Microsoft

Even Microsoft has heavily invested in telecommunications but with a very different angle. In 2011, it acquired Skype Technologies in an $8.5 billion deal; according to Trefis, in 2018 Skype had an estimated user base of 1.43 billion worldwide. In 2014 the telephony company accounted for 39% of the combined international volume of calls for every telco in the world (TeleGeography 2014), so Skype itself was a source of disruption for the telecommunications sector. Since then, things have changed dramatically and even got worse for telecom operators.

Today there are many alternatives to Skype: WhatsApp, WeChat, Facebook Messenger, Viber, Line, Tango, Google Hangouts, and Samsung's ChatOn. But none of them was conceived as Skype to have also a telephone number from the public switched telephone network (PSTN) to substitute a fixed telephone line using software. Moreover, Microsoft has not stopped investing in Skype, adding new features such as artificial intelligence with the ability to translate calls into 12 different languages in real time.

What's more, in recent years, Microsoft has continued to invest in international submarine cables like New Cross Pacific (NCP) Cable Network, Hibernia Express Cable, AcquaComms, to be autonomous in connecting its data centers over long distances.

---

[15]Free-space optical communication is a form of optical communication technology that uses light propagating in free space (that is, in the air, outer space, a vacuum, or something similar) to wirelessly transmit data for telecommunications or computer networking. This is an alternative to optical transmission using solids such as optical fiber cable, and is also a substitute for radio transmission.

Table 4.4 A comparison between OTT as a whole and a typical telco operator profile

	OTT	Internl. telco	Telco incumbent	National telco	
App & Services	Yes	Marginal			
OTT Comm. App	Yes				
Int. cables	Yes	Some	Some		
Data centers	SW	Yes			
	HW	Hypescale	Small	Small	Very small
Satellite Network	SW	Yes			
	HW	Yes	Marginal	Marginal	
Wireless network	SW	Yes			
	HW	Yes	Yes	Yes	Yes
Wireline network	SW	Yes			
	HW	Yes	Yes	Yes	Yes

4.3.4 Amazon

Amazon made many investments to turn a profit from telecommunication disruption. In September 2018, Amazon Web Services announced a partnership with Iridium Communications to develop a satellite-based network called CloudConnect for IoT applications. In January 2019, Iridium completed its $3 billion satellite network Iridium NEXT, consisting of 75 satellites launched by SpaceX for which Iridium is its largest non-government customer.

Moreover, Amazon Web Services (AWS) announced AWS Ground Station, a plan to build a dozen satellite transmission facilities throughout the world. Ground stations are essentially antenna-equipped facilities that can send and receive data from satellites orbiting the earth. Amazon will let customers rent access to these stations in the same manner that they lease access to its cloud data centers. Using this new service, companies that are too small to build and operate their own satellite transmission infrastructure will be able to access satellite services on-demand. Amazon will make it low cost and very simple, so as to replicate the key success factors of its cloud computing platform.

4.3.5 An Evaluation of the OTT Approach in the Telecom Business

Some of the moves by OTTs are aimed at putting pressure to the telecom industry, as in the case of Google, to speed-up fiber investments, or Facebook, to improve quality and reduce the cost of telecom equipment. The aim of the latter is to spread Internet broadband in every remote location on the planet. Others, however, have the goal of substantially changing the telecommunication world by creating new forms of communication, as is the case with Microsoft's Skype, or offering access to a completely new communication network, as with Amazon's satellite network, to create a different kind of communication wherever possible. A comparison between OTTs and traditional telco operators is summarized in Table 4.4.

Everyone has learned that in technology, realizing a desired effect takes more than just investing; it is more effective to apply the right kind of pressure. What experience has shown in recent years is that OTTs are much more adept at achieving their objectives than telecommunication companies are in defending their own markets. But the real difference is that OTTs are playing on their home field, in a more favorable position. They have more technical skills, move faster and are less worried about failing in the struggle to innovate. They look at physical infrastructure as an unbearable burden that should be reduced to a minimum. All the key components of their products or services should use proprietary technologies or adhere to an open standard.

Traditional telecom operators, on the contrary, have been delegating innovation to equipment vendors for years. Being complex giants, they move slowly. Because they have a make-no-mistakes culture, they are used to levels of reliability the Internet world cannot afford. Traditional telcos are intimately linked to physical infrastructure, which they consider an entry barrier and a source of competitive advantage. They are recent converts to open standards, just because they have seen the positive effects on OTTs, but they never controlled their key technologies. In the end, their playing field is becoming more and more the increasingly problematic one of the internetization, a world dominated by the standards of the Internet, with its technical solutions and its disruptive business models.

4.4   Evolution of the Telecom Industry and Regulation Issues

4.4.1   The Telecom Industry Evolution

Despite an increasingly stronger global demand for data and mobile telephony, sustained by a steady proliferation of fixed broadband connections, this magic moment of a favourable market has not materialized in revenues in the same way all over in the world (Fig. 4.14). Since the 2011 crisis, telecommunications revenues have risen by 8% on a global scale. Nonetheless, due to more intense regulatory and competitive pressure, this trend has not been seen across the board. In other words, revenues are up everywhere except in Europe. The Middle East and Africa saw the best of this trend, with revenue growth of 29%, almost double that of Latin America and Asia but more than triple that of North America. In the same period, on the contrary, in Europe revenues decreased by 8%, with a minimal trend reversal in 2017.

In the European scenario, mobile revenues (representing 51% of total telecom revenues) dropped by 13% and fixed telephony revenues (18% of the total) by 36%. These trends were not fully compensated by a 15% increase in fixed broadband, which unfortunately represented only one-third of industry revenues (Fig. 4.15).

But how was that possible if demand for telecommunications services was so strong, as we have seen above? The answer is a generalized downturn in prices in Europe. This happened in fixed broadband, where average revenue per user (ARPU) fell by 6% (Fig. 4.16), although growing volumes managed to offset this decline.

Fig. 4.14 Telecom revenues by region, 2011–17, index numbers (source: iDate 2018)

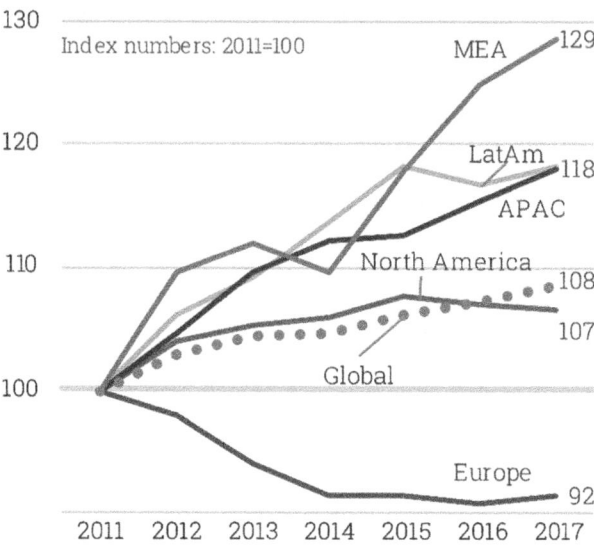

Fig. 4.15 Telecom revenues in Europe (EU 28) by service, 2011–17, index numbers (source: iDate 2018)

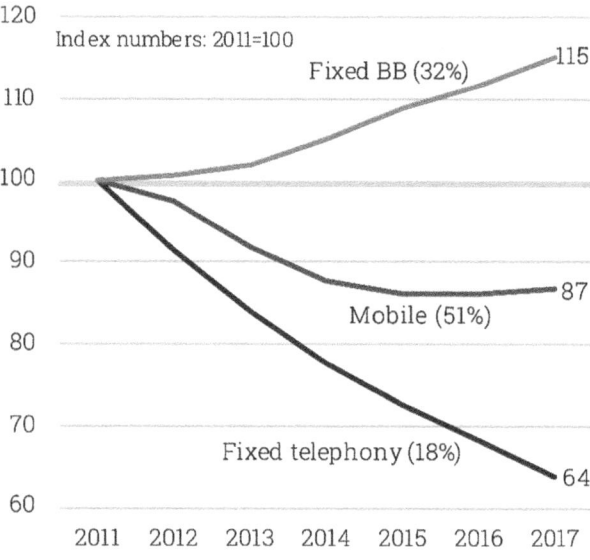

The mobile sector saw a much stronger decrease in average prices (13%), which volumes did not compensate for, leading to a sharp drop in revenues.

Because of this negative trend, European telecom operators devoted an increasingly higher share of their sales to infrastructure investments compared to their peers; European incumbents even more (Table 4.5). The capex-to-sales ratio was 14.1% in the USA in 2018 while for European telecom incumbents the figure was 17.5% and for European telecom challengers 15.2%.

Fig. 4.16 Telecom ARPU in Europe according to European Telecommunications Network Operators' Association (ETNO) by service, 2011–17, index numbers (ETNO perimeter includes EU 28 plus Albania, FYR Macedonia, Iceland, Norway, Switzerland and Turkey. Source: iDate 2018)

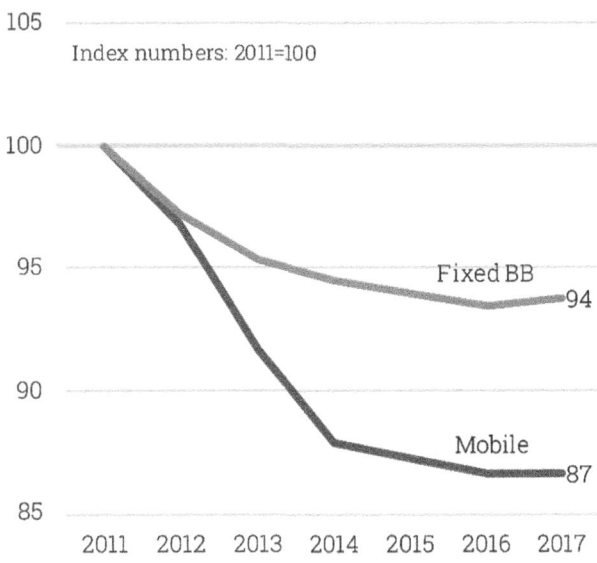

Table 4.5 Capex to sales ratio for main telecom operator aggregations, percentage

	2017	2018	2019
European telecom incumbent	16.4	17.5	16.7
European telecom challengers	15.5	15.2	14.5
LATAM	18.2	19.9	16.8
USA	13.3	14.1	14.1

Source: Patrick et al. 2018

Despite this, in relative terms American operators from 2010 to 2016 boosted their investments by 21%, while this figure for their European counterparts was 17% (Fig. 4.17). That was possible, in absolute terms, thanks to the more favourable evolution of revenues in the US, which sustained an increase in investments that rose from 51.8 billion € of capex in 2010 to 62.8 billion € in 2016. This number was almost 33% higher than in the European Union, where the 28 member states (EU 28) stepped up their efforts to 47.2 billion € from 40.5 billion in 2010. In terms of spending per capita, this meant that American operators invested 193.9 € per capita of capex, twice the 85.0 € in the ETNO perimeter. In the meantime, Japan had just completed its investment cycle, after creating a state-of-the-art infrastructure.

Europe is struggling to find a way to overcome its problems of slow investments, and prospects are not terribly promising. The profitability of European telecom operators has been sliding since 2011 in all the main countries (Fig. 4.18). In fact, profitability is at much lower levels than the USA. Case in point: Italy's profitability is just one-third that of the US and falling. Even if in France and in Germany the situation is expected to improve, unfortunately levels still remain too low to justify and support the new investment cycle of 5G in front of the shareholders of telecom companies.

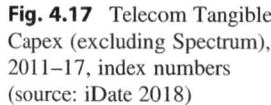

Fig. 4.17 Telecom Tangible Capex (excluding Spectrum), 2011–17, index numbers (source: iDate 2018)

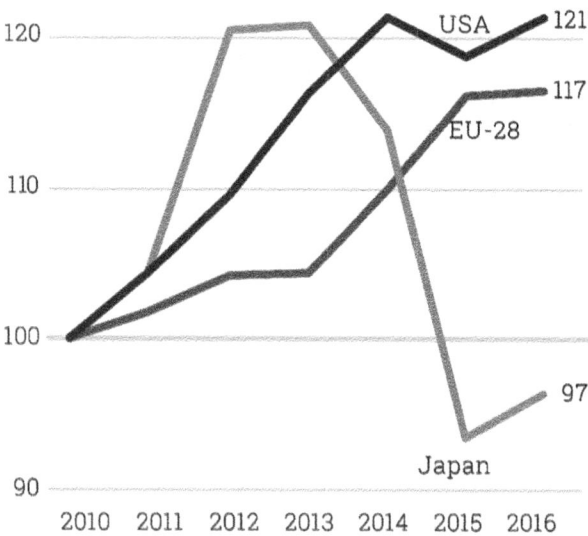

Fig. 4.18 Country ROCE of telecom operators (excluded specialized), 2011–19 (source: Patrick et al. 2018)

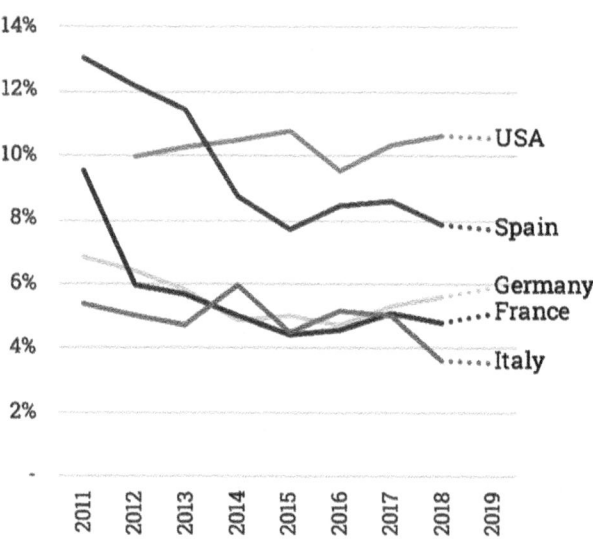

However, a more detailed analysis of telecom profitability shows wide differences across Europe. The Nordic countries stand out as the most profitable, with a ROCE ranging from 11.9 to 10.4%, well above the sample average of 7.9%. This is because of smaller national size, stable competition, solid profitability and

Fig. 4.19 Country ROCE of telecom operators (excluded specialized): a comparison USA vs. selected European countries (source: Elaborations on Venkateshwar et al. 2019a)

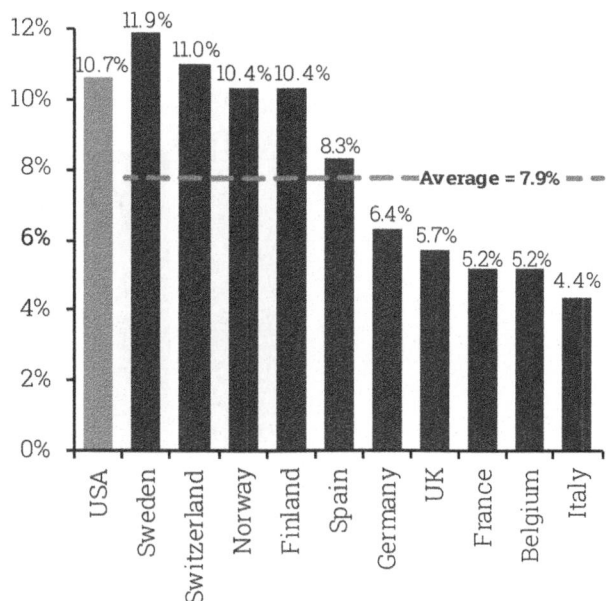

relatively low spectrum costs. Due to lower capex and much lower spectrum spend, profitability in Spain is much higher than other EU markets while Italy represents the worst case (Fig. 4.19), with high spectrum costs and intense competition.

Estimates by BCG (Bock and Wilms 2016), Accenture (2017) and the European Commission (2016) indicate that in Europe the actual pace of investments will not be sufficient to be able to achieve the Gigabit Society objectives set for the European Union[16] by 2025. These objectives are as follows:

- All schools, transport hubs and main providers of public services as well as digitally intensive enterprises should have access to Internet connections with download/upload speeds of 1 Gigabit of data per second.
- All European households, rural or urban, should have access to networks offering a download speed of at least 100 Mbps, which can be upgraded to 1 Gigabit.
- All urban areas as well as major roads and railways should have uninterrupted 5G wireless broadband coverage, starting with fully-fledged commercial service in at least one major city in each EU member state by as early as 2020.

The cost of reaching the EU connectivity objectives is estimated at 500 billion € in investments from 2016 to 2025. These funds would come largely from the private sector, but under current investment trends, there is a 155 billion € investment shortfall, according to European Commission calculations.

---

[16]Broadband Europe, https://ec.europa.eu/digital-single-market/en/broadband-europe.

Fig. 4.20 International
Telecom Operators, share of
respondents that chose
"Business case" as top
challenge for 5G, by national
area (source: Grijpink et al.
2019)

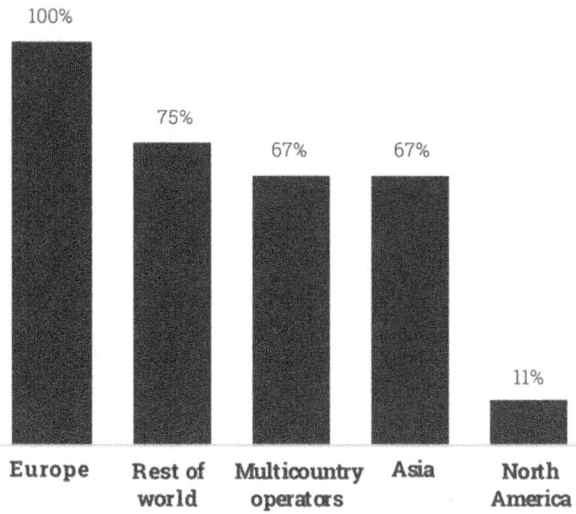

Even in a scenario in which the telecom sector will continuously inflate the capex/
revenue ratio to the benefit of investments, it is difficult to sustain this position
without incremental revenues. Indeed, according to a survey by McKinsey &
Company (Grijpink et al. 2019) based on interviews with 46 chief technology
officers at large telcos around the globe, while the majority of North American
telecom operators (56%) will have large scale 5G deployment before 2020, no other
region is above 40%. What is the explanation of this difference? Most operators
surveyed (60%) think that the biggest challenge to their 5G strategies is identifying a
business case. But this was the answer of 100% of European operators and of only
11% of North American operators (Fig. 4.20). This viewpoint is a sharp departure
from the rollouts of earlier mobile generations, such as 2G and 3G, when Europe led
the technology's introduction. It is not a problem of confidence in the technology,
that is high, but of uncertainty about whether and how soon 5G can fuel new
products and services that customers are willing to pay for.

There are three other elements that emerge from the research that are equally
noteworthy and will have an impact on the future of telecom infrastructures:

- The uncertain economics of 5G are spurring telcos to consider some alternative
  business models. About 93% of the respondents said they expect network sharing
  to expand with efforts to bring 5G to areas where it does not make sense to have
  multiple networks. Moreover, approximately 90% anticipate that third-party
  neutral hosts will supply a part of the network to run for several operators
- While the top reason for investing in 5G is network leadership, that means pure
  competitive pressure, at least at the outset, the majority of the telecom operators
  see enhanced mobile broadband, IoT, fixed wireless access (see Sect. 4.4 for more
  details) and mission-critical applications as the most prevalent applications for
  5G. These are not the revolutionary use cases mentioned by 5G enthusiasts,

nonetheless in the eyes of telecommunications operators these are the most credible applications.

- From a global perspective, the survey confirms a new scenario in regional technological leadership. Although North America is still in the lead, Asia is keeping pace and Europe is waiting for a clearer view on use case economics to accelerate.

Is this last point another proof of the beginning of a new and negative phase for European telecommunications? European telecom operators no doubt face pressure from regulatory bodies and competition. At the same time, they are loading their balance sheets to undertake investments while trying to meet shareholders' expectations of preserving the historical dividend distribution. They are also defending their position from the potential threats of a long-awaited industry consolidation through mergers or acquisitions. As a result, the European Commission is struggling to incentivize the start of a new investment cycle in the telecom industry.

4.4.2 Regulation Issues in Europe

The European Commission is in a difficult position, as declarations about Gigabit society, the strategic importance of digital connectivity for European competitiveness and results are not tightly coupled. The European role in the digital arena remains very weak and technological leadership is losing ground while prices and competition have favored European citizens, as seen above.

Following the proposal for a new Electronic Communications Code from the European Commission in September 2016, in June 2018 a political agreement was reached[17] to update the EU's telecom regulatory framework (after the previous update in 2009). Adopted by the Parliament and then by the Council in November 2018, member states have until 21 December 2020 to transpose the new directive into national legislation.

The code sets a new regulatory objective of promoting access to, and take-up of, very high capacity connectivity (fixed and mobile) across the European Union. This in addition to the existing objectives of promoting competition, contributing to development of the internal market and fostering the interests of EU citizens.

The Commission proposal addresses four existing directives, on the Framework, Access, Authorization and Universal Service. The code would amend these directives and integrate all four into a single new legal text with two major objectives:

---

[17]Proposal for a Directive of the European Parliament and the Council establishing the European Electronic Communications Code: http://data.consilium.europa.eu/doc/document/ST-10692-2018-INIT/en/pdf

1. Enhance the deployment of 5G networks by ensuring the availability of 5G radio spectrum by the end of 2020 in the EU and provide operators with predictability for at least 20 years regarding spectrum licensing;
2. Facilitate the roll-out of new, very high capacity fixed networks by:

- Making rules for co-investment more predictable and promoting risk sharing in the deployment of very high capacity networks;
- Promoting sustainable competition for the benefit of consumers, with a regulatory emphasis on the real bottlenecks, such as wiring, ducts and cabling inside buildings;
- Creating a specific regulatory regime for wholesale-only operators (see Sect. 4.4).

The last point is in part a new proposal that could open sizeable investment spaces to institutional investors in telecommunications, especially if the whole set of guidelines included in the code is matched with the opportunities arising from the evolution of the telecom infrastructure.

4.4.3 The Geopolitical Role of Telecom Investments

The evolution of telecom infrastructure is so critical for OTTs that they are actively involved in trying to influence it. But they are not the only ones.

Telecommunication infrastructure is a general-purpose technology (Bresnahan and Trajtenberg 1995) that, as such, has a big impact on potential productivity gains and economic growth across major economic sectors and on a large scale. So, governments are paying more attention to their comparative position in the deployment and adoption of telecommunication infrastructures while there is growing evidence of the socio-economic impact of this kind of investments on economic growth, local development, labor market, firm productivity and entrepreneurship, (Alizadeh 2017; Edquist et al. 2018; Oughton et al. 2018; Abrardi and Cambini 2019).

This is even more palpable because the most recent developments in manufacturing and IT (Internet-of-Things, artificial intelligence, augmented or virtual reality, blockchain, big data, additive manufacturing, etc.) have ever-increasing telecommunication needs, both fixed and wireless. Further, given the importance of cloud computing, which is "where" most of the most advanced technologies are located, an obsolete telco infrastructure could delay or reduce the impact of these innovations.

To quantify the economic relevance of telecommunications, consider this: reaching the objectives set by the European Commission for the "Gigabit Society by 2025" will trigger investments that could boost European GDP by an additional

910 billion € ($1.023 trillion). In addition, 1.3 million new jobs will be created by 2025, according to European Commission evaluations.[18]

Likewise, mobile technologies make a significant contribution to socioeconomic development around the world. In 2018, these technologies and related services generated $3.9 trillion of economic value (4.6% of GDP) globally. This contribution will reach $4.8 trillion (4.8% of GDP) by 2023 as countries derive ever greater benefit from the improvements in productivity and efficiency brought about by more widespread take-up of mobile services. The global mobile ecosystem generated $1.1 trillion of economic value in 2018 with infrastructure providers accounting for $80 billion (7%). Further ahead, 5G technologies are expected to contribute $2.2 trillion to the global economy over the next 15 years (GSMA 2019a).

Moreover, in every national plan to improve competitiveness in manufacturing (and all the major countries have one), the role of telecommunications is critical. This is true for "Industrie 4.0", the German national plan launched in 2013 that will leverage on Cyber-Physical Systems (CPS) to defend the future of Germany in manufacturing. It is also true for "The Next Wave of Manufacturing" in Australia (2013), "Made Different" in Belgium (2013), "Make in India" in India (2014), "Produktion 2030" in Sweden (2014), "Smart Industry" in the Netherlands (2014), "Manufacturing Innovation 3.0" in South Korea (2014), "Industrial Value Chain Initiative" in Japan (2015), "Made-in-China 2025" in China (2015), "Industrial Internet of Things" in Canada (2015), "Industrie du Futur" in France (2015), "Industrial Strategy" in the UK (2015) and "Industria 4.0" in Italy (2016). This is also the reason why China, Korea and Japan had such a strong government push to lead the world in fiber adoption and in 5G plans.

However, this industrial perspective views the telecom infrastructure as a means to improve competitiveness in manufacturing. But there is also an industrial opportunity that sees telecom infrastructure from the opposite standpoint. Leading the adoption of a technology (e.g. 5G or fiber networks) gives a country the opportunity to develop and nurture national champions up to a point in which they can develop the underlying products to a level of maturity to be competitive in exporting them to other countries.

This was China's strategy in fiber optics, for example. China had 347 million subscribers to FTTH or FTTB (Fiber-to-the-Building) lines in 2018 while in North America were 19 million and in Western Europe 26 million (iDate 2018). 2021 forecasts set that number at 421 million in China, but only 26 million in North America and 52 million in Western Europe. Consuming 58% of the total fiber optic produced in the world, China has successfully become the worldwide leader in passive fiber, the *de facto* global standard in optical networks.

China is trying to implement the same approach in mobile networks. In 2G, China had none to speak of, but developed a China-only standard in 3G and had some marginal participation in 4G research. But after LTE (4G), which was the first global telecommunication standard, 5G will be the first real universal standard, redesigning

---

[18]European Commission (2016) http://europa.eu/rapid/press-release_IP-16-3008_en.htm

Table 4.6 Standard-Essential Patents (SEPs) for 5G and 5G Standard Proposals, owners and contributors by country

Country	5G Standard-Essential Patents (SEPs), owners by country	%	Number of 5G Standard Proposal submitted by country	%
China	2081	31	25786	40
Korea	1787	27	6992	11
Others	1461	22	1482	2
US	1321	20	11590	18
Europe	–	–	15669	24
Japan	–	–	3481	5
Total	6650	100	65,000	100

Source: IPlytics GmbH 2019; Lee and Chau 2019

telecom networks from the ground up. In 5G, China is in first place for patent owners, controlling 31% of the Standard-Essential Patents (SEPs) for 5G networks. This country also leads the world as contributor to research with 40% of the total standard proposal submitted (Table 4.6). Plus, the number of Chinese representatives in the International Telecommunication Union (ITU),[19] technical specification groups (TSG) and sub-groups has increased from 8 out of 57 in 2013 to 10 in 2017 (Lee and Chau 2017, 2019).

Once 5G networks begin to be built and deployed, the control of technical standards will influence which companies will win lucrative equipment contracts. Whoever owns a significant portion of the patents in the underlying technology should be able to be more effective in bidding for network projects. It is a commercial advantage which parlays itself into a security advantage: whoever controls the technology has an intimate knowledge of how it was built and where all the doors and buttons are (Zhong 2018).

Finally, if China ends up dominating 5G networks, the authority will also shift toward China to set standards for future network technologies such as 6G, which is already under development. Furthermore, whoever dictates the standards will dominate future products because early developments will be faster and work better than others. In sum, commercial power almost directly translates into standard-setting power.

Actually, the market leaders in telecom equipment are already Chinese (Huawei and ZTE): in a few years they managed to surpass Nokia Networks and Ericsson, contending for some of Cisco's niches too. Since 2012, when a US congressional report revealed that the Chinese government could potentially use Huawei's equipment to spy on Americans, telecom security is a top concern in the United States.

---

[19]ITU is the United Nations (UN) specialized agency for information and communication technologies. Founded in 1865, it is the oldest among all the 15 specialized agencies of UN. It is responsible for facilitating international connectivity in communications networks, allocating global radio spectrum and satellite orbits, and developing the technical standards that ensure networks and technologies seamlessly interconnect. The agency also strives to improve access to ICTs to underserved communities worldwide.

Both ZTE and Huawei have been effectively blocked from major US telecom networks due to fears that their gear could be used for espionage. In addition, US authorities have pulled the companies' smartphones from US military bases and stopped all sales by ZTE and Huawei to the government.

In August 2018, Australia excluded Chinese telecommunications equipment manufacturers from the countries' 5G rollout over fears of possible cyber espionage. The decision was based on the belief that 5G networks will be more vulnerable to security breaches because they will be less centralized than current networks, with more sensitive network activity occurring in a multitude of locations closer to users (Strumpf and Cherney 2018). Japan, the UK, Germany and Italy have also started studying the prospect of a similar ban with restrictions on Huawei and ZTE ahead of the rollout of their 5G networks. It is impossible to imagine the outcome of this battle on the control of technology, but it is already clear that it has changed forever the perception of the consequences of technology choices.

Clearly, in the future the geopolitical impact of telecommunications investments will be stronger than in the past. Most likely investments in mobile and fixed networks are destined to do the same. Moreover, almost all the big telecom incumbents, with a few exceptions, are controlled by national governments with heightened sensitivity to competitiveness issues linked to technology and cyber-safety. This will make government interventions more and more likely in the technological infrastructures of their countries, even in Europe.

Therefore, in the future there will be huge investments in fiber networks and 5G, pushed by a strong demand by users. To face this investment cycle telecom companies should commit a huge amount of resources, but they also need new skills and a fresher approach. Considering the negative trend in Europe in terms of profitability and revenues, we can anticipate a probable outcome: soon in Europe there will be very interesting opportunities to invest in the telecommunications infrastructure that were unimaginable in the past. But most likely that will not be good news for telecom operators.

4.5   Emerging Investment Opportunities in the Telecom Industry

As explained in the previous sections, for different reasons, telecom operators face an extraordinary number of critical challenges, and will continue to do so. These challenges, listed below, often call for decisions that cannot be postponed, and almost always require new investments despite growing uncertainty on returns.

- Mobile networks' transition to 5G in a scenario of uncertainty as far as the sustainability of the business cases;
- Mounting competitive pressure from the OTTs on different arenas increasingly targeting some cornerstones of telecom business;
- Improving fixed/mobile network quality to guarantee a lower latency and more reliable connections, with or without edge computing;

- Creating a business case on edge networking or leaving the floor to operators like OTTs that can further weaken telecoms traditional business and harm the future profitability of 5G networks;
- The decommissioning of a large number of central offices and the transformation of the remaining ones in data centers;
- Peak time traffic increasing faster than average traffic, adding to the problem of a greater need for backhauling capacity due to rebound effects from faster connections on mobile and fixed networks;
- Geopolitical issues delaying and potentially making every answer to telecom infrastructure challenges more critical and expensive;
- Additional investments in submarine transcontinental cables if telecom operators want to compete with OTTs on network performances.

Traditionally, telecom operators have always been very jealous of their business, especially incumbents. They take great pride in controlling their network and every aspect of their operation. But things are changing. Telecom companies are in second place as the industry most reliant on outsourcing: 72% of their executives currently outsource or offshore services. Moreover, in 46% of these companies, demand for outsourced technology is boosted by an in-house lack of talent (Nash 2017). Furthermore, as we have seen, there is growing pressure on the telecom industry about financial results. Therefore, telcos can be less effective in defending their business from outside investments or be tempted by opportunities for containing their capital commitment.

In this scenario, especially in Europe, where decreasing revenues and thinner margins are coupled with a tighter procompetitive regulation, there could be a proliferation of new opportunities for investing in the telecommunication industry. These range from fixed to mobile networks, but the 5G transformation could create even more lucrative opportunities across the two networks.

4.5.1 Emerging Infrastructure Investments in Fixed Networks and from Network Evolution

In fixed networks, given the existing configuration, there could be four major cases of separable infrastructures, giving rise to different models (Fig. 4.21):

1. Vertically Integrated	In a vertically integrated infrastructure, the separable infrastructures may include the access to ducts and poles, sometimes other structural passive elements of the network; this is the case in Japan. The separation of ducts and poles is a complex operation with a high execution risk because it is difficult to manage contractually and even in day-by-day operations. With this model, incumbents try to exert tight control over the value chain and to improve their cash flow profile. Duplication of vertical infrastructures creates a high barrier for new entrants which, in turn, after the initial investment, works as a barrier against other

(continued)

	potential entrants This model tends to be very closed to external investments unless forced by the national regulator.
2. Passive sharing	As with Openreach in the UK, this model is easier to realize and can capture a large part of the revenue potential. The infrastructure owner lacks direct control over the revenue stream and marketing to the end-user, but this model can ensure stable cash flows. An effective and credible regulator is needed. Interesting opportunities can open up for investments if vertical service providers are able to differentiate their services.
3. Active sharing	This model, diffused in Asia and in India, creates large infrastructure providers with stable cash flows. It creates additional margins for modest incremental investment, giving an incentive for continuous updates. It must be technically credible yet flexible. With an effective and credible regulator, this is the model that best fits into the technological evolution taking place. Small retail service providers may struggle if there are no commercial and operational standards for wholesale.
4. Full separation	This model, realized in the Netherlands, is the most difficult to implement. It creates additional margins for modest incremental investment to the infrastructure owner and network operator. It must be technically credible yet flexible. This model can catalyze many resources, especially from local entities, but needs an effective and credible regulator. Theoretically, this is the perfect pro-competitive model, but it is difficult to manage in practice. Small retail service providers may struggle if there are no commercial and operational standards for wholesale.

Since the vertically integrated model is the natural monopolistic starting point in developed countries for fixed networks, most of the evolutions towards other models are driven by a need to facilitate investment in new technologies. Broadband, ADSL, but mostly FTTx[20] are the real triggers that could open up new spaces for investments in telecom networks. But, due to the delay accumulated in fiber deployment, mainly in rural areas and in Europe, there could be even more investment opportunities.

Therefore, political pressure for investments in fiber will likely intensify. The primary reason for this is that in a 5G future, fiber densification is a mandatory requirement to ensure backhauling connections to the thousands of new micro cells, creating the service umbrella for this extremely promising evolution. But the

---

[20]FTTx is an abbreviation that stands for all the different combinations of infrastructures based on fiber: FTTH, FTTB, and so on.

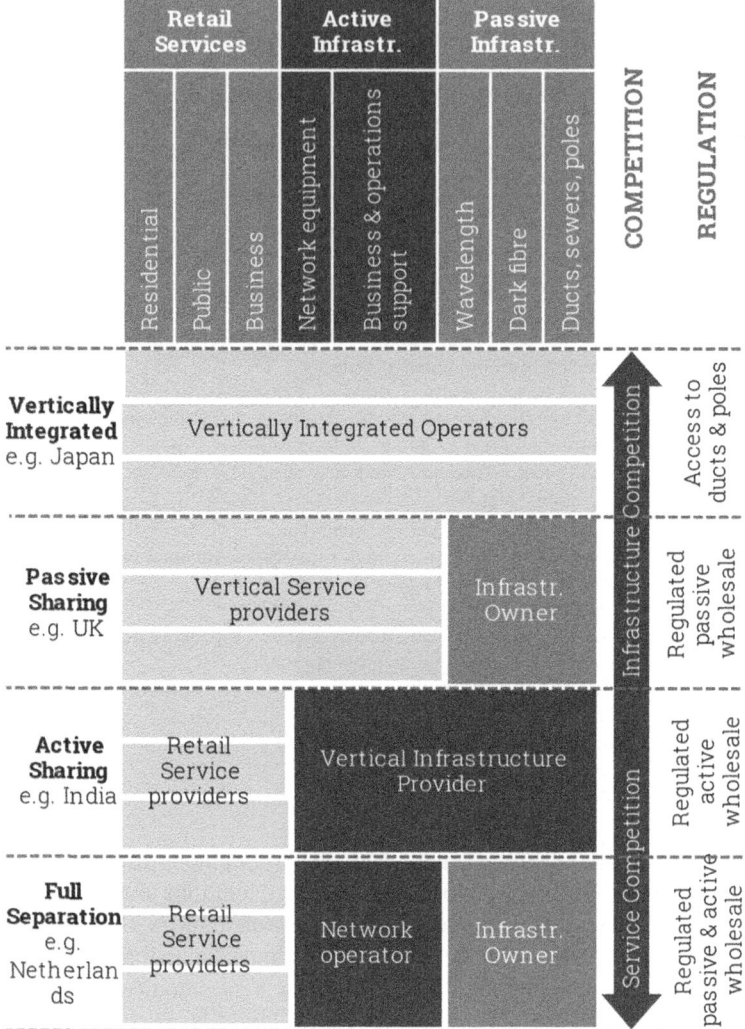

Fig. 4.21 Separable infrastructures in the traditional telecom infrastructure (source: Adapted from Alcatel-Lucent, FTTH Council)

changing structure of the network (whether or not it supports 5G communications) is in itself a source of new kinds of investment opportunities in telecom infrastructures, as illustrated in Fig. 4.22.

Starting from the physical infrastructure, closer to the final user, there is the pure **(1) fiber wholesaler**, which provides the fiber lines (the grey lines in the figure), with or without the FTTB or the FTTH connections (the green dots in the figure). This model has been codified for the first time by the European Commission in the new regulatory framework. The first real example of this new business model is the

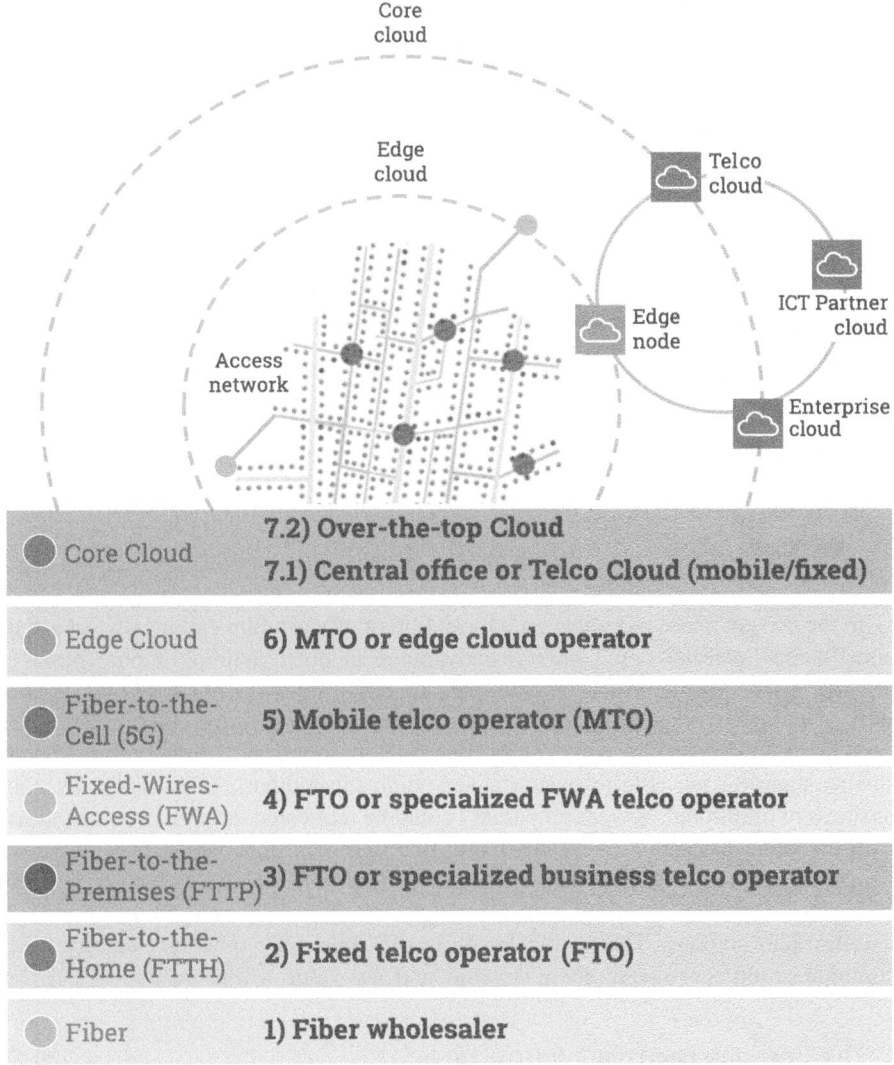

Fig. 4.22 Separable infrastructures in the telecom infrastructure formed by ongoing and future network evolutions

Italian Open Fiber, financed by private and public money. The aim here is to realize a fiber network in areas under-served or far from the coverage plan of the main operators but also in areas already served by other fiber providers without a FTTH or FTTB infrastructure. It is too early to judge the sustainability of this business model, but it looks promising. Its weakest points, being almost greenfield, are the timing of the coverage, which requires effective and timely execution, and the ability to transform this coverage into subscribers at a fast pace leveraging the appropriate marketing approach.

Vouchers and Incentives for FTTH/FTTB Take-Up

Governments in Europe have just started to give financial incentives, funded by the EU, especially to families to increase the user base of fiber networks. In the new European communications code, promoting access to, and take-up of, very high capacity connectivity is a new regulatory objective. The incentives are not directly linked to the market structure, but when there is a pure fiber wholesaler it is much easier to satisfy the regulatory requirements. The first proposal in 2014 came in Italy; since then it was approved but never launched. On the contrary, since 2016, Denmark is fully operational with a tax break of up to 1600 € per family. Since 2018, the United Kingdom and Greece are in a pilot phase, the UK with a voucher up to £3000 for SMEs and up to £500 for individuals. Greece offers a 48 € discount on installation plus a discount of 13 € per month for 2 years on the subscription cost for a FTTH connection in selected areas. Germany is moving in the same direction. Here in 2018 some telecom associations proposed that the government adopt a voucher program to incentivize FTTH or FTTB connections, offering up to 1500 € per installation.

In the present phase of radical transformation of telecommunication networks, the pure fiber wholesaler could have an advantage in not remaining a pure passive provider of infrastructures. For example, an opportunity in 5G networks is the shift of radio coverage from macro cells (a few very powerful cells, covering a very large area) to small cells (many more cells, about 6–10 times more, much smaller than 4G but able to ensure a very high throughput). For small cells, the business of traditional "tower companies" could be replicated through infrastructures with a smaller scale but a vast coverage, like that of a fiber wholesaler network. Every point along the fiber network with a minimum of space, having a fiber connection and easy access to a power supply, could readily be used as a base for mobile radio stations. This is the business of "enercom": wherever energy plus communication is available, there is value, and this value will grow.

The Emerging Enercom Infrastructures

The evolution of energy and telecommunication infrastructure, both in a phase of turbulent change change (see Di Castelnuovo and Biancardi 2020), is partially overlapping. Wherever there are electrical infrastructures, the presence of a form of communication adds value, enabling new business models or different kind of services. Just to mention some: smart grids, demand-response systems, V2G (Vehicle-to-Grid), EV recharging points, smart street lights, and smart lighting. Wherever there is a source of communication or a communication device, there are electrical needs to be met in different ways and forms.

(continued)

Some examples are: low or high voltage power, batteries, battery back-up, solar panels and batteries for power autonomy, redundant supply of energy, and surge suppression systems. Therefore, every public site equipped with both energy and communication, (hence the term "enercom site") will have a different value in the future from a strategic perspective. In fact, each enercom site is a potential piece of a larger infrastructural telecom network (for example, a small cell for 5G, a point for FWA distribution, or part of a network using unlicensed spectrum).

Moreover, the telecommunication industry has a problem with energy cost and supply because the proliferation in communication traffic analyzed in Sect. 4.1.3 will also lead to a substantial hike in energy consumption. Over the next few years, in fact, global energy consumption of telecommunication networks will surge from $40 billion in 2011 to $343 billion in 2025, with wireless networks accounting for over 70% of the total (Weldon 2016). Telecommunications represent about 2% of the worldwide electricity consumption, whereas the entire ICT sector (including data centers, devices, computers and peripherals) accounts for about 6%. The network energy bill typically runs between 7 and 15% of the operational expenses of telecommunication service providers in developed countries and up to 40–50% in some developing countries (Intelligent Energy 2012; GSMA 2014; Kim 2017). A major European network operator stated that its energy bill would hit the $1 billion mark by 2020 (Le Maistre 2014), whereas that of some of the large operators in the USA had already topped this price point in 2012. In the UK and Italy, telecommunications operators are the largest consumers of electricity, utilizing about 1% of the total electricity generation of their countries. For these reasons, the energy problem has become critical in telecommunications as well as any form of energy saving or any potential use of renewable sources of energy. This leads to the opportunity to develop an "enercom business" that manages and optimizes all the energy needs of telecom infrastructure.

In any case, there is a third possible business for enercom infrastructures. IoT devices and sensors, mostly equipped with batteries, individually tend to consume relatively small amounts of energy in absolute terms, but as we have seen earlier, there will be an enormous number of such devices deployed. Therefore, all the activities related to enercom management are key to monitor and manage such networked infrastructures, replacing and recycling batteries while maintaining devices.

Another option to enrich the business of a fiber wholesaler is the **Open Service Exchange Operator (OSEO)**. To a dark fiber infrastructure, the OSEO adds a technical layer that simplifies the day-by-day operations of monitoring fiber lines. This operator also provides a business support system for selling, delivering, invoicing, administering and managing the final users of fixed fiber operators (see Sect. 4.2.2). The OSEO can increase the revenues of the wholesaler and enlarge its market by changing the billing operator without any physical intervention, greatly improving opex. The OSEO also makes it possible to offer innovative, customized subscription plans with time-based service, for example, for vacation homes. Such a plan might work over the weekend with a full bandwidth, and at a reduced speed during the week, solely for security and monitoring purposes.

The pure fiber wholesaler, that sells to the **(2) fixed telco operator (FTO)**, share with it a large part of its destiny. The FTO is a relatively new business model. For its success the key appears to be its ability to execute and to differentiate its offer with a convincing service proposition. Its business could be relatively poor or rich in terms of infrastructure, depending on whether or not the fiber wholesaler manages the fiber connection from the basement of a building to the home (the green dot in the figure) in a FTTH scheme, or to the building for FTTB. The natural evolution of this model is to enrich the fiber connection with a "triple play" (telephone, Internet connection and media services), but other services such as Internet security can complement the offering too.

Just a little further away from the final user, we find the **(3) specialized business telco operator** which works on mainly with business customers and on their premises (the red dots in the figure). These customers are served with fiber connections to distribute other telecom or IT services, which might include network management, security, wifi or more sophisticated forms of wireless connections such as Multefire, Sigfox, Lora, CBRS or other services in the IoT market that work on the unlicensed spectrum. Some of the business models enabled by the OTTs (and described in Sect. 4.3) could belong to this category even if they offer their final users fixed wireless access service or a form of mobile connection. The specialized business telco operator could be a small-scale enterprise or part of a larger network with a sizeable infrastructure.

The **(4) Fixed Wireless Access (FWA)** operator (the yellow dots in the figure) is an emerging business model that has a proprietary infrastructure connecting a point-of-presence (POP), linked to the FWA with leased fibers or lines, to its users in a fixed position with a wireless link. In some cases, this is the solution to coverage problems in rural areas, but sometimes it is also a cheaper alternative in densely populated areas as well. AT&T and Verizon are using the FWA model in urbanized areas where a low population density does not justify more investments to bring other forms of high-speed connections. Google Fiber, instead, after the acquisition of WebPass, a specialized FWA operator, is using it in some very dense urban areas, such as in San Francisco. FWA could be delivered in many ways. Usually, the fixed wireless broadcasting equipment is installed on the roofs of buildings, on balconies or out of a window to ensure an obstruction-free connection, since most FWA receivers are conceived to be connected in line of sight for better signal reception. FWA could also be implemented as a point-to-multipoint or multipoint-to-multipoint infrastructure, as with 5G.

Fixed Wired Access has still a business model in evolution without a dominant technical solution. The most promising one appears to be 5G, which is so flexible that it can also serve fixed installations with a special equipment, ensuring a connection quality that is similar to a fixed connection but at a much lower cost. Exploiting beam-forming and millimetre wave spectrum (which are part of the 5G technology) provides a considerable performance boost to wireless broadband services. As of 2018, Verizon already has a 5G FWA program up and running on a small scale in Sacramento and Cincinnati, but forecasts are that in 2024 more than 12 million households in the US will receive home Internet service via 5G through FWA points (Newman 2019b).

In this scenario, traditional **(5) mobile telecom operators (MTO)** can choose to take advantage of fiber densification and improve their network density (the dark blue dots in the figure). Since expectations for 5G mainly center on performances, the most critical requirement to ensure this promise is cell densification, which means having much more cells, covering a smaller area, and bringing fiber to every micro cell. From this perspective, as anticipated above in this section, there could be space for a new kind of tower company. In fact, fiber wholesalers or specialized business telco operators can form a new kind of infrastructure, without owning big towers but having access, control or simply installation rights on enercom points like public lampposts, electric or telephone poles, electric substations or telecom secondary stations. The development of this kind of infrastructure is only beginning, but with ongoing progress in 5G deployment, many owners of small urban infrastructures may realize they are sitting on a truly valuable asset for them and for MTOs.

At a similar stage is the business model of the **(6) edge cloud operator** (the small light blue cloud in the figure). Also known as fog computing, it is partially linked to 5G networks and still under development. The edge cloud operator is a data processing model that uses sensors and connected devices to transmit data to a nearby computing device for processing, instead of sending it back to the cloud or a remote data center. Edge computing solutions are located close to where applications or data are utilized, so users do not need to deal with the time that it takes for communication to travel back and forth to the cloud or a server and delays due to latency are minimized. This allows edge computing users to make real-time decisions and to automate processes, since it takes almost no time to create and analyze data and then take a decision on it. There is a second reason that makes edge computing so important: by using an edge computing solution, companies process their data locally, meaning they can extract what is useful out of raw data and store only the insights in the cloud. This cuts down on the volume of data they need to send to the cloud (reducing networking needs) as well as the amount of data that is being kept on cloud storage.

Edge computing has many use cases. It could greatly improve efficiency when processing the growing volumes of data-rich video from security cameras and other camera-based monitoring solutions, for example. Business Insider Intelligence forecasts that smart city systems, which include connected cameras, will generate nearly 180 billion terabytes of data a year by 2023 (Newman 2019a). A Gartner research (van der Meulen 2018) reports that around 10% of enterprise-generated data is created and processed outside a traditional centralized data center or cloud, but by 2025, this figure is predicted to reach 75%. Besides, the augmenting complexity of vehicles and the amount of data they record pose a problem for automakers and operators looking to process that data. A connected car generates thousands of GBs of data every day, without taking into account additional autonomous features. In fact, an autonomous vehicle could churn out 4000 GB of data every day, according to Intel's estimates. Moreover, total data exchanged between vehicles and the cloud could reach 10 billion GB per month, based on Toyota's forecasts. This raw data streaming to the cloud can be critical for improving autonomous driving capabilities, but the volume is staggering and could overwhelm both cloud systems and cellular networks. By 2023, vehicles in the US will generate 8 ZB annually, up from 0.72 ZB in 2018 (Business Insider Intelligence, The EDGE Computing Report 2018), creating an opportunity for edge computing.

Edge servers can form clusters or micro data centers giving processing power or data storage where more computing power is needed locally. With local processing, telcos could reduce data loads on their networks and generate additional revenues while companies can choose to send only meaningful insights to the cloud. With edge computing, the more technical structure of 5G networks moves away from the core of the network but not necessarily into the hands of telecom companies. Edge computing act as if it were part of cloud computing, only closer to the final user. But the OTTs are much better at managing and operate the cloud, they created it, and they are also better equipped to take profit of it than telecom operators. For example, since 2017 Amazon AWS has been selling edge computing solutions connected to its cloud computing infrastructure. Since 2019 all the services on its Elastic Compute Cloud have been available at the edge of the network through a relatively small but powerful device. This development has two infrastructural implications. First, unless OTTs accept to have in edge computing the role of pure technology providers, the business case of edge computing with great difficulty could become a separate infrastructure to develop, which was totally unanticipated at the inception of 5G. Second, small enercom points could instead serve to support edge computing, especially if they can form a capillary infrastructure.

Finally, there is the **(7) cloud computing** level (the small grey clouds in the figure), which is becoming a different and more effective computing paradigm for all the players that intend to leverage IT: telecom and IT companies and the clients of both. At the moment, from a business point of view, there is no question that OTTs have been more successful in the cloud business than telecom operators. In fact, the latter tried to compete for cloud services, but with poor results in terms of market share (which is still negligible) because telcos struggle to keep pace with OTTs in competitiveness and innovation. Global leader Amazon AWS, for example, has lowered its prices by as much as 65 times since its launch in 2006 (every 2 months and 6 days approximately). This translates to an average price reduction of around 14% per year over the period from 2008 to 2018, which means in 10 years prices have plunged to less than a quarter of the original starting price. What's more, only in 2018, Amazon AWS was launching 1985 new functionalities on its cloud platform, an average of almost five new functions every day.

However, from the infrastructural point of view, for telecom companies, along with fiber densification, the transformation of their central offices into data centers could be a saving opportunity. The number of offices will drop; the capex of every central office will be much lower, using commoditized hardware such as cloud computing data centers; even the opex will be lower in a re-engineered architecture. Therefore, the old central offices could be sold or repurposed as a different infrastructure.

4.5.2 Emerging Infrastructure Investments in Wireless Networks

The huge investments needed to deploy 5G networks and the opportunities it opens will transform the whole mobile industry landscape.[21] But since now, they create incentives to find alternative solutions to the traditional proprietary model of mobile operators (see Sect. 4.4.1). This opens a large opportunity window to infrastructure investors willing to contribute to financing the 5G infrastructure, in whole or in part. As specified in the box below, infrastructure sharing is already being put into practice, although at the moment, it is limited only to agreements between peers.

A Common Infrastructure for 5G Networks
Some countries are already exploring a single infrastructure across different operators for 5G networks:

- In South Korea, wireless carriers and Internet Service Providers (ISP), with a combined annual capex of $6 billion, are pooling resources to build out 5G with an expected capex savings of around $1 billion in 10 years.
- In China the largest enercom agreement in the world is ongoing. China Mobile, China Telecom and China Unicom jointly own China Tower, controlling about 2.5 million towers. This partnership stipulated a deal with State Grid Corporation of China (SGCC, the country's largest state-run electric utility company) to share resources in telecommunications infrastructure and electricity. By sharing telecommunications towers, the deployment of 5G and smart grids is accelerating, lowering installation and operative costs of Chinese mobile infrastructure. A similar agreement has already been negotiated with China Southern Power Grid, another state-owned electric utility, to share resources and establish regular cooperation.

(continued)

---

[21]See for this Section also the study commissioned by Berec, the association of the European national regulatory agencies (DotEcon and Axon Partners 2018).

According to the Chinese press, feasibility studies and applications on power and communication infrastructure resource sharing have already been carried out by the companies in Fujian, Yunnan, Hainan and Hubei.

- In the USA, the National Security Council (NSC) proposed a state-owned 5G infrastructure involving AT&T, Verizon, T-mobile and Sprint, with a combined annual capex of $30 billion.
- In Italy, Telecom Italia (TIM) and Vodafone Italy have agreed to an active 5G network sharing project and are examining a move to share 4G infrastructure. The two companies would combine their respective mobile tower networks which together cover some 22,000 sites to support faster deployment of 5G over a wider geographic area, at a lower cost.

In general, since 2012 there has been growing interest in negotiating agreements involving fixed and wireless infrastructures. This trend could result in synergies and savings on mobile networks, improving the offering profile. In total, 26 partnership have been negotiated, of which 20 (77%) in Europe followed by 2 (8%) in Asia, involving 29 different countries. Four proposed partnerships have been abandoned, 2 are pending and 20 are signed, for a total declared value of 180 billion €, on average 7 billion € per deal (Venkateshwar et al. 2019a).

The antenna site is the easiest component to share in a mobile network. A typical as-is model, illustrated in Fig. 4.23, has an antenna positioned in an authorized site. The site may be exclusively available to a mobile network operator (MNO) or shared with another MNO. This way the MNO can reduce costs by giving up an alternative site and placing its antenna, connected to its network, in the same site. A mobile virtual network operator (MVNO), hosted on the network of the second MNO, does not need another antenna on the same site, but being only a virtual operator, can leverage the existing equipment.

To enhance performances, 5G networks are denser in populated places, because of the greater use of small cells, covering a smaller area compared to the typical macro cells of 3G/4G. Thus, 5G networks require a great number of small sites within urban areas, either outdoor or indoor, in shopping centers or stadiums, for example. These sites can be shared basically in two ways. First, as in Fig. 4.24 Model 1, with an MNO physically controlling a privately owned site that can be shared with another MNO. Since 5G is more flexible in terms of configurations, another antenna is not needed, almost as would be the case with an MVNO. Second, as in Model 2, the site can be controlled by an intermediary, which rents the site as a neutral host. The site itself can either already be equipped as an enercom point, or be equipped by the MNOs, which can share the site and the antenna.

Especially in rural areas, a backhaul is needed for 5G cell sites. This can potentially represent another service sold to the MNOs by the site owner, increasing its revenues. Edge computing or energy back-ups could be other potential services.

Fig. 4.23 The as-is model of
a mobile network

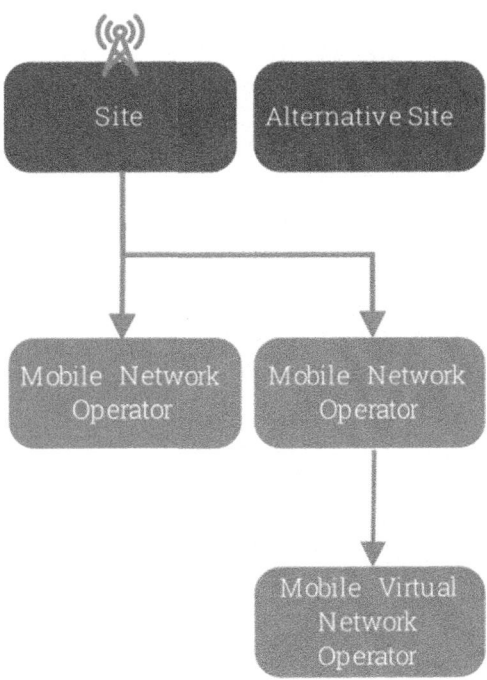

A different approach to sharing telecommunications infrastructures is based on services. Vertical markets with specialized requirements could be an opportunity for intermediaries who are familiar with relative requirements and industries (DotEcon and Axon Partners 2018). These intermediaries could be in an optimal position to assemble connectivity services targeting industry needs, bundling them with other specialized services to differentiate their offering from the non-specialized communication services of a typical MNO (Fig. 4.25). For example, intermediaries could serve hospitals with low latency services for remote surgical interventions. Being able to identify and address their specialized needs, these companies can develop an infrastructure able to complement medical equipment that can be used in emergencies, bundling together 5G connectivity with edge computing and other supporting hardware to offer a service capable of operating a portable ultrasound system or an electrocardiograph. Differentiation by price may allow niche services to develop and be paid by users with specific needs, whilst avoiding price increases for users who do not require these additional functionalities.

Therefore, in specialized vertical markets there could be other business models for 5G deployment. In a typical as-is model, MNOs use their spectrum to provide connectivity and negotiate with a vertical and/or an original equipment manufacturer (OEM) customer to provide a bespoke connectivity (Fig. 4.26, As Is Model).

A variation of this paradigm is represented by Model 1 in Fig. 4.26. A vertical industry and/or a specialized OEM customer uses a self-supplied private 5G network solution due to concerns regarding public network security, quality or cost. A private

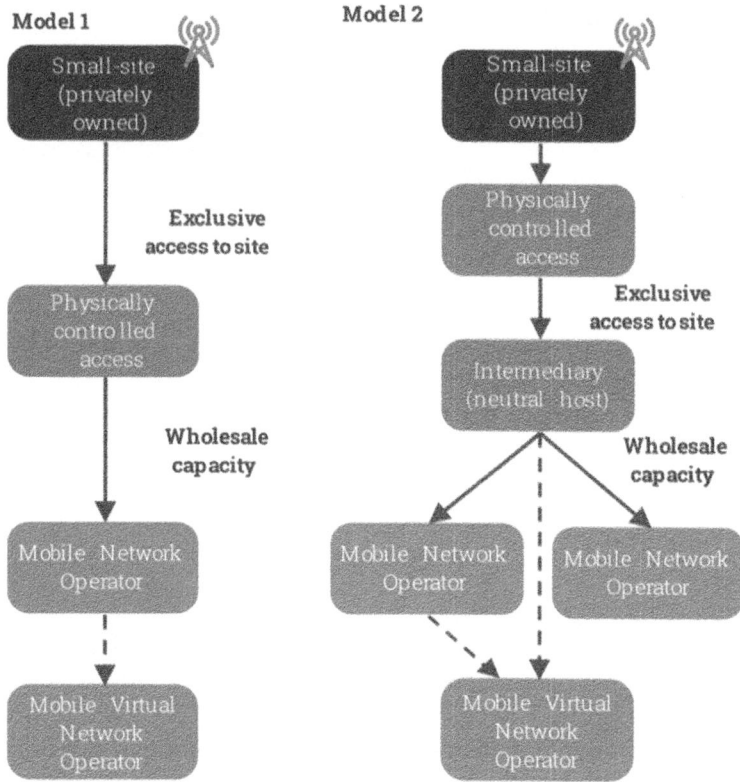

Fig. 4.24 Two models of site sharing in 5G

infrastructure can be developed that leverages 5G standards but uses the unlicensed spectrum, avoiding in this way traditional MNOs. This approach could be successful in highly specialized industries like oil, for example, and may be a likely scenario especially in case of slow deployment of 5G networks. But, once developed, these wireless private networks will remain, reducing the potential 5G market for traditional operators.

On this model there could be a variation (Model 2): a joint venture in a vertical industry (or in part of the industry), eventually between some OEM customers and network operators to share the cost of 5G network deployment. In this way the infrastructure would be deployed more quickly, but it would remain under the control of an MNO that could still sell other services.

This approach, on a larger scale, could work as in Model 3. In this model there is an opportunity for new intermediaries to enter the market who can negotiate deals with a large number of mobile operators. Then they could market a single "connectivity solution" to the vertical and/or to the OEM customers.

The distinctive technical characteristics of 5G networks result in the ability to manage a large number of devices simultaneously, with low latency or particularly

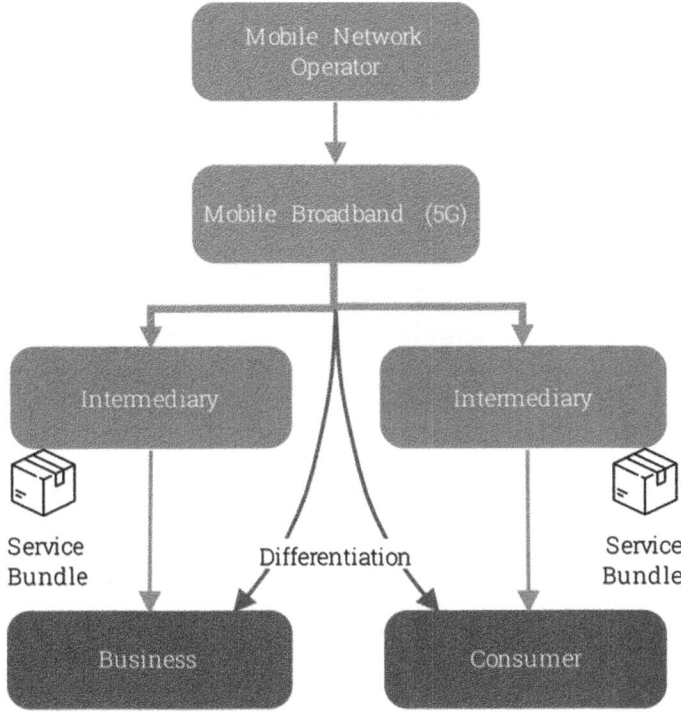

Fig. 4.25 Sharing bundled services through intermediaries in vertical industries

high data transmission rates. There are many areas of application for 5G, from healthcare to the automotive sector to logistics. Mobile operators will be able to configure networks in different ways to offer tailored solutions. But telecommunication services will simply be an ingredient, and sometimes a small ingredient, of the recipe that wins over the market.

The 5G era opens the prospect for telecommunication operators to provide differentiated services for a number of different verticals simultaneously. Furthermore, service innovation should become faster and more effective. Thus, the emergence of 5G could lead to significant changes within the value chain for mobile data connectivity, both by modifying the traditional business models of telecom operators, and by providing new opportunities for intermediaries of various types. It may be even possible to create new "merchant markets" where various connectivity services are exchanged on the wholesale level between operators and orchestrated physical networks to create a certified communication service for customers.

There are several changes to the current telecom business that may emerge with extensive 5G deployment. Each change can potentially create great risks to telcos and service providers, but together, with a staff reskilling and a suitable supporting infrastructure, those risks can also be transformed in valuable opportunities.

Fig. 4.26 Different approaches in vertical industries or for specialized OEM

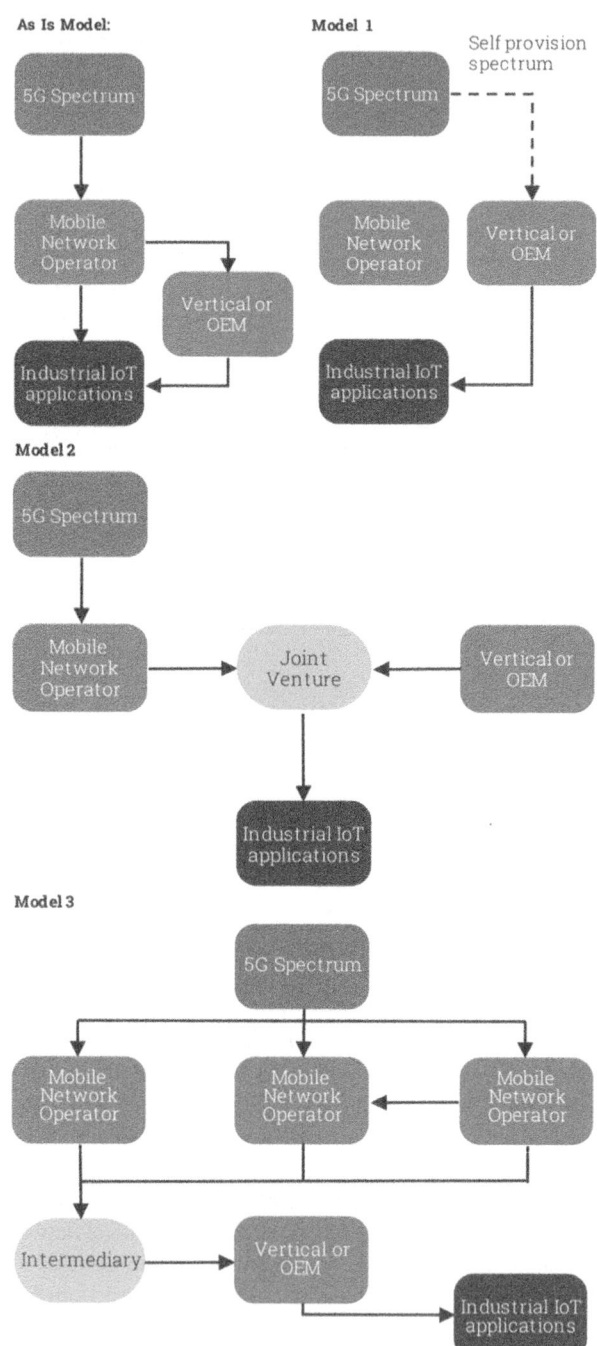

4.6   Conclusion

Telecommunication companies are in the midst of many overlapping transformations. Telecommunication operators, traditionally rich and enjoying solid financial resources, have never left large investment spaces open within their sector. Thanks to the evolution of regulation, competition and technology, this will no longer be true.

Soon, there will be great room for investments, which may differ in size and quality, but this space will emerge at the intersection of:

- New definitions of "investable assets", identified by technology;
- New business models, designed by the competition; and
- New roles defined by both technology and competition.

From the point of view of a potential investor in telecommunication infrastructures, the discriminating rule to distinguish between mature, promising and risky opportunities is not easy to identify. But being that technology is the source of this reshaping of the traditionally slow-moving world of telecommunications, technology itself could be the possible key.

Compared to the past, telecom infrastructure presents two distinguish evolutions:

1. There is a sort of Cambrian explosion in the number and variety of assets that can form an asset base or be part of a larger definition of an asset base (e.g. pure passive fiber to be used by a pure fiber wholesaler, a specialized business telecom operator or an edge cloud operator; enercom points that could be an asset base to rent to service providers, MNOs or specialized business telecom operators).
2. There is a clear trend in transforming basic telecommunication assets (e.g. unlicensed radio spectrum, satellite communications, edge computing sites, enercom sites) using software to create different business models and potential disruptions.

Despite many discussions on the topic of 5G, the evolution of telecommunication networks and their seducing promises of extraordinary performances, the business case for 5G is still vague for telecom operators while it is already popular among their potential customers. And this is a significant potential risk. Indeed, the monetization of innovation is always risky. As far as the growing demand for communication services, 5G, fiber and satellite will provide an enormous technical improvement, creating great opportunities. But no one will have any guarantee regarding economic returns. The forces surrounding these incredible improvements will decide for everybody. On one side there is the actions of the OTTs, which are intently interested and investing in telecommunication technologies. They dominate the software component along the entire value chain of telecommunications and are in the best position to judge and influence its evolutions. On the opposite side there are traditional telecom operators struggling to keep pace with innovation imposed by the OTTs, but without the right set of skills to impact the fight for dominance in the future of telecommunication. In the middle there are the current and future customers of this evolution, both companies and individuals.

Assets that have a software component (e.g. FWA, low-power wide-range devices, solutions in the unlicensed spectrum) look riskier because these assets could be disrupted by new business models, new evolution, new combinations of assets. More traditional and essential assets, like naked fiber, or small urban locations equipped with power or poles, appear to be components of a structure that will be complex and always evolving, but that is starting to have some solid, even if minimal, cornerstones. New assets, like the enercom infrastructures, based on the recombination of more traditional assets but answering to a widespread need in the industry, instead will have a bright future.

The ancient alchemists believed that does not exist emptiness in nature. Maybe that is also true in the highly competitive market of telecom services, because every market space left unfilled will be served in some other way by someone else. In this perspective, the telecom industry could benefit from the contribution of other industries in keeping pace with the market, following the evolutions and the transformations of the market, and giving its best to create the best of possible futures.

References

Abrardi, L., & Cambini, C. (2019). Ultra-fast broadband investment and adoption: A survey. *Telecommunications Policy, 43*(3), 183–198.

Accenture. (2017). Lead or lose—A vision for Europe's digital future. Accenture.

Alizadeh, T. (2017). Political economy of telecommunication infrastructure: An investigation of the National Broadband Network early rollout and pork barrel politics in Australia. *Telecommunications Policy, 41*(4), 242–252.

Baumgartner, J. (2019, February 14). Google fiber: A timeline of the good, the bad & the ugly. *Light Reading*.

Bock, W. & Wilms, M. (2016). Building the gigabit society: An inclusive path toward its realization. BCG.

Bresnahan, T. F., & Trajtenberg, M. (1995). General purpose technologies 'Engines of growth'? *Journal of Econometrics, 65*(1), 83–108.

Case, S. (2016). *The third wave: An entrepreneur's vision of the future*. New York: Simon & Schuster.

Cisco. (2017). Cisco VNI Global IP Traffic Forecast, 2016–2021.

Cisco. (2018). Cisco VNI Global IP Traffic Forecast, 2017–2022.

Di Castelnuovo, M., & Biancardi, A. (2020). The future of energy infrastructures: Brace yourself for a bumpy ride! In S. Gatti & C. Chiarella (Eds.), *Disruption in the infrastructure sector: Challenges and opportunities for developers, investors and asset managers*. Heidelberg: Springer.

Donovan, J., & Prabhu, K. (2017). *Building the network of the future : Getting smarter, faster, and more flexible with a software centric approach*. Boca Raton: CRC, Taylor & Francis.

DotEcon and Axon Partners. (2018). Study on implications of 5G deployment on future business models, Berec.

Edquist, H., et al. (2018). How important are mobile broadband networks for the global economic development? *Information Economics and Policy, 45*, 16–29.

European Commission. (2016). Communication from the commission to the European Parliament, the Council, the European Economic and Social Committee and the Committee of the Regions Connectivity for a Competitive Digital Single Market—Towards a European Gigabit Society, European Commission.

Gallagher, D. (2019, February 9). Google watching its cable bills. *Wall Street Journal.*

Gartner. (2019). *Vendor revenue from the public cloud services IaaS market worldwide 2015-2018.*

Gatti, S., & Chiarella, C. (2020). The future of infrastructure investing. In S. Gatti & C. Chiarella (Eds.), *Disruption in the infrastructure sector: Challenges and opportunities for developers, investors and asset managers.* Heidelberg: Springer.

Grijpink, F., et al. (2019). Cutting through the 5G hype: Survey shows telcos' nuanced views. McKinsey.

GSMA. (2014). Green power for mobile, GSMA.

GSMA. (2019a). The mobile economy 2019, GSMA.

GSMA. (2019b, February 26). Modernise regulation to deliver Europe's digital future calls GSMA. GSMA.

Harbor Research. (2018). The private LTE opportunity for industrial and commercial IoT, Harbour Research.

Harris, M. (2019, January 21). Facebook's plans for space lasers revealed. *IEEE Spectrum.*

iDate. (2018). Annual Economic Report 2017. European Telecommunications Network Operators Association.

iDate. (2019). DigiWorld Yearbook 2019. iDate.

IDC. (2017). *Share of IT infrastructure spending worldwide 2014-2021 by deployment type.*

Intelligent Energy. (2012). The true cost of providing energy to telecom towers in India. White Paper.

IPlytics. (2019). *Who is leading the 5G patent race? A patent landscape analysis on declared SEPs and standards contributions.*

Kim. (2017). 5G Economics—The numbers. *Techneconomy Blog.* https://techneconomyblog.com/2017/07/07/5g-economics-the-numbers-appendix-x/. Last accessed 28 Apr 2019.

Klinkenborg, V. (2003, November 12). *Trying to measure the amount of information that humans create.* The New York Times.

Lee, E., & Chau, T. (2017, January 4). The geopolitics of 5G and IoT. Jefferies.

Lee, E., & Chau, T. (2019, January 4). 5G: The geopolitical game continues. Jefferies.

Le Maistre, R. (2014, September 24). Energy bill shocks orange into action. *Light Reading.*

Nash, K.H. (2017). Future of outsourcing—Outsourced tech. Raconteur.

Newman, P. (2018). *Business insider intelligence.* The EDGE Computing Report 2018.

Newman, P. (2019a). The Internet of Things 2019: How the IoT continues to transform business, homes, and cities through next-generation digital solutions. Business Insider Intelligence.

Newman, P. (2019b). Telecom and technology forecast book 2019. Business Insider Intelligence.

Oughton, E., et al. (2018). Towards 5G: Scenario-based assessment of the future supply and demand for mobile telecommunications infrastructure. *Technological Forecasting & Social Change, 133*, 141–155.

Patrick, M., Robilliard, M., Morris, D., Coles, S., & Challawala, A. (2018). *European telecom services. Make up or break up.* Barclays: Barclays Research.

Strumpf, D., & Cherney, M. (2018, September 12). Australia's actions against Chinese firms ignite 5G security debate. *Wall Street Journal.*

TeleGeography. (2014). Skype traffic continues to thrive. TeleGeography.

TeleGeography. (2019). *Global internet geography.*

The Economist. (2019, March 23). The future of big tech: Why big tech should fear Europe. *The Economist.*

van der Meulen, R. (2018). What edge computing means for infrastructure and operations leaders. Gartner.

Venkateshwar, K., et al. (2019a, February 28). Understanding convergence. Barclays Research.

Venkateshwar, K., et al. (2019b, February 28). CBRS: The convergence band. Barclays Research.

Venzin, M., & Konert, E. (2020). The disruption of the infrastructure industry: How investment decisions in the infrastructure industry are expected to change and how to prepare. In S. Gatti & C. Chiarella (Eds.), *Disruption in the infrastructure sector: Challenges and opportunities for developers, investors and asset managers*. Heidelberg: Springer.

Weldon, M. K. (Ed.). (2016). *The future X network: A Bell Labs perspective*. Boca Raton, FL: CRC.

Zhong, R. (2018, March 7). China's Huawei is at center of fight over 5G's future. *The New York Times*.

The Disruption of the Infrastructure Industry

5

Coming Changes in Investment Decisions and How to Prepare for Them

Markus Venzin and Emilia Konert

5.1 Small Disruptions, Big Impact

Firms in all industries operate in an increasingly complex ecosystem. As opposed to well delineated and relatively stable sectors, these business environments are more diverse, dynamic and interconnected, and as a result are less predictable than in the past. But many companies still approach strategy with the same methods that they used decades ago, often reacting instead of observing the changing environment of their industry and planning for these changes. An ecosystem may be defined as a complex of living organisms, together with their physical environment, and all their interrelationships in a unit of space. How does this relate to business, or any industry for that matter? Anyone who has worked in a firm, especially in a large multinational corporation, knows that a business environment can feel as complex and interconnected as a natural ecosystem. Industries can also be viewed as complex systems, the behavior of which is intrinsically difficult to model due to the dependencies and competition between different players within them. A major factor in the difficulty of predicting business ecosystems is that they can be described as nonlinear—meaning that they respond in different ways to the same input, depending on the context. Another feature of complex systems is that they have emergent behaviors which result from the relationships that develop over time within a system. Take for example a colony of ants, who each react to a series of stimuli (e.g. chemical scent from larvae, food, other ants, waste, etc.) and act as autonomous units. These properties result in a complex system, an adaptive one as well, where individual and collective behavior eventually self-organize in response to any tiny

M. Venzin (✉)
Innovation, Bocconi University, Milan, Italy
e-mail: markus.venzin@unibocconi.it

E. Konert
Inovation Catalyst, Corporate Hangar, Milan, Italy
e-mail: emilia@corporate-hangar.com

change in events (Holland 2006). An industry as a complex system is already intricate and responsive to internal changes, but imagine the disruptive individual firms that enter from the periphery of an ecosystem, and what a huge effect that they can have. Just think of Uber—a firm that entered the transportation sector with a completely unconventional approach and challenged the current business models, resulting in total disruption and the firm's own great success.

A Harvard Business Review study examined the longevity of more than 30,000 firms in the US over a 50-year span, and found something surprising: public companies have a one in three chance of being delisted in the next 5 years. This is six times the delisting rate of companies 40 years ago. And it seems there is no correlation between size, age, or sector and this shortening lifespan (Reeves et al. 2016).

To survive, firms need to be able to improve their understanding of how their environment is changing. The title of the book written by the Chairman of Nokia, Risto Siilasmaa, indicates that success can be toxic: "Transforming Nokia: The power of paranoid optimism to lead thorough colossal change." Managers need to hold on to the optimistic belief that things will turn out fine, but at the same time they need to be paranoid enough to avoid being overoptimistic. Tali Sharot suggests that most humans show a bias towards overestimating the likelihood of positive events while underestimating the likelihood of negative ones (Sharot 2011). In other words, we expect changes in the ecosystem to be positive for the performance of our firm—but often, they are not.

5.2   Creating Industry Adaptability

Complex systems do not allow precise predictions of future states, but it is possible to detect patterns and make educated predictions by observing the entire industry ecosystem and tracking the changes. One way to do this is by actively monitoring industry trends, activities, and the success of new or innovative companies that have the potential to disrupt an ecosystem. When firms focus on tracking these alterations, they gain valuable knowledge about how their own business models could be impacted or disrupted. They create industry foresight, or the ability and acceptance of the fact that their industry is not static. The learn to adapt to their complex environment.

The goals of this process are distinct from mere prediction or forecasting. Prediction is a confident statement about the future state of affairs, best confined to systems that can be fully measured or understood. Forecasts, instead, extrapolate from the past into the future by applying "if ... then" relations (Slaughter, Futures concepts 1993, p. 293). Organizations are therefore likely to predict mechanisms that can be fully measured or understood, such as the production process or the system-breakdown point caused by data overload in a computer network. But what if the system under observation is perceived as complex, non-linear, dynamic and unpredictable? What if no patterns of the observed system can be extrapolated from past to future? What is the goal, if not fairly accurately predicting or forecasting the future?

5.2.1 Experiencing the Future

Firms need to improve their ability to experience emergent futures. The ultimate way to adapt is to create awareness and clarity with regard to the dynamics of an emergent situation (Slaughter 1993, p. 801). Inherent to this view is an open attitude towards the future that we perceive as increasingly important in the light of highly dynamic industry ecosystems as described by Weick:

> In a fluid world, wise people know that they don't fully understand what is happening at a given moment, because what is happening is unique to that time. They avoid extreme confidence and extreme caution, knowing that either can destroy what organizations need most in changing times, namely curiosity, openness, and the ability to sense complex problems...In this sense, wisdom, understood as simultaneous belief and doubt, improves adaptability (1996, p. 148).

Consequently, the first goal of this adaptability is to increase one's ability to "experience" the future, and to acknowledge one's inability to collect 100% of the relevant information necessary to completely understand an (emergent) situation. If every situation is perceived as emergent, and if any situation can only be filled with meaning after it has occurred, the importance of prediction or forecasting will be much reduced. Prediction and forecasting undervalue the dynamics and the ambiguity inherent in these situations. Some authors in the field of strategic management or organizational behavior argue that it might be problematic to think about the future before it has occurred. Karl Weick (1995) uses the term "Future Perfect Thinking" to describe a different attitude needed to talk about the future. One of the main goals of our process is to develop an awareness of the future by thinking in the "Future Tense" (James 1996; Morrison 1994) and by challenging prevailing mindsets. Firms need to develop the capability to think about the future as history. To what extent is the future inherent and rooted in the present? What experiences do we undergo now that will be intensified and become more relevant in the future? To find important experiences which may seem negligible at the moment, and to live through them or at least seriously consider these scenarios as if they were of utmost importance: the priority goals of becoming an adaptive firm.

5.2.2 Reducing Uncertainty and Ambiguity to Create a Preferred Future

In order for adaptability to provide results, a critical element is the desire to reduce uncertainty and ambiguity. Uncertainty arises from the perceived inaccuracy in "estimates of future consequences conditional on present actions" (March 1994, p. 174). While predicting and forecasting the future are essential to long-term survival, these activities might not be sufficient in themselves, because the future is highly uncertain. In order to cope with uncertainty, a complementary approach to strategy must be adopted. Firms need to develop the capability to shape their ecosystems and develop processes that make them responsive to unpredictable events.

Ambiguity makes the task of shaping the environment even more difficult. Even if managers can predict with a decent level of certainty that certain events will happen, they still might not be able to understand clearly what these events mean for their business. Ambiguity refers to the confusion created by different interpretations of the same concept at the same time (Weick 1995, p. 91). Hence management teams need to engage in the social construction of what they think is going to happen. In addition, ambiguity may include the ignorance arising from insufficient information, which would call for more careful scanning and discovery.

The point we want to make here is that management teams can collect all possible data about the future development of their business ecosystem, but they still risk getting it all wrong. To increase the probability of survival in today's ecosystems, firms need to create rich experience about future events. The true purpose of developing industry adaptability is to have a role in shaping the futures one prefers, rather than having to simply be ready to accept likely futures created by others. This process emphasizes the possibility of influencing/creating one's own system. Hamel and Prahalad (1994, p. 105) state that: "Although potentially useful, technology forecasting, market research, scenario planning, and competitor analysis won't necessarily yield industry foresight. None of these tools compels senior management to reconcile the corporation and the industries in which it competes."

The objectives of Hamel and Prahalad's concept of industry foresight approximate most closely our perception of the nature of adaptability: to develop a new strategy framework that creates a seemingly unbridgeable gap between ambition and resources, to go beyond imitation, and to draw the future back into the present to generate a sense of urgency. Foresight processes ensue from an attempt to be guided by our own preferences rather than external forces: the idea is to motivate people by promoting a sense of shared expectations. The foresight process involves the entire organization and attempts to create awareness of changes in the system. If there is no consensus about the future role and activities of the company, it may be hard to commit the staff to daily work. Foresight processes may therefore create such a consensus and combine individual and organizational goals. "Experience is not merely a product of past events, or simply a passive record of elapsed time. Experience is the interaction of memory and foresight, of identity and purpose" (Slaughter 1996, p. 156). If the purpose of the company interferes with the individual or organizational identity created in the past, organizational members may have a low motivation to work in this company. This in turn mar the attractiveness of the company as an employer. Hence, to make a company fit for the future, managers need to get the opportunity to experience the future before it arrives.

5.3   Where Is Disruption Coming from, and Why Is it So Difficult for Incumbents to React?

Industry innovation in many sectors has been considered an oxymoron for many years. The infrastructure sector is not generally noted for its willingness or ability to embrace innovation. Francesco Starace, CEO of ENEL, explained this stereotype honestly, "A utility is not the most fertile ground for innovation. For decades the industry has selected people that had a certain mind set for skills of obedience, order, compliance, rather than to change or innovate. Those are the people owning the system—in an environment with a low stress for change." (Chesbrough 2016, p. 1). But suddenly things have changed, and the environment is no longer low stress, now there is a very high demand for change, and it is clear that more and more often, large and previously stable companies are failing to do so.

As discussed in other chapters of this book, the infrastructure sector is being disrupted by several megatrends. Understanding these trends is the first step in focusing on the changes, challenges, and disruptions that the infrastructure ecosystem will face.

- *Convergence* refers to the merging of distinct technologies or industries into a unified whole as depicted in Fig. 5.1. Michael Porter and James Heppelmann (2014) outlined how the first wave of industry transformation revolutionized the order process and resource planning, resulting in standardized processes across companies. The second wave was triggered by the rise of the internet, which reshaped how firms coordinate and integrate globally. These two points increased

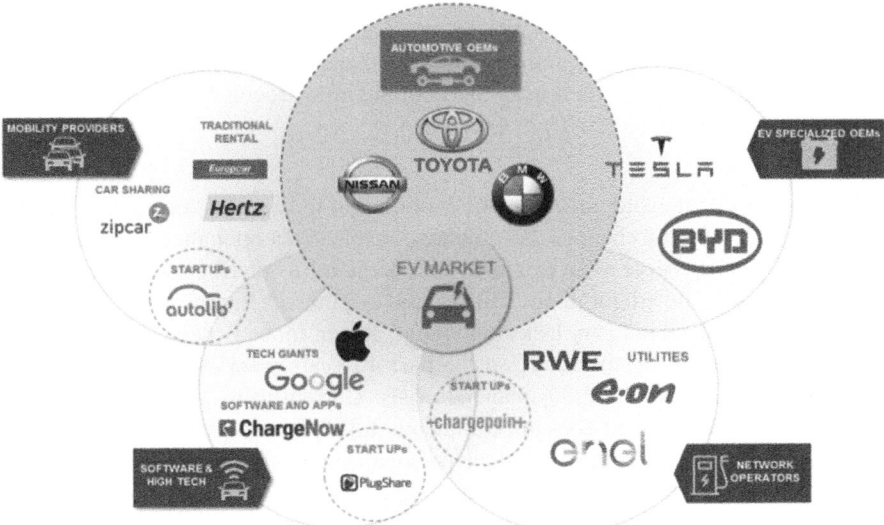

Fig. 5.1 Example of an industry ecosystem—illustrated with the electric vehicle industry

productivity and spurred growth in the economy, but products remained unaffected. The third wave saw the rise of smart products with IT as their integral components. The technological landscape has made the invention of smart products feasible: miniaturization, energy efficiency, low cost processors and data storage, low cost wireless connectivity, rapid software development, big data analytics. All these new technologies are now able to converge to become the product. The impact of all this has already reshaped industry landscapes by making separate industries overlap and enabling players to operate in multiple segments. Consider energy, telecom, and mobility, for example. Traditionally these segments were separate and no one dared to tackle them all at once. Now ENEL has become an industry leader competing in all three, something that would have been impossible even a decade ago.

- *Digitalization and servitization* are the natural consequences of equipping objects with sensors that provide data. The availability of data has increased exponentially, and as a result this has the ability to change the infrastructure landscape. Knowing exactly how, when, and why assets are used can guide intelligent infrastructure planning. Once the right data are compiled, important and potentially cost-saving decisions can be made to manage the overall network. As seen in many industries, business models have begun to shift quickly to adding services to their products. This allows companies to create an additional competitive edge and greater value in an increasingly competitive market. Looking at the market capitalization of these firms, it seems that value has shifted from owning assets to owning transactions. In fact, the top five most valuable firms in the world are all firms that deal in data, not in assets.

- Enhancing the *sustainability* of business operations is increasingly important. Particularly for energy infrastructure, drastic environmental changes (natural resource shortages, such as oil, water, etc.) and political commitments (e.g. EU 2030 targets) will accelerate major changes in the energy system. As discussed already, the lines between infrastructure industries are blurring and these new regulations will begin affecting all facets of the infrastructure world, as discussed by Gatti and Chiarella (2020) in Chap. 6.

These and other megatrends shape the evolution of the business ecosystems. Most firms are aware of these changes, but still are not able to act upon them. The financial services sector may serve as an example. Like large infrastructure companies, banks are not generally noted for their willingness to embrace innovation. The rather conservative financial industry lacks innovative power. Indeed, many of the financial innovations which have characterized the past 40 years were called into a serious question during the 2007–2009 financial crisis. Currently, many banks still offer only online banking, which does not completely fulfill the expectations of customers who want innovative solutions for their personal financial management. There are many reasons for the lack of entrepreneurship:

- Data protection makes Big-Data approaches very difficult to implement for financial services: data protection levels and processes are so high and complex that it becomes difficult to share large amounts of data. Other industries (i.e. internet, telco) are characterized by less constraints.
- Financial services are not customer-centric: a proliferation of requirements and domestic and international regulations call for expert managerial competencies, which have led to a decreased focus on customers. The implementation of these requirements and regulations takes up important resources, both human and monetary, since large investments in IT infrastructure are needed.
- Financial services are risk-averse: The decision-making structure generally avoids risk and does not encourage innovation. Due to a strong risk-averse decision-making structure, banks act very passively with regard to change. Innovations are seen as a risk here, since banks need predictable income and returns on any investment, partially due to the fact that banks have to satisfy their shareholders.
- Financial services are highly regulated: Compliance requirements in the banking sector significantly exceed those in other industries. Hence, understanding the role of regulation is crucial, first because it limits the strategic decisions of the managers and thus their opportunities to innovate. Second, because the strict regulation of the sector has left financial services with a legacy of a conservative culture hostile to change.
- Financial services lack internal technological competencies: Costs and lack of know-how and competencies hinder in-house development. Financial services have not developed technological competencies as a part of their core business, so now other industries have a competitive advantage. Acquiring or internally developing these kinds of competencies could be expensive in terms of time and money.

Infrastructure companies can learn from the financial services sector as there are many similarities between the two industry ecosystems. Who would have thought 10 years ago that banks might be replaced by Facebook or Apple? Many banks attempt to cope with the challenges posed by digital start-ups by adopting what Chesbrough (2003) labeled an "open innovation approach," i.e. openly collaborating with external partners to favor speed of innovation, instead of trying to retain full ownership of ideas and intellectual property.

Infrastructure firms need to boost their capability to innovate and investors in infrastructure must be able to understand which companies in the infrastructure universe are the most disruptive. Generally speaking, the rather conservative infrastructure industry lacks innovation power. Firms like ENEL have shown how former state-controlled utility firms can become innovation powerhouses. ENEL's key to success was open innovation.

There are potentially numerous answers to the question of how innovation processes can be organized in infrastructure firms. Only a few companies are able to realize the potential of each new finding internally. Projects may therefore sit on a shelf for years unless an internal champion of the project leaves the company to develop the idea elsewhere (Chesbrough 2003). Collaborative R&D may be particularly well-suited to the current globalized and interconnected innovation environment. Scholars have identified several advantages for businesses that engage in open innovation (i.e., shorter time to market with fewer costs and risk, more innovations over the long term, increased quality of products and services, exploitation of new market opportunities, greater flexibility). The need for open innovation came about through the failure of financial services firms to successfully bring innovations developed by their in-house R&D facilities to the market. With open innovation, the boundaries between the business and the environment in which it operates have become more permeable; innovations can easily be transferred inwards and outwards.

In particular, we believe investing in start-ups is the most effective way for firms to deal with digitalization and other megatrends. A start-up investment (or the creation of a start-up accelerator) can move faster and more flexibly, and is more cost effective than traditional R&D to help firms respond to changes in technologies and business models. However, the main goal of the investment is not to increase market value but to utilize early strategic investments to expand the infrastructure firm's business model and to secure its long-term competitiveness.

Hence, infrastructure investment firms could and should do more than just monitor start-ups and analyze how they could impact the business model of firms they have invested in. In our view, these investment firms should investigate the opportunity of setting up an investment accelerator to identify, track, and potentially invest in disruptive companies. This would allow infrastructure investment firms to: (1) protect their core investments; (2) use their core investments to accelerate the business of start-ups; and (3) increase the profitability of their investments within an acceptable risk level. The development of an investment accelerator will be discussed in our closing section. Next, we focus on the potential benefits of investing in disruptive start-ups.

5.4   Benefits of Investing in Disruption

5.4.1   Protecting Core Investments

The market segments where many infrastructure firms invest are admittedly more stable than many other industries. However, as we have discussed those segments are still subject to substantial change. Firms do keep this in mind and carefully develop their investment criteria to select the safest harbors in the infrastructure industry. Yet they still have a lot to lose if there is no action or evolution to confront these trends, especially because the investment horizon of most infrastructure investment firms is 5 years. This means we need to look at an investment horizon of 10 years, as assets are usually sold to other investors with a 5-year investment

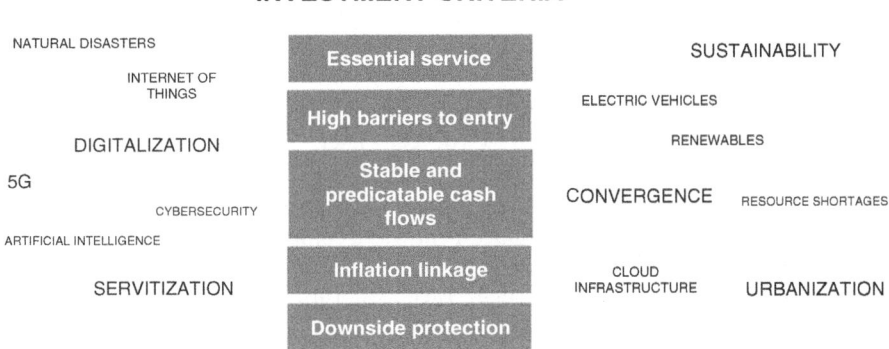

Fig. 5.2 Examples of investment criteria and potential trends that could challenge them

horizon. And with the evolution of the infrastructure ecosystem rapidly changing, firms need to be more prepared to make quick decisions (Fig. 5.2).

Consider solar farms. Renewable energy is becoming increasingly vital, as discussed by Di Castelnuovo and Biancardi (2020) in Chap. 2, and infrastructure firms are wisely investing. It is well known that the cost of solar panel installation has decreased exponentially, and at the same time, technological milestones are being achieved more and more rapidly. Harvesting solar energy doesn't have to mean using huge solar panels anymore, thanks to innovations in solar thin film technology. These solar films can be 'printed' in rolls, which greatly reduces both the cost and the installation, as well as opening up more opportunities for placement of these solar power producers. This new technology allows for the integration of solar panels directly into roofing material, at nearly the same power generation capability of standard solar panels.

How will this impact the future of solar farms? Is it feasible for individual homes to gradually begin switching to solar roofs to supply their own energy? Research shows an incredible trend where this is entirely possible. It is not so distant a possibility that entire buildings could become their own power generators, utilizing solar roofs, solar windows, and other renewable energy sources. These disruptive technologies have the capability not just to disrupt the solar farm industry, but the entire energy industry.

In the United States the total nationwide technical potential of photovoltaic energy across all buildings is 1118 GW of installed capacity and 1432 TWh of annual energy generation, which equates to 39% of total national electric sales. This is significantly greater than previous estimations of 664 GW of installed capacity and 800 TWh of annual energy generation. The state of California has the greatest potential to implement solar power for use on rooftops, and in total potential could generate 74% of the state's total electricity sold by utilities in 2013. A cluster of New England states could generate more than 45% of their needed electricity, despite these states' below-average solar resource. Washington, with the lowest population-weighted solar resources in the continental United States, could still generate 27%. (Gagnon 2016). All these numbers assume full acceptance and implementation of rooftop solar panels but regardless it is clear that household energy generation is a huge market that cannot be ignored.

The first big player in the rooftop solar world was Tesla with the unveiling of their Solar Roof tile prototypes in 2016. Two years later, Tesla is struggling to meet demand in California. Meanwhile, Tesla, who itself is a disruptor in the industry, has already been disrupted in less than a year. Lost in the information tsunami surrounding Tesla's solar roof announcement was a competing solar roof technology launched by the Palo Alto, California based startup, Forward Labs. Its solar roof offering costs about one-third less than Tesla's and the company claims it can be installed in half the time, with a more minimal appearance that mimics a metal roof. And already there are players disrupting the (already disrupted) solar roofing industry, such as Polysolar and Solar Window, who have developed solar windows offering increasing efficiency every year. In university labs, research has produced solar panels that have doubled in efficiency from 20% to over 40% in just 2 years.

All these technological developments are happening at a completely different pace than the traditional energy industry- and have the power to affect how renewable energy develops in the coming years. By tracking these innovations and identifying firms who are commercializing disruptive technologies and business models, infrastructure firms will be able to adjust their understanding of segments that until now have all been relatively stable.

5.4.2   Use Core Investments to Accelerate the Business of Start-Ups

The accelerator can not only serve to protect core investment, but also to help those investments to thrive and grow in value. As discussed, the value system of the infrastructure (and most industries) has begun to shift, and most high-value activities generally involve a great deal of digitalization. Infrastructure investment firms have considerable market power in many areas, and by identifying and investing in relevant disruptors, they could greatly complement their investments with high value players. Furthermore, the scale of infrastructure investment firms can help start-ups commercialize their offer more quickly and create market champions.

For example, the transportation sector will see great changes in the coming years, as discussed by Baccelli in Chap. 3. Electric vehicles and autonomous vehicles will significantly shape the traffic of roads and cities. Certain elements of our current transportation world will always remain, such as roadside rest stops, but they will certainly be impacted by the new realities of transportation. For example, service stations along highways, like Roadchef in the UK and Autogrill in Italy, will see their business transformed by many technologies. Increasingly, cars will rely less on traditional fuel and begin switching over to electric batteries. Charging systems or battery swapping stations will have to be installed in order to serve this new market.

Service stations could substantially boost the business of companies such as Ubitricity, an electric vehicle charging company that that develops low-cost mobile electric charging systems by integrating them into existing energy infrastructure such as lamp posts.

Another example is virtual reality, a key technology that will transform many sectors, for example social infrastructure. Special needs homes, assisted living homes [see Gatti and Chiarella (2020) in Chap. 6], and various educational segments can benefit greatly and boost their competitive advantage through adopting new technologies. In addition, virtual reality has proven to have great potential in the education sector, especially to complement special needs learning. (Jeffs 2009) Though not a critical infrastructure segment, digital services such as virtual reality or augmented reality could become essential in the offer of many infrastructure investments, and infrastructure firms can selectively find disruptors in these fields that complement their current investments.

5.4.3 Increase the Profitability of Investments with an Acceptable Risk

The above examples show that there can be strong ties between infrastructure disruptors and the core investments of infrastructure investment firms. So the clear question now is how to engage with those disruptors. Simply monitoring them and developing contractual agreements where it makes sense is clearly an option. Another strategy is to create a low risk infrastructure technology fund of less than 20 million. Based on their infrastructure radar, infrastructure investment firms could acquire minority stakes in companies that have the potential to either enhance or disrupt their core investments. In a period of 6 to 9 months, these investments have the chance to prove their value in relation to the core investments, either by demonstrating they can help protect the core business, or they can accelerate those start-ups to complement the core businesses of the investment firm. If the links between the core business and the start-up in question are not strong enough, the investment firm has the possibility to divest. Such a fund clearly has a higher risk profile, but also a better chance to yield higher returns.

Many infrastructure investment firms have the industry expertise which is necessary to adapt to shifting ecosystems. But clearly this cannot be done at the expense of the success of their current business. Adapting does not mean a drastic change, but instead being able to embrace trends without necessarily changing core investment strategies. Creating a separate investment unit like an investment accelerator would allow a firm to develop expertise in the industry, form partnerships with disruptors and other key players, externalize uncertainty, and to gain the flexibility to react quickly to disruption.

5.5   The Infrastructure Radar: How to Create a Disruption Map

An innovation radar is a theoretical framework that firms may use to (a) scan the market, and (b) select relevant start-ups in which to invest.

Screening
Screening involves scanning and coming up with a pre-selection of promising start-ups to support and in which to potentially invest. It can be organized as follows:

- Analysis of relevant markets. This is the first step, and includes both domestic and international markets. It implies active monitoring of relevant areas (universities, crowd-investment platforms, start-up centers).
- Platform creation. A passive search could be implemented by creating a development platform for capital-seeking companies. Start-ups could apply for investments or grants through an online platform.
- Identification and selection of different fields of innovation. Firms can scan and identify which field of innovation is most suitable for their purposes.
- Identification and selection of assessment criteria. These may include soft factors such as the degree of innovation as well as the magnitude of the potential threats posed by the innovation (Fig. 5.3).

To structure their screening efforts, firms have many analytical tools at their disposal:

Ecosystem analysis: To understand how disruptions will take place it is necessary to establish an ecosystem perspective in order to recognize how technologies and business models combine, and how the profit pools are distributed within the ecosystem. This approach will pinpoint those players who have the potential to influence the dynamics of the industry, directly or indirectly, or even coming from different sectors. The result: identification of the disruptors.

Once the disruptors are identified, they can be more thoroughly investigated and mapped in relation to each other and the respective business ecosystems they could impact (Fig. 5.4).

Competitor intelligence: Promising start-ups can be evaluated and selected according to some specified criteria (see an example in Appendix 1). The result of this step is an investment decision. Firms should consider hard factors such as

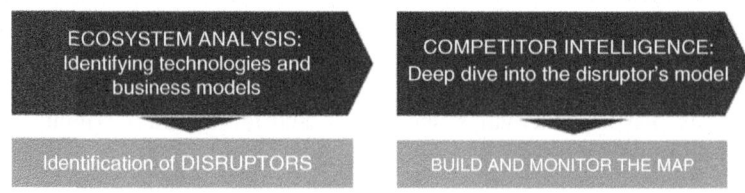

Fig. 5.3 Methodology for mapping disruption

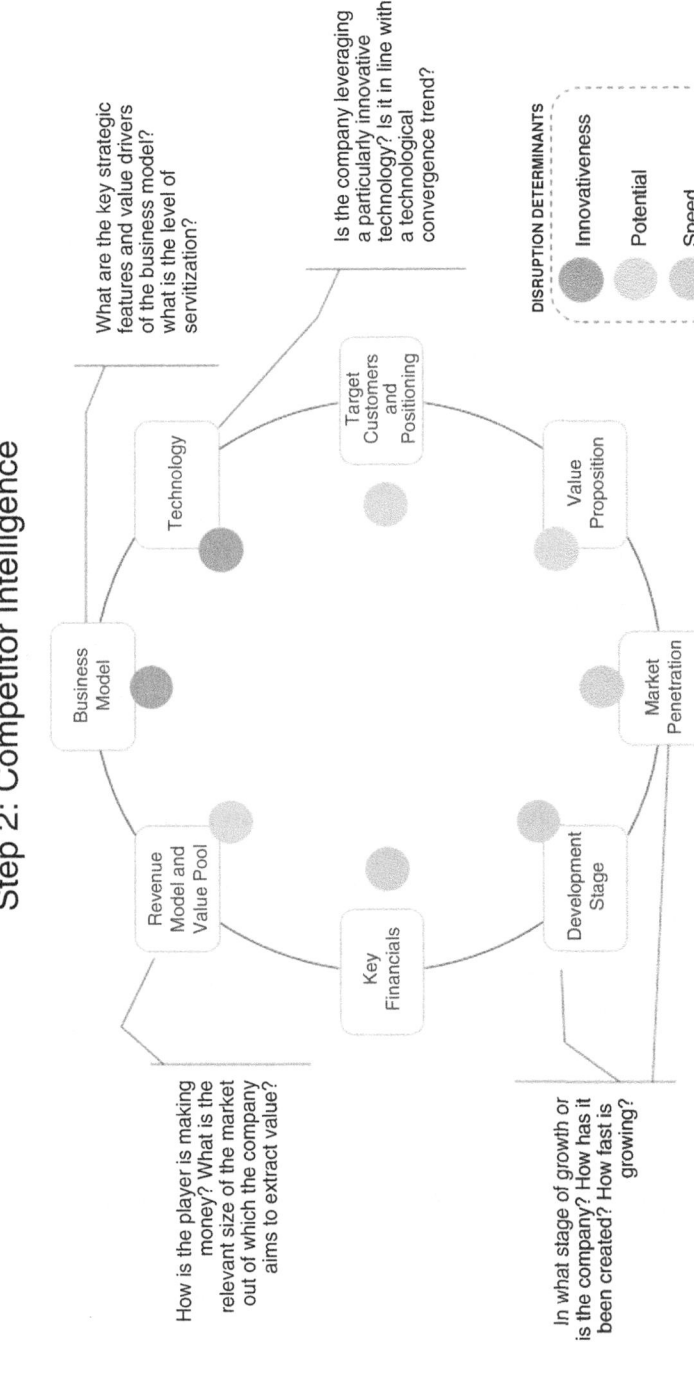

Fig. 5.4 Qualities of a firm to evaluate during competitor intelligence

plausibility checks of the business plan or the adherence to key performance indicators, along with strategic criteria such as potential threats, as well as market and development predictions for the start-up. The following questions may be used to guide the evaluation process:

- Will the firm generate competitive advantages through the investment?
- Is an integration into existing investments possible?
- How will the investment affect long-term revenues?
- What influence does the innovation have on existing business fields within the firm?

5.6 Learning from Disruptors: Alternative Investment Strategies

We have described the tools required to learn about industry ecosystems and to discover new opportunities by identifying infrastructure trends and developments in this industry, by active monitoring relevant markets, and by recognizing potential industry disrupters. We argue that infrastructure investment funds should invest in creating an infrastructure radar to understand where the next disruption is likely to come from. By discussing these insights with the management teams in charge of running infrastructure firms, investment funds can substantially contribute to preparing contingency plans and protecting investments. But are contingency plans enough?

5.6.1 Creating Industry Adaptability Through an Innovation Accelerator

As discussed, an innovation accelerator is a practical tool that firms can use to assist and finance start-ups, obtaining the biggest returns and moving faster to embrace megatrends such as digitalization. There are different options for financing the selected start-ups. The investment can be made by establishing a traditional venture capital firm, or by creating an incubator or an accelerator. However, since the goal of the investment is to secure and develop the firm's own business, the creation of a classic venture capital firm is unsuitable for this purpose. (From now we will refer to this type of venture capital firm as an 'incubator'.) We propose the creation of an investment 'accelerator' as the most suitable solution for infrastructure investment firms to follow through with data collected on disruptors and to implement some degree of adaptability into their investments. The substantial difference between an incubator and an accelerator is the business stage of the company. Incubators focus on the so-called seed-phase, which involves coming up with an idea for a product or a service. The business plan is not yet in place, and the company still does not exist.

Consequently, this means that the duration of the project is significantly longer and more extensive compared to an accelerator. Additionally, external competencies, especially in the area of IT, have to be brought in to evaluate the feasibility of the project.

In contrast, the investment focus of the accelerator is on the start-up or the expansion phase, which means that market maturity has already been reached. The accelerator supports companies only for a few months during the realization of their business ideas. In this case, the type of support can be versatile and would depend on the focus of the accelerator. To get an overview of the diversity of accelerator models, we briefly describe three of them in Appendix 2.

5.7   Implications for Infrastructure Investment Firms

An accelerator is a practical tool that infrastructure investment firms can use to assist and finance start-ups, to obtain the biggest returns and to move faster towards digitalization and other industry trends. Accelerators help ventures define and build their initial products, identify promising customer segments and secure capital and human resources. More specifically, accelerator programs are limited in duration (lasting approximately 3 months), and assist cohorts of ventures with the new venture process.

Now is the time for infrastructure investment firms to use and adapt their investment and management capabilities to finance smaller industry disrupters. It is not too late for traditional infrastructure firms to escape the innovation trap and to face their digital competitors. It is crucial, however, that they take a systematic approach to innovation. In this chapter, we highlighted the need for infrastructure firms to address barriers to innovation in the face of the major trends that are shaping the industry ecosystem. To do so, we suggested that these firms create an innovation radar to be used by an investment accelerator. By doing so, infrastructure firms will be able to protect their core investments, use these investments to accelerate the business of start-ups, and increase the profitability of their investments within an acceptable level of risk.

Appendix 1. Sample of Basic Screening of a Selection of Potential Disruptors Within the Port, Road, Solar, and Rail Ecosystems

Example disruptor identification and intelligence

Company	Brief Description	Problem to be solved	Key people	Investors	Funding	Notes
VesselBot	Vessel owners and cargo charterers rely on brokers to match goods with ships. Vesselbot uses algorithms to match parties at less than half of the 2.5% fee charged by brokers.	The world's 24000 cargo ships often travel empty in one direction.	• Constantine Komodros (Co-founder/CEO) • Anastasia Panagiotopolou (co-founder/CMO)	• PortXL (accelerator) • Egg-THI Excellence Award Pitching Competition	N/A	Similar start-up Shipomax raised $2.5M. Planned full launch by the end of 2016 and to reach breakeven by 2018.
StaffaIPI	UCLS: Universal twist-lock mechanism that is compatible with current mechanism and can still be used during integration period.	Container industry needs a standard, safe and automated system for securing containers to one another. UCLS can provide estimated savings of USD 2k per upgraded well.	• Norman Kaiser (co-founder) • Peter Walker (co-founder)	• Paul Jansen • Marc Stroetmans • PortXL (accelerator)	N/A	N/A
NYSHEX	Ocean shipping through digital contracting. SaaS created to increase reliability in the shipping industry.	Currently, process of contracting includes face-to-face negotiations between multiple parties and is resource-intensive.	• Gordon Trouncer Downes (Founder and CEO) • Matt Bornstein (Board observer)	• Goldman Sachs • GE Ventures	$13,000,000	N/A
Parkofon	Device for park-and-pay (to be integrated in tolls, meters and gates)	Due to outdated paying system, Americans yearly overpay USD 20 billion for parking time they don't use.	• Evgeny Klochikhin (Co-founder and CEO) • Vladimir Klochikhin (Co-founder and chief engineer)	• Conscious Venture Lab (accelerator/incubator)	N/A	Product is market ready and has been tested - company interested in raising funds from accredited investors.
Alchera Technologies	Machine learning software that provides data to safer, cleaner and less congested cities	Cities have become congested, polluted and inefficient 'beings' due to poor planning of infrastructure & mobility systems.	• Emil Hewage (Founder and director)	• Cisco (incubator) • Nitrous London (incubator/accelerator)	N/A	N/A
Arrivo	High-speed super urban network	2D structure of traffic which leads to congestion, pollution and negative economic spillovers.	• Brogan BamBrogan (Co-founder and CEO) • 6 other co-founders	• Plug and Play Ventures • Trucks VC	N/A	Competitors Hyperloop Transportation technologies and Virgin Hyperloop One raised USD 69M and 300M, respectively.

Example disruptor identification and intelligence

Company	Brief Description	Problem to be solved	Key people	Investors	Funding	Notes
Oxford PV	Perovskite-silicon solar cells	Breaking the theoretical efficiency limit of silicon solar cells using perovskite thin-film solar cells.	• Frank P. Averdung (CEO) • Prof. Henry Snaith (co-founder and Chief Scientific Officer) • Michael Rowley (CFO)	• Legal & General Capital • Equinor • Parkwalk Advisors Ltd. • MTI • Longwall Venture Partners	$39,900,000	Oxford PV announced in December it has been granted €15M from the European Investment Bank (EIB).
Aquion Energy	Safe and sustainable saltwater batteries	Batteries made from abundant, safe materials that remove the hazards of lithium-ion batteries	• Scott A. Pearson (CEO & Board of Directors) • John Connolly (CFO) • Prof. Jay Whitacre (co-founder & CTO) • Ted Wiley (Co-founder & VP of product & Corporate Strategy)	• Foundation Capital (lead) • DNS Capital (lead) • Bill Gates • Total Energy Ventures • Shell Technology Ventures • 12 others	$183,200,000	"Emerged" from Chapter 11 bankruptcy in July, 2017. Company is now regrouping, refining and reshaping sales and supply chain. CEO's LinkedIn page says he is not the CEO anymore.
1366 Technologies	New standard in wafer manufacturing	Silicon wafers is the most expensive part of the solar module, representing almost 40% of the total price. 1366's technology cuts the cost of producing the wafer by more than half.	• Frank von Mierlo (Co-founder and CEO)	• WACKER Chemie • Hanjin Capital • Tokuyama • Polaris Partners • North Bridge Venture Partners & Growth Equity • US Department of Energy	$96,500,000	Japan's IHI Corporation has announced it will feature more than 120 thousand Direct Wafer® products in one of its 500kW solar installations.
Hedgehog Applications	Regenerative braking systems for metros, trains and trams	Recharging batteries with energy that was previously wasted while still braking the train.	• Arjan Heinen (Founder)	N/A	N/A	N/A
Cylus	Rail Cyber-security	Provide cybersecurity to a system of increasingly automated railways	• Amir Levintal (CEO) • Boaz Zafrir (President)	• Zohar Zisapel • Magma Venture Partners • Vertex Ventures Israel • SBI Group	€4,700,000	N/A
GreenRail	Energy generating, ecological sleepers	Sleepers made out of recycled materials with integrated solar panels used to power analytics and sensors providing diagnosis of the railroad line.	• Giovanni Maria De Lisi (CEO) • Firas Bunni (COO)	• SME Instrument	€2,290,000	In January 2018 Greenrail signed its first contract with a client. The deal consisted of a €75 million contract with an American company
Kinergizer	Asset monitoring through sensors powered by motion energy harvesters	Reducing costs of maintaining/disposing/powering batteries used in the IoT. Company plans to achieve its goals by creating systems which are self-sufficient energetically.	• Oleg Guzyi (CEO) • Nima Tolou (CTO)	N/A	N/A	Recently attempted to raise €1.8M through Acess to Capital in The Hague

Appendix 2. Benchmark Innovation Accelerator Models

ENEL

ENEL was organized as a collection of quasi-independent companies until 2014. Each country's operations were led by a country manager, who had full P&L responsibility for operations in that country, covering the whole value chain from generation to distribution to sales and services to customers. The company had different lines of business along geographies and products, with a culture that was very hierarchical and structured in organizational silos, each relying on their own individual knowledge. In fact, innovation activities of the company followed the organizational silos approach. To manage the transformation of the company's innovation process, new CEO Francesco Starace recruited Ernesto Ciorra, who worked on projects at ENEL previously as a consultant and knew the company from the outside. He soon realized, though, that transformation would need to reverberate throughout the organization and would require significant time and CEO support. Ciorra became the Head of the newly-created Innovation and Sustainability Department reporting directly to the CEO, to concentrate innovation efforts and strategy, and to overcome the issue of organizational silos. All innovation functions in the company's business lines and countries were now grouped together into a central innovation hub, which reported directly to the CEO of ENEL. This structure was supported by new tools that allowed innovations to be more widely known throughout the company and be more closely connected to the businesses. As each project was initially established, it would be evaluated for its innovative potential. Initially, funds to support the project would be kept small, to keep them agile. But as progress was made, if it was substantial more money would be provided.

Clearly, ENEL's current strategy is driven by an innovation perspective that aims at looking beyond the traditional electricity sector. The company has developed an approach based on a framework that spots innovative projects coming from the external environment that could be new for ENEL or for the entire industry, combining both technology and business model innovativeness. The final aim was to detect interesting opportunities in adjacent markets to build on leveraging the company's strategic assets and capabilities. The combination of technology innovativeness, business model innovativeness and asset fit made business intelligence possible that could overcome the industry myopia. What is more, a new unbiased lens gave a measurement of the risk and uncertainty and the potentially disrupting effects associated with each innovative initiative.

RWE

In 2014 RWE created a centralized task force called the "Innovation Hub" with the aim of developing new business models and scouting outside technologies to contribute to RWE turnover over the next 10 years. The main difference with standard RWE innovation is the unprecedented focus on the customer, the search for new business models rather than simply technologies, and a conscious effort to look beyond the energy sector. The Hub is led by InkenBraunschmidt, in RWE since 2004, with extensive experience in reorganization, restructuring, mergers and acquisitions, and business transformation. The organization of the Hub centers on the collection of small teams emulating start-up environments. It does not have an organizational chart. Instead the hub is considered a network organization, with people from inside and outside the company, and from different countries, working on proof-of-concept in small start-up teams.

The Hub also makes an effort to scout ideas and set up partnerships. A "small, hand-picked" team had been dedicated to drive forward a change across European markets and to identify new partners, technologies and solutions so that RWE could come up with an initial business model for its markets in Europe. Teams also moved in Berlin and Israel. In Berlin, they demonstrated via the 'Accelerator Programme' that concepts can be brought to market quickly and successfully in such a dynamic market environment. In just 2 weeks, a team from the RWE Innovation Hub and several young entrepreneurs developed and tested a concept for a social network to help senior citizens to live independently. Recently, following the reorganization in 2016, RWE decided to move the Hub inside Innogy, a wholly-owned subsidiary with the core business of developing the digital energy market. In this contest, the Hub started to manage the Innogy's venture capital fund, with 130 million in start-up funding, and continued in the development of a network of partnerships with start-ups to get promising ideas and projects onto the market as quickly as possible. To do so they created the "Innogy Generator Programme", providing consulting and support to start-ups. The programme offers the partnership, coaching and infrastructure to help start-ups become high performance, high-growth businesses.

Fintech Europe
A new approach in the financial sector is to combine forces and use this combined expertise and market power to approach the need for innovation. For example, Aareal Bank, BNP Paribas, Deutsche Bank, DZ Bank and NETS Group have joined with Silicon Valley-based innovation platform "Plug and Play" to create a hub for financial tech, or fintech, in Frankfurt, Germany. The hub, called Fintech Europe, aims to provide the infrastructure and support for start-ups to work with and present their products to Europe's leading banks. Naturally the selected start-ups will benefit greatly, but advantages for the banks will be significant as well. Funding and working closely with disruptive start-ups will strengthen the banks, allowing them to understand the rapid digital changes in the financial world, to develop expertise in evolving technologies, and to quickly adapt (and possibly even lead) the disruption in their industry.

References

Chesbrough, H. W. (2003, Spring). The era of open innovation. *Sloan Management Review, 44*(3), 34–41.

Chesbrough, H. (2016). *Innovation @ ENEL: From monopoly power to open power.* Berkeley, CA: University of California.

Di Castelnuovo, M., & Biancardi, A. (2020). The future of energy infrastructure: Challenges and opportunities arising from the R-evolution of the energy sector. In S. Gatti & C. Chiarella (Eds.), *Disruption in the infrastructure sector: Challenges and opportunities for developers, investors and asset managers.* Heidelberg: Springer.

Gagnon, P. (2016). *Rooftop solar photovoltaic technical potential in the United States: A detailed assessment.* Golden, CO: National Renewable Energy Laboratory.

Gatti, S., & Chiarella, C. (2020). The future of infrastructure investing: Challenges and opportunities for investors and asset managers. In S. Gatti & C. Chiarella (Eds.), *Disruption in the infrastructure sector: Challenges and opportunities for developers, investors and asset managers.* Heidelberg: Springer.

Hamel, G., & Prahalad, C. (1994). Competing for the future. *Harvard Business Review,* 384.

Holland, J. H. (2006). Studying complex adaptive systems. *Journal of Systems Science and Complexity, 19*(1), 1–8.

James, J. (1996). *Thinking in the future tense: Leadership skills for a new age.* New York: Simon & Schuster.

Jeffs, T. L. (2009). Virtual reality and special needs. *Themes in Science and Technology Education,* 253–268.

March, J. G. (1994). *A primer on decision making.* New York: Free Press.

Morrison, J. (1994). *Future tense.* New York: Morrow.

Porter, M. E., & Heppelmann, J. E. (2014, November). How smart, connected products are transforming competition. *Harvard Business Review,* 65–88.

Reeves, M., Levin, S., & Ueda, D. (2016, January–February). The biology of corporate survival. *Harvard Business Review,* 1–11.

Sharot, T. (2011, December). The optimism bias. *Currrent Biology, 21*(23), R941–R945.

Slaughter, R. (1993). Futures concepts. *Futures, 25*(3), 289–314.

Slaughter, R. (1996). Foresight beyond strategy: Social initiatives by business and government. *Long Range Planning, 29*(2), 156–163.

Weick, K. (1995). Sensemaking in organizations. *Scandinavian Journal of Management, 13*(1), 113–116.

Weick, K. (1996, May–June). Prepare your organization to fight fires. *Harvard Business Review,* 143–148.

The Future of Infrastructure Investing

6

Challenges and Opportunities for Investors and Asset Managers

Stefano Gatti and Carlo Chiarella

6.1 Introduction

According to estimates by the McKinsey Institute (Woetzel et al. 2017), filling the world infrastructure gap would require investing at least 4.1% of global GDP though 2035 in economic infrastructure, such as roads, railways, ports, airports, power, water and telecoms. An average annual investment of \$3.7 trillion would be just enough to keep pace with projected GDP growth, while meeting the sustainable development goals proposed by the UN for universal access to drinking water, sanitation and electricity, would require an additional \$1 trillion invested annually. Almost two-thirds of the needed investment will be in emerging economies. Figure 6.1 compares historical spending with investment needs. Unless infrastructure spending gains substantial pace, a spending gap of approximately 50% of the investment need would emerge between 2017 and 2035. Power and roads are the two most important sectors: together they account for more than two-thirds of global investment needs. The gap is proportionately largest for emerging Latin America economies such as Mexico and Brazil.

With public finances already stretched, private investors are called to fill this gap, precisely when the industry is undergoing a process of transformation as it matures. This poses crucial questions for investors and asset managers about the long-term changes that the sector will experience in the next few years, which take on even more importance given the long-term nature of infrastructure investments.

Historically, infrastructure was viewed as one of the safest harbors in the universe of alternative investments. The regulation of the various sectors, high barriers to entry, rigid demand, and hedges against inflation were factors that allowed investors

S. Gatti
Department of Finance, Bocconi University, Milano, Italy

C. Chiarella (✉)
Colegio Universitario de Estudios Financieros, Madrid, Spain
e-mail: carlo.chiarella@cunef.edu

© Springer Nature Switzerland AG 2020
S. Gatti, C. Chiarella (eds.), *Disruption in the Infrastructure Sector*, Future of Business and Finance, https://doi.org/10.1007/978-3-030-44667-3_6

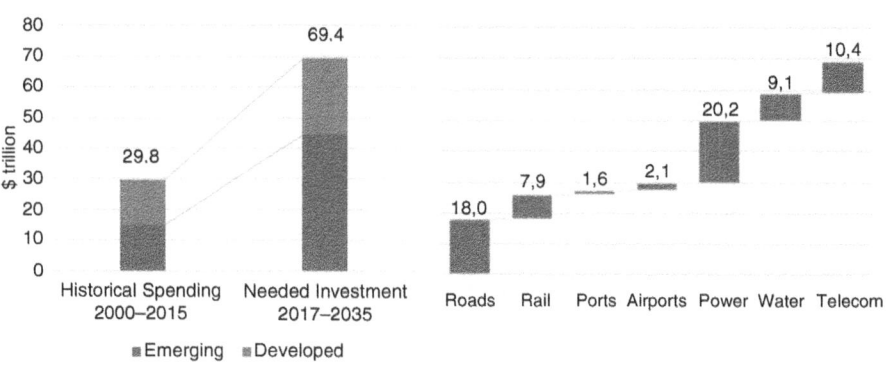

Fig. 6.1 The Infrastructure Spending Gap, Spending vs. Need. (Source: Exhibit from "Bridging infrastructure gaps: Has the world made progress?", October 2017, McKinsey Global Institute, www.mckinsey.com. Copyright © 2020 McKinsey & Company. All rights reserved. Reprinted by permission.)

to benefit from stable and inflation-linked cash flows for extended periods of time. However, changes in demographics, technological advancements, and a growing awareness of the importance of protecting the planet are only a few examples of the megatrends that investors and asset managers expect will reshape the established business model of infrastructure. A deep understanding of these megatrends is essential for long-term investors.

In this chapter, we first provide an overview of the status of infrastructure investing and look at how investors are approaching this alternative asset class. Then, in the second part of the chapter, we identify and discuss the key megatrends that we expect to reshape the established infrastructure business models, both within and across sectors. Finally, with this in mind, we analyze the infrastructure landscape from the perspective of the asset management industry. In particular, we highlight the main challenges posed by the radical changes that the asset class is undergoing. Our analysis is based on sector-specific skills and knowledge, and we propose new levers of value creation to succeed in an increasingly competitive market.

Indeed, the ultra-loose monetary policies put in place by central banks after the collapse of Lehman Brothers in 2008 and the consequent compression of yields have contributed to piquing interest in the infrastructure asset class among investors. Fundraising for unlisted infrastructure has experienced remarkable growth recent years and despite the turbulence brought on by the financial crisis, infrastructure has proven to be a very resilient asset class. With some differences among the sub-classes of this asset type, infrastructure has offered investors relatively good yields, also compared to private equity. Yet, as investor appetite for this asset class held strong and the *dry powder* available to infrastructure asset managers reached record highs, transaction prices have steadily risen. With scarcer and more expensive opportunities in *core infrastructure*, asset managers are called to rethink their investment process and investment philosophy, taking a broader and more forward-looking view of infrastructure.

Adapting to the new landscape, characterized by compressed yields, risk of overpayment and a looser discipline toward risk taking, requires moving from core investments to higher-return strategies. To do so, the selection criteria that asset managers use to identify the investment with the best long-term potential need to be redefined in light of the long-term megatrends that will reshape the way modern society works and lives. For example, just to name a few, the population is getting older, social dissatisfaction with existing infrastructure is growing and the attention of public opinion is shifting more and more towards environmental, social and governance (ESG) issues. Thanks to technological progress, digitalization and shared economies are gaining widespread diffusion, impacting different fields. Urbanization and demand for smart cities are rapidly growing trends. Considering all this, we propose, therefore, a new approach to infrastructure investing by which the traditional *silos* framework, based on sectorial/industry specialization, is replaced by an *eligibility criteria* approach. In this scenario, infrastructure is no longer defined based on industries but on features/characteristics of the needs it serves. The rationale we advance for this change is twofold. First, the proposed approach fits better with investors' hunt for long-term sustainable returns that are supported by transformative macrotrends driving demand for new and better infrastructure. Indeed, investors would be able to make better assessments of the long-term potential of different investments and avoid the trap of investing in stranded assets. Moreover, they would also have greater flexibility to selectively modify the risk profile and pursue emerging investment *themes* such as green (i.e. sustainable and environmental) infrastructure and intangible data-powered infrastructure.

Yet the proposed approach is not per se a guarantee of success. Long-term strategic views need to be complemented with tactical optimization in the short-term. In this respect, as the barriers between infrastructure investment and private equity blur and the two asset classes converge, we highlight the need for infrastructure asset managers to strengthen their ability to spot undervalued assets and to assess the quality of management teams in investee firms. Moreover, with weaker barriers to entry and new competitors challenging incumbents, we argue that infrastructure is no longer the safe harbor of alternative investments it once was. Revenue increases and cost optimization through well-designed strategic rethinking have become the keys to ensuring a solid, sustainable long-term yield for investors.

6.2   Infrastructure Investing

The big picture as far as the status of infrastructure investing is characterized on the positive side by the heightened interest in this asset class among investors. In recent years, positive and continued investor sentiment has been a key contributor in making infrastructure a mature and established asset class and engendering a greater specialization among asset managers. Yet, on the negative side, maturity has been accompanied by more intense competition for capital and deals; this poses increasing threats to the ability of asset managers to continue offering investors attractive yields.

In this section we first highlight the elements that have contributed in the past to paint a bright picture for the infrastructure asset class. Then we introduce the current elements that could potentially tarnish its prospects in the years to come.

6.2.1   A Resilient Asset Class

With some differences among its sub-asset classes, infrastructure has offered investors relatively good yields. Data provided by Preqin indicate that over the 10 years between 2007 and 2017 unlisted infrastructure has provided investors with yields comparable to private equity and well above listed infrastructure equities. Figure 6.2 compares the performance of the Preqin Infrastructure Index with its private equity equivalent and the S&P Global Infrastructure Total Return Index in the period from January 2008 to June 2017. The compounded annual growth rate (CAGR) for unlisted infrastructure over this almost 10-year-long horizon is 8%, just below the 8.3% CAGR obtained by private equity and well above the 1.7% CAGR of listed infrastructure. Consistently, then, 93% of the infrastructure investors surveyed by Preqin in 2017 reported that the performance of the unlisted infrastructure

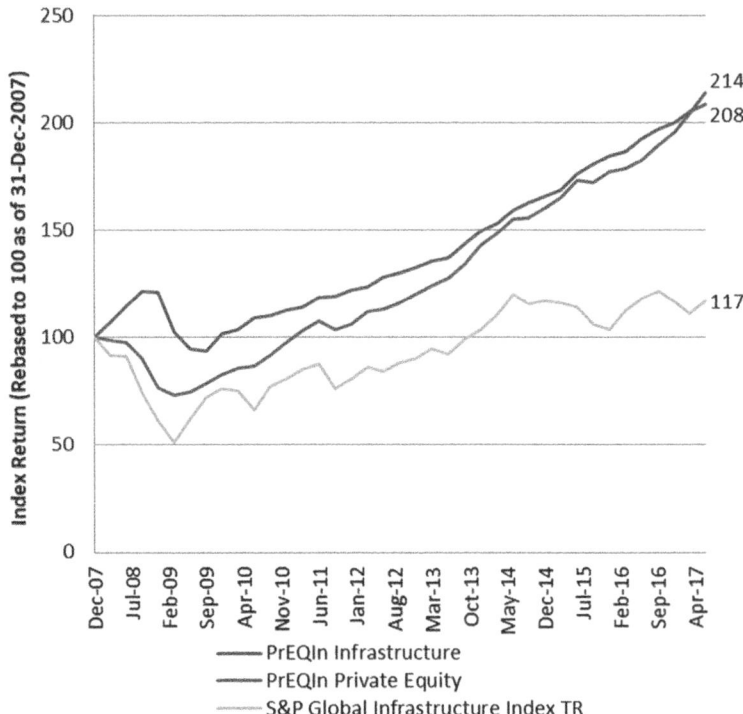

Fig. 6.2 Unlisted Infrastructure vs. Private Equity and Listed Infrastructure Indices (Source: Authors' elaboration of data provided by Preqin)

asset class met or even exceeded their expectations (Preqin 2018d). Indeed, among the funds with vintages between 2007 and 2015, the median net IRR ranged from 7% to 12%, according to Preqin data.

6.2.2 Investor Appetite on the Rise

The compression of yields due to the ultra-loose monetary policies put in place by central banks after the collapse of Lehman Brothers in 2008 and the European sovereign debt crisis in 2012: these are key contributors to a renewed interest in the infrastructure asset class among investors. Since then, investor appetite for infrastructure has been consistently on the on the rise. Figure 6.3 shows the results of a survey conducted by Preqin among fund managers in 2017 on their views with regard to investor demand (Preqin 2018d). Approximately 83% of the respondents report that they perceived an increased appetite for unlisted infrastructure, and especially so for unlisted infrastructure funds targeting North America, Europe and Asia. Private and public pension funds together with insurance companies and sovereign wealth funds are the types of investors whose interest in the infrastructure asset class has grown the most.

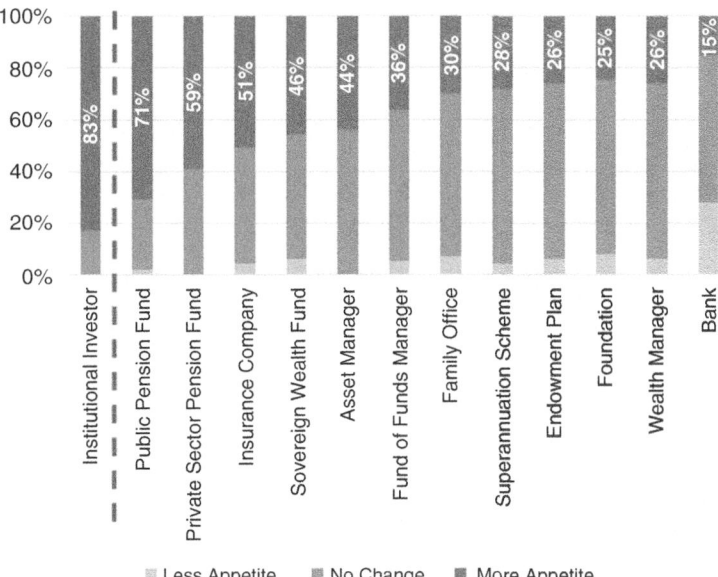

Fig. 6.3 Investor Demand According to Fund Managers (2017) (Source: Authors' elaboration of data provided by Preqin)

6.2.3   Fundraising for Unlisted Funds on the Rise Too

Consistent with the heightened interest on the side of investors, fundraising for unlisted funds is also on the rise. The $81 billion aggregate capital targeted by the 145 funds in the market as of January 2013 is only approximately two-thirds of the $128 billion targeted by the 177 funds in the market as of January 2018, which implies an 11.6% average annual growth (Preqin 2018c). Figure 6.4 reports the aggregate funds actually raised between 2008 and 2017, by fund investment style. The core category includes investments in regulated industries with low exposure to market risk; these returns are characterized by low volatility and a large income component. Core-plus and value-added categories refer instead to investments in less regulated industries that involve rising market risk, whose returns are more volatile and progressively more dependent on capital gains (Table 6.1).

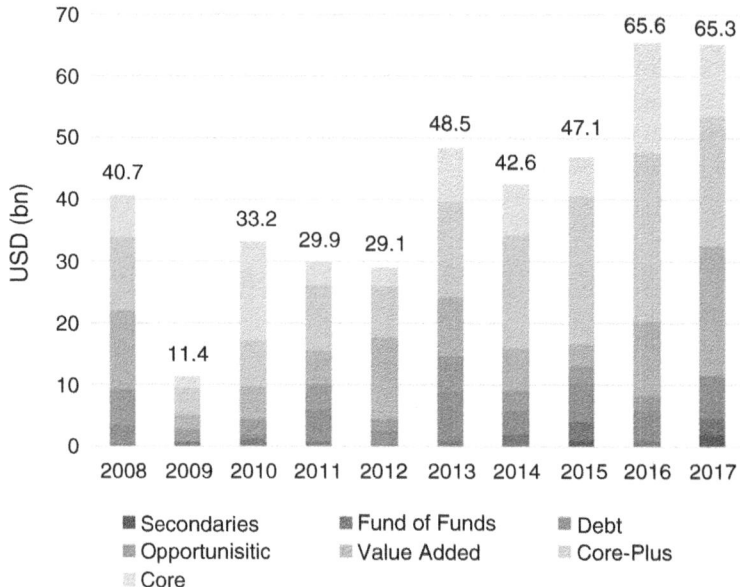

Fig. 6.4 Unlisted Infrastructure Funds: Aggregate Fundraising by Investment Style from 2008 to 2017 (Source: Authors' elaboration of data provided by Preqin)

Table 6.1 Fund investment styles

	Regulated industries	Exposure to market risk	Income return	Capital return	Return volatility
Core	●●●	●	●●●	●	●
Core-plus	●●	●●	●●	●●	●●
Value-added	●	●●●	●	●●●	●●●

Fundraising has been growing at a rate of approximately 7% a year since 2013 and has reached $65.3 billion in 2017. No less than 50% of the capital raised in each year since 2013 has been directed towards core and core-plus strategies. However, in more recent years core-plus and value-added strategies have been gaining weight consistent with a style drift towards riskier transactions in less regulated industries with lower income streams but more capital upside potential.

6.2.4   Assets Under Management at Record Highs

Not surprisingly, with both fundraising and investor demand on prolonged winning streaks, assets under management have reached record highs. Figure 6.5 shows that unlisted infrastructure fund assets under management have soared more than four-fold since 2007, from $99 billion to almost $426 billion in 2017. The pattern is similar, but the pace is much more pronounced compared to that of private equity, which hit a record high of approximately $3.1 trillion at the end of 2017, from just below $1.5 trillion in 2007. Yet according to a 2017 survey by Preqin, fund managers expected assets under management to grow even more (Preqin 2018d). This as investors largely reported being below their target allocations (67%), and ready to commit more.

6.2.5   Dry Powder Piling Up

The drawback of such a large flow of capital towards the infrastructure asset class is that dry powder has been piling up, as fund managers are unable to deploy capital in

Fig. 6.5 Unlisted Infrastructure Assets Under Management from 2007 to 2017 (Source: Authors' elaboration of data provided by Preqin)

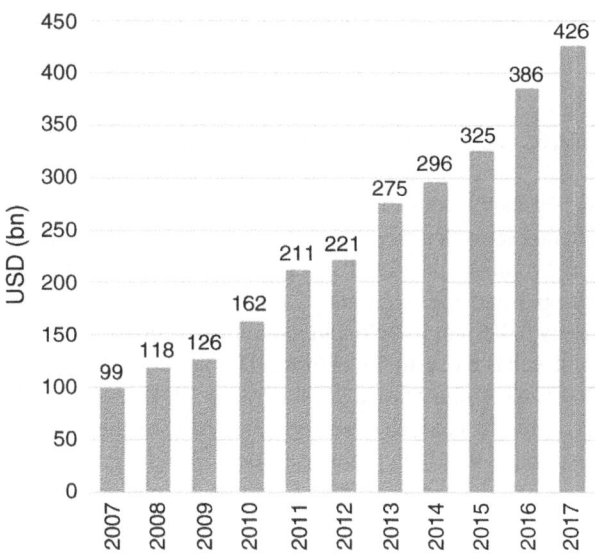

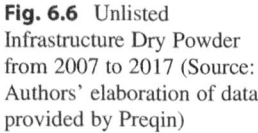

Fig. 6.6 Unlisted Infrastructure Dry Powder from 2007 to 2017 (Source: Authors' elaboration of data provided by Preqin)

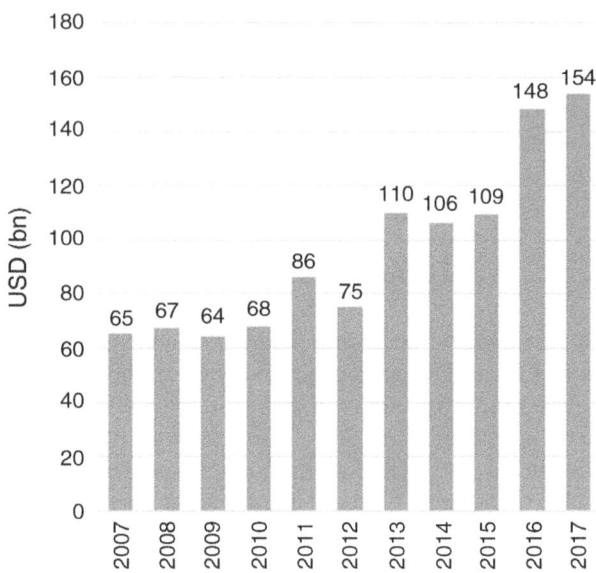

attractive investment opportunities as quickly as they can raise funds. Figure 6.6 shows the evolution of dry powder for unlisted infrastructure funds between 2007 and 2017. According to Preqin data, dry powder has more than doubled since 2007 scoring a record high of $154 billion in 2017. Larger funds, i.e. those with assets under management in excess of $1 billion, account for approximately 70% of this pile of unused capital, and 76% is concentrated in funds focused on North America and Europe (Preqin 2018c). The accumulation of dry powder has been more pronounced in the infrastructure asset class than for private equity, which hit a record-breaking $1 trillion in 2017, from approximately $650 million in 2007.

6.2.6 More Intense Competition for Deals

A key factor contributing to the inability of funds to deploy capital and the consequent rise in dry powder is the intensified competition for deals. Figure 6.7 reports the evolution of global infrastructure deal volumes between 2013 and 2017. The number and the aggregate value of infrastructure deals have increased by respectively 5.4% and 9.7% on an annual basis, up to 2809 deals for an estimated aggregate deal value close to $1 trillion. The average deal size has reached $378 million in 2017, the highest since 2008 (Preqin 2018b). Nonetheless, dealmaking activity was expected to heat up even more, as 74% of the fund managers surveyed by Preqin responded that they planned to deploy more capital (Preqin 2018a).

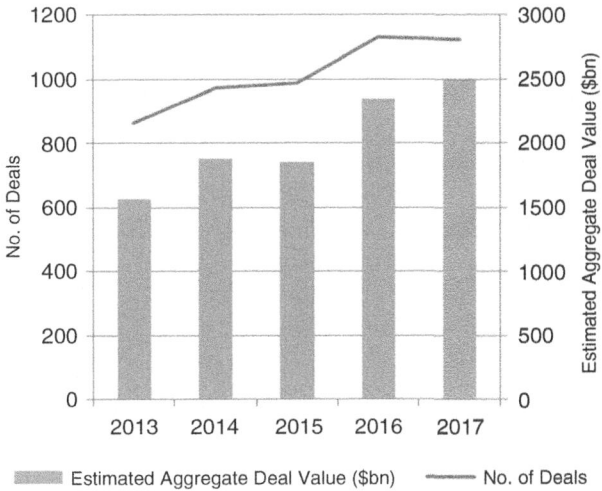

Fig. 6.7 Global Infrastructure Deal Volumes from 2013 to 2017 (Source: Authors' elaboration of data provided by Preqin)

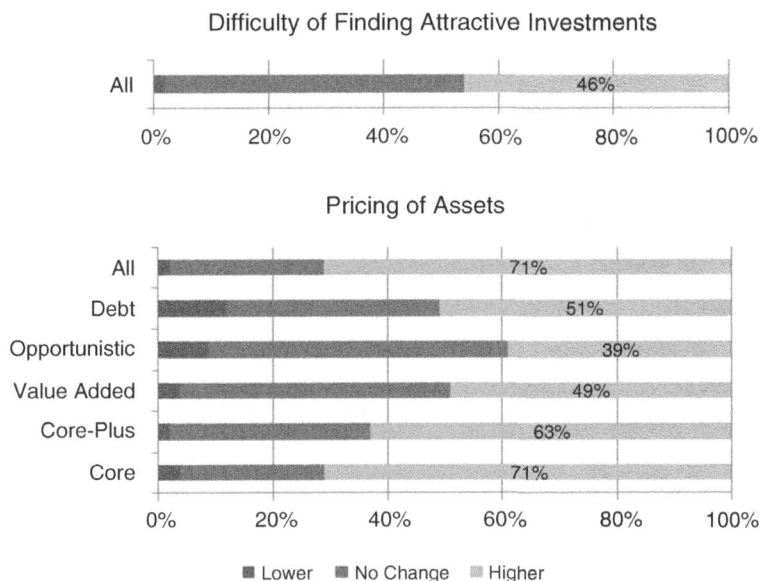

Fig. 6.8 Fund Managers' Views on Investment Opportunities and the Pricing of Assets in 2017 (Source: Authors' elaboration of data provided by Preqin)

6.2.7   Transaction Multiples and Prices also on the Rise

Increased competition for deals puts pressure on valuations. This brought transaction prices closer to record highs. Accordingly, Fig. 6.8 shows that 46% of the fund managers surveyed by Preqin in 2017 responded that attractive investment opportunities were turning scarcer, as core and core-plus assets have become more expensive (Preqin 2018d).

6.2.8   Future Yields Are Under Threat

Looking ahead, then, intensified competition for transactions and increased over-payment risk put the pressure on performance. In fact, transaction prices have steadily risen since 2015 when J.P. Morgan estimated that the average yield for infrastructure investment had already declined by 3–3.5% from 2010 due to higher valuations. Accordingly, there was a consensus among 60% of the investors and 59% of the asset managers surveyed by Preqin in 2017 on viewing asset valuations as their key concern for the years to come (Preqin 2018d). The risk for the asset class is then twofold. On one hand, high valuations add to overpayment concerns. But, on the other, high valuations may also induce a looser discipline toward risk taking. Indeed, in the face of compressed returns, investors and asset managers are forced to move from core investment towards more remunerative investment styles to meet targeted returns. Nonetheless, as infrastructure investors and asset managers become more aggressive with their investment style, capital appreciation becomes a larger component of their returns, as for public and private equity. In this respect, infra-structure as an asset class may lose some of its appeal to investors as it becomes more closely correlated with other risky assets and investors see their diversification benefits reduced.

6.3   The Changes Ahead: Megatrends and the Infrastructure Universe

Long-term investors, and among them infrastructure investors, do not base their decisions on short-term ups and downs of the financial markets but seek to profit from the predictability and sustainability of multi-year trends. The key to success involves understanding how these trends will influence the way infrastructure assets are built and operated. Indeed, any investment decision made today will have lasting repercussions, since many infrastructure assets have a lifespan of 50 years or more.

In this section we discuss the technological and socio-cultural trends with the strongest potential impact on infrastructure investment in the years to come. For each megatrend we first present evidence that indicates the effect on infrastructure and then we highlight the possible consequences and implications for investors, asset managers and policymakers.

6.3.1   Sustainability and the Environment

Overall, modern societies are raising their awareness of environmental, social and governance (ESG) issues. A recent study conducted by the Boston Consulting Group

(Beal et al. 2017) shows that, all else being equal, companies that outperform in important environmental areas achieve higher valuations and higher margins. More specifically, the companies whose products, services, operations, core capabilities and activities have a larger economic, social, and environmental impact are also the ones that provide larger returns to investors.

As a consequence, investors, bankers, insurers and policymakers are becoming more cautious about the environmental challenges and the need for a better relationship between economic activity and environmental sustainability. With regard to the latter, Mark Carney, Governor of the Bank of England, has repeatedly warned of the threat climate change poses to the financial system through physical risk, liability risk and the transition risk of moving to a low carbon global economy. Consistently, in a speech at the International Climate Risk Conference for Supervisors in 2018, he remarked that the largest providers of shareholder services and several of the world's largest asset managers and long-term investors have been calling for disclosures of material, decision-useful climate-related financial risks. As a result, 2017 was a record year for climate-related shareholder resolutions, with a threefold increase in motions (184 vs. 63) and investment managers controlling over 45% of global assets under management backing shareholder actions on carbon disclosure.

Greater attention to ESG issues is being accompanied by fast technological progress, making clean and renewable energy a valid, cost-effective substitute for fossil fuels.

In the past, the transition to renewable energy was driven by policy actions, as it was not economically efficient. However, renewable energy is now showing clear signs of increased competitiveness with traditional fossil fuels for purely economic reasons. According to a 2017 report by the International Energy Agency, new solar photovoltaic capacity worldwide grew by 50% in 2016 to more than 74 GW. For the first time in history, solar photovoltaic additions rose faster than growth in any other fuel, surpassing the net growth in coal. In addition, the production cost for utility-scale solar PV is expected to fall by 25% in the period from 2017 to 2022, while 15% and 33% reductions in costs are expected for onshore and offshore wind, respectively. Furthermore, many countries are abandoning government-set tariffs in favor of competitive auctions based on long-term purchase agreements. The dynamics of auction prices indicate a steep reduction in the costs of solar, onshore wind, and offshore wind.

The rapid deployment and falling costs of clean energy technologies, the growing share of electrification in consumption, climate change awareness and the action of policymakers to decarbonize the economic system are the key trends that Di Castelnuovo and Biancardi (2020) identify in their analysis of the future of energy infrastructure in Chap. 2. They indicate these factors as the drivers of the major ongoing transformation of the energy sector, in particular electricity.

This transition to renewable energy calls for the redesigning of the business model of utilities and opens up new business opportunities. Indeed, the intermittency of renewable energy requires new solutions for storage and distribution, such as the development of smart grids and more efficient batteries. Consistently, utilities are becoming less asset intensive and more service intensive. Moreover, they have started expanding in downstream businesses, like charging and renting electric vehicles. Understanding these changes is key to identifying the opportunities with the highest potential and avoiding investing in stranded assets. For example, the widespread proliferation of efficient energy storage technology could have profound effects on the power and transport sectors. The rise in popularity of electric vehicles threatens oil demand, which could plausibly peak before 2030. In fact, technological advances (such as the continued decline in battery costs), a greater product awareness, consumer preferences and environmental policy could lead to annual sales of 10 million battery-powered electric vehicles by 2025. Such an acceleration of the electrification of the transportation infrastructure would be resoundingly negative for the oil sector. Indeed, this trend could change the economics of power plants facing new peak loads, potentially polarizing electric utilities and the automotive sector into winners and losers.

Another sector with strong environmental implications is water and sanitation. McKinsey Institute (Woetzel et al. 2016) estimates that the percentage of the population of sub-Saharan Africa with access to clean water is less than 30%, while it is slightly less than 40% in South Asia. The OECD estimates that 4 billion people will live in areas seriously affected by water supply shortages by 2050 (see Gurria 2017). This implies a need for sustainable water projects, as well as water-sanitation, sewage-treatments and sand desalinization plants.

As a result, building supply, treatment, storage and reuse systems to ensure a sustainable flow of safe water has become a significant opportunity for investors. A growing portion of investment opportunities in the water sector is opening up in systems for capturing water, related technologies and systems for processing wastewater to varying levels of purity, and the infrastructure to deliver water to industrial, agricultural and residential customers. The focus on efficient use is a global trend, involving utilities, infrastructure investors, and scientific researchers who are developing new treatment technology. In particular, the need to reuse wastewater could create investment opportunities as new technologies enable advanced wastewater treatment techniques to be used by smaller and mid-sized treatment plants.

6.3.2 Inequal, Angry and Scared Societies

After years of hyper-globalization, the great financial crisis, and job losses the financial healthiness of the middle class has worsened and inequalities in terms of revenue distribution have proliferated. In the US, for example, the middle-income tier no longer accounts for the majority of the adult population. According to a study by Credit Suisse (2017), the proportion of the adult American population falling in the middle-income tier has dropped from more than 60% in 1971 to slightly less than 50% in 2015. This expanding inequality has pushed growing portions of the population towards lower standards of living and has led to an increased feeling of anger and greater insecurity.

6.3.2.1 A Growing Sympathy for Populism

With larger inequalities within countries, higher flows of immigrants and refugees, less security in big cities, fear of terrorism, and widespread disenchantment, sympathy for populism is growing especially among millennials and older people. Indeed, Hofrichter (2017) shows that support for populist parties in Europe has grown hand-in-hand with the Gini index of income inequality. The polarization of society and its disillusion with the political status quo are now pushing politicians in developed economies towards economic policies which are more protectionist. These measures aim to support sectors with high domestic employment and to appease the middle class.

Remarkably, in many developed countries disillusion is also growing towards infrastructure, privatized infrastructure in particular. The poor quality of roads and railways in the USA, the water emergency in Australia and South Africa, the excess cost and poor quality of water in the UK are all used as the posterchild of a new anti-private infrastructure attitude. As politicians act more proactively to tackle these issues, understanding the impact of the emergence of populism on infrastructure takes on paramount importance.

On the positive side, growing nationalism should lead to more domestic investments in sectors with strong growth potential for a country, and infrastructure is a key sector in this respect together with military defense. Moreover, income redistribution, which is often supported by populist parties, tends to decrease savings and increase inflation, favoring infrastructure over less inflation-linked asset classes. Yet while deglobalization implies more domestic rather than international investments, a lower general growth outlook would have an offsetting effect. But there are also other marked negative implications.

- Stronger national identities could reduce the attractiveness of cross-border infrastructure due to the erection of trade barriers among states. Furthermore, increased protectionism could hamper the possibility of cross-border acquisitions from foreign investors in strategic sectors and those related to the security of the country, such as transportation, power and defense. Recent decisions in the USA by the CFIUS-Committee for foreign investments, in particular against investments coming from China, as well as the anti-takeover measures adopted in the European Union, the UK and Australia are all clear signs of the potential effect of protectionism on the infrastructure sector.[1]
- The active intervention of the State in a strategic sector like infrastructure is a flagship of radical political movements and could jeopardize investments in infrastructure that are already in place. Populist could then pressure governments against the privatization of infrastructure or excessive rents that private investors extract from concession agreements in water, and power utilities. Curiously, this

---

[1]In Australia, the situation is even more pernicious. Not only is the Australian Government paying attention to acquisitions of strategic infrastructure by foreign investors, but it also scrutinizes the composition and ownership of consortia in joint bids. See Chong (2018).

is happening in established and developed economies, once considered safe harbors in terms of political and regulatory risk. In the UK, one of the most liberal countries in the world and the first to enact a massive infrastructure privatization process in early 1980s, there is a growing tendency to revise original agreements. This in light of the supposed extra returns that private investors have gained from infrastructure, particularly in the water and energy sector. More radical proposals are calling for more intense supervision of private counterparties in PFI contracts, and for resolution mechanisms in case of bankruptcy. These mechanisms would be similar to those banks have been subject to in the years following the Great Financial Crisis.[2]

The implications for long term investors are evident: as governments prioritize investments, some sectors will benefit more than others, very likely shifting the spotlight to national champions and brands, defense and security. Therefore, the intensification of these political pressures makes countries where populist movements are emerging less attractive for investors. Looking ahead, this means that infrastructure investors and asset managers must pay ever closer attention to political and regulatory risks. Indeed, according to a survey conducted among European investors by Deloitte (2016), 38% of investors report that the most worrying risk they perceive when considering whether to invest or not is political risk, while another 35% cite regulatory risk. Interestingly, regulatory risk is perceived as particularly high in Western Europe, with investors identifying the UK (for the first time), Spain and Italy as jurisdictions where regulation is considered to be both excessive and lacking stability and consistency. In these countries, a clear desire from infrastructure investors emerges for more stable regulatory regimes, and for regulators to be more independent and less susceptible to the influence of changes in the political landscape. Indeed, an overwhelming 84% of infrastructure investors responding to a survey by DLA Pipers (2018) agree that infrastructure project proposals in the UK have become too politicized. Tellingly, more than half (55%) believe over-politicization has a direct effect on the value for money of project proposals, with as many as seven in ten having been deterred from investing due to political concerns.

---

[2]Two recent examples are striking. In the UK, Ofgem (the regulatory authority for power and energy) has recently started a renegotiation with the National Grid on a major project to connect the Hinkley Point Nuclear Plant to the electricity network. Estimates point out the need for a grid upgrade costing around £800 million. While this extra cost would be shifted to end users via energy bills, about £100 million would be put on the National Grid, limiting its return on investments. The second example is the recent debate proposed by Shadow Chancellor John McDonnell on the extraction of rents under the price cap mechanism in the Water Sector. See Ford and Plimmer (2018), Megaw (2018) and Jenkins (2018). In Sect. 6.4.3 of this paper we cite one public speech by John McDonnell to analyze infrastructure investors' response to emerging political risk. We also provide evidence of the relevant threat political risk poses to the prospects of this asset class.

6.3.2.2 A Growing Sense of Uncertainty

Aside of the growing sympathy for populism, today's more inequal and polarized society is also characterized by a heightened sense of unsafety. Not only are developed societies becoming angry societies, but also scared societies. Defense and security are turning into political priorities. In this respect technology is expected to play an increasingly important role for civil and military security, as urban safety, traffic safety and the protection of health of human life become essential services. In particular, explosives detectors, infrastructure protection and surveillance of public places are among the areas where IT hardware and software such as drones, robotics and artificial intelligence algorithms come into play to enhance homeland security to protect from traditional threats. In addition, significantly improved semiconductors and the expansion of the Internet of Things (IoT) provide new means for protecting societies against new security threats. Indeed, governments and infrastructure owners are called to sharpen their focus on cybersecurity, as cyber threats evolve beyond simple thuggery to include misinformation campaigns and political muckraking as well. Therefore, for an investor putting money into infrastructure, cybersecurity may become an interesting opportunity. Indeed, according to research and consultancy firm MarketsandMarkets (2018), the information security market will grow to $170 billion by 2020 from $70 billion at the time of the study.

6.3.2.3 Unaffordable Housing

Finally, growing inequality combined with urbanization are making housing unaffordable for lower- and middle-income groups. Several housing markets around the world show warning signs. The World Bank and the United Nations define affordability of housing as a function of the median house price divided by the median household income. Any housing market with a median multiple of above 3 is defined as unaffordable. According to the 14th International Housing Affordability Survey conducted by Demographia in 2017, by this measure, the housing markets of China (18.1), New Zealand (10.0) and Australia (6.6) qualify as plagued by severely unaffordable housing. Other major housing markets with relevant affordability issues include Japan (4.1), the UK (4.5), Canada (4.7), Ireland (4.7) and Singapore (4.8).[3]

According to the McKinsey Institute (Woetzel et al. 2016), if the current urbanization trend continues, the number of households that occupy unsafe and inadequate housing or are financially stretched could reach 440 million (or approximately 1.6 billion people) by 2025. To fill this gap, the investment needed in construction alone would amount to $9 to $11 trillion. With the cost of land, the total market value estimated could be as high as $16 trillion. The largest markets for low income housing units would be China, India, Russia, Brazil and Nigeria. However, urbanization is becoming an issue in European countries as well.

---

[3]See Cox and Pavletich (2018).

Governments have started to take action. Given the limited space in many cities, urbanization has resulted in public authorities relaxing change-of-use rules to increase the supply of residential accommodation. The case of UK permitted development rights (PDR) introduced after 2013 to allow office buildings to be converted to residential use without the need for planning consent is a clear example of a move in this direction (Fixsen 2018). The UK has also announced a proposal for a £2.3 billion housing-infrastructure fund to unlock land for housing and a further £1.4 billion for the construction of affordable housing. In a similar vein, Canada has earmarked $11.6 billion for affordable housing over the next decade, while Australia plans to spend close to $11 billion a year on affordable and social housing. Meanwhile, the Indian government has launched the "Housing for All" scheme, which aims to build approximately 22 million low-cost homes across urban areas by 2022. But the affordability gap is too large to be met with government subsidies and income support alone. Market-based approaches are also needed, presenting therefore interesting opportunities for infrastructure investors.

6.3.3 Demographic Change and Demography Trends

The structural change of the world's demography has a twofold effect on infrastructure, as very different lifestyles and needs clash. The percentage of the young population is growing, but at the same time the population as a whole is ageing. On one side are millennials, who are more attentive to ESG issues. These eco-friendly, digital natives are more oriented toward using rather than owning durable goods in a shared economy logic. On the other side is the silver society, who is more affluent than young people and spends more, especially in healthcare and assistance, and has specific housing needs.

Generation Y refers to those people born between 1981 and 1995. Generation Z refers to those born from 1996 onwards. Overall, they are the millennials. They will become one of the largest generations in the world and, as they grow old, will become the majority of investors and consumers (Gapper 2018). An increase of the percentage of millennials implies that the values and needs of this segment of the population will become pivotal in the years to come. Millennials are much more attentive than past generations to ESG issues, to clean energy consumption, to more ecologically-friendly means of transport like electric vehicles and motorcycles. Consistently, a number of surveys and market analyses indicate that these sectors will grow in importance in the near future. This, however, is not only a generational shift, but also a change in ethnicity and nationality. The millennial generation is dominated by developing countries. Gapper (2018) reports that 43% of US millennials are non-white, and millennials in Asia vastly outnumber those in Europe and the US. Indeed, despite China's former one-child policy, it has 400 million millennials, more than five times the US figure (and more than the entire US population).

Millennials show a clearer distrust for the status quo. Distrust is also driven by the fact that millennials will be poorer than the previous generation and will have less possibility to accumulate wealth during their lifetimes. So, millennials' sophistication and ambition is not matched by their security.

Furthermore, millennials are digital natives. They have a strong inclination to information search, they spend more time being connected to information and social networks. Accordingly, data compiled by Credit Suisse (2017) show that the 18–29 age group scored the highest growth rate in internet access among emerging consumers between 2012 and 2016.

This lifestyle influences their consumption patterns: millennials prefer to use— rather than own—durable goods in a shared economy logic. For example, according to data compiled by Boston Consulting Group (Bokkerink et al. 2017), from 2011 to 2016, large US consumer groups lost $22 billion in sales to smaller brands.

A shared economy, in turn, is supported by connectivity. Speed and availability of an internet connection open new opportunities for infrastructure like fiber networks and telecom towers. Data treatment, data storage and data protection against cyberattacks are additional areas of business in which new opportunities for infrastructure investors are opening up.

The impact of the new consumer habits on the Telecom infrastructure is thoroughly discussed by Sacco (2020) in Chap. 4, who shows how the telecommunication network is evolving in response to the evolution of demand.

On the other hand, population is ageing and by 2020, the spending power of 60+ people is expected to reach an estimated $15 trillion according to Credit Suisse (Hechler-Fayd'herbe 2017).

Fertility rates have been progressively dropping and they are already below the population replacement level of 2.1 in many countries. By 2050, the population aged 60+ will rise to 2.1 billion globally from 900 million in 2015. The median age worldwide will be 36.1 in 2050 compared to 29.6 today. Life expectancy will increase by one year every five years. Six out of 10 women and slightly over 5 of 10 men born between 2000 and 2005 can be expected to live to 80. Unlike today, demographers estimate that 80% of all people 60+ will live in emerging markets by 2050.

The implications of the ageing population for welfare spending and housing are considerable. Indeed, 80% of older people have at least one chronic disease, and an estimated 75% of healthcare spending is on the elderly. But, while today there are 7 workers for every retired person, in 2030 there will be only 4.9 workers.

During active adult life, housing preferences are defined by choice and usually by a low need for care. Thus, households stay in their housing situation often for many years. With age, the needs and level of care can change rapidly along with demand for housing. One out of seven older people spend on average the last 12–18 months of their lives in residential care facilities (Fixsen 2018).

Senior housing typically starts with barrier-free apartments, equipped with smart house devices, easily accessible by public transport and close to medical care, dining, shopping and recreation facilities. The support of social contacts within the community is important as well. When assisted living services are available (e.g. out-patient care, household assistance, emergency services), this supports a household's independence and delays relocation to care facilities or nursing homes.

Senior housing which is close to care homes, hospitals or medical centers can also generate considerable synergies. Furthermore, senior living operators increasingly run facilities made up of multiple units and allow residents to age in place. The higher life expectancy not only boosts demand for such homes, it also shifts the disease pattern from physical weaknesses to dementia cases as the lifespan of the human brain is more frequently the limiting factor. This opens new investment ideas in both the hospitals/health care sectors via Public-Private-Partnership models and in the real estate business with housing solutions suitable for an aged population, not to mention assisted living, memory care facilities and nursing homes.

An older population will also influence urban development, with the need to create urban areas served by a more efficient and extensive network of public transportation and more support services for this portion of the population (Take for example the case of remote monitoring solutions for elderly people who live on their own). The impact of demographic changes and population ageing on the European transportation infrastructure is analyzed in depth by Baccelli (2020) in Chap. 3. In light of these trends, solutions for assisted transportation (public transport/light rails) will be preferred to highways because elderly people drive less.

6.3.4   Urbanization, Transportation and Smart Cities

Megacities are expected to attract even larger shares of the population. Currently, 54% of the global population lives in urban areas. The United Nations estimates that this percentage will grow to 60% by 2030 (United Nations 2018). In China alone, over 600 million people are expected to move from the countryside to megacities in the next 10 years. In Africa, the population is expected to double from 1 billion to 2 billion people by 2050. By 2030, with the exception of Cairo, Mexico City and Lagos, the ten largest cities in the world in terms of population will be located in Asia.

Increasing urbanization questions the current business models for providing city services, such as power distribution, commerce, transportation and logistics. Cities must become energetically more efficient; they need to improve their capacity for absorbing higher traffic volumes by moving people and goods more efficiently; and they need to become better able to withstand the impact of more severe weather that comes from climate change.

On the logistics side, new consumption habits combined with pressure on land prices, urban congestion and demand for rapid delivery of goods may open up new opportunities for infrastructure investors interested in a new breed of warehouses. Emsden (2018) argues that the increased pollution of megacities coupled with the need of customers to have access to goods real time (home delivery) will lead e-retailers and e-grocers to move big warehousing facilities to the outer edges of big cities. This would mean that shipping costs (both explicit (fees) and implicit (carbon emissions and pollution)) can be minimized thanks to the optimization of the supply chain.

Transportation also needs to adapt to higher passenger volumes and physical constraints. By 2030, 95% of passenger miles travelled are expected to be served by on-demand autonomous electric vehicles (Meggiolaro 2018; Emsden 2018; Pressi 2018) owned by companies providing transport as a service. Most of the energy these vehicles use is expected to be produced by solar panels and stored thanks to extremely efficient batteries.

Multiple advantages derive from the move towards green cities connected by low-impact highway and rail systems effortlessly moving people and products. Car sharing and localized production will result in less traffic and fewer parking areas as well as less demand for cement and asphalt, all of which will reduce greenhouse gas emissions and air pollution. The entire ecosystem will rely on clean energy. Much of it will operate autonomously, without direct human guidance, and will be much more efficient than what exists in most places today. Moreover, reduced amounts of pavement will allow for more natural water flows and drainage; green areas will absorb greenhouse gasses and naturally cool nearby areas. Yet, all this transformation is expected to happen essentially for purely economic reasons, not for environmental or ethical ones (Meggiolaro 2017).

The impact of urbanization as well as international tourism on transportation infrastructure is further discussed by Baccelli (2020) in Chap. 3. Such a future will no doubt differ dramatically from the world we live in today, opening up new opportunities for infrastructure investors positioned to take advantage of this trend.

6.3.5 Digitalization and Shared Economies

Digital transformation is radically changing products, business models and value chains. The growing use and consumption of data imply that infrastructure is no longer a physical asset like in the past. Infrastructure is becoming more immaterial. Indeed, managing infrastructure has less to do with physical goods, and more closely resembles the management of intangible assets like data, information, and services.

A fundamental role is played by the diffusion of the web and web-connected devices. As a consequence, wireless traffic and use of data flow is expected to expand significantly. Forecasts by Cisco (Visual Networking Index) in 2017 indicated that traffic on internet capable devices was growing at a 57% CAGR and was expected reach 6.2 exabytes per month by 2019. This data traffic is increasingly moving from laptops to portable devices, such as smartphones and tablets.

The impact of these new consumer habits on the telecom infrastructure is thoroughly discussed in Chap. 4 by Sacco, who shows how the telecommunication network is evolving in response to the evolution of demand.

Digitalization is also remapping the boundaries between sectors and the way firms operate in modern economies. They are shifting to digital business models that make things smarter by using connectivity (Internet of Things), analyzing the collected data in a more sophisticated manner (big data), and managing and sharing data via the cloud (Internet of Services—IoS).

This represents a disruptive change in the infrastructure industry ecosystem. Venzin and Konert (2020) discuss in Chap. 5 how investing in infrastructure today is more complex than it has ever been before. Not only does technology change more rapidly, but regulations, internationalization, consumer behavior, and ·business models can quickly shift profits and alter social and environmental impact. In this renewed ecosystem the ability to identify disruptors, as well as firms or assets with embedded adaptability, will become central to the investment process.

For example, Internet Platform (IP) companies could be among those who benefit most, in our view, due to their network and scale. In fact, they already have a huge customer base that provides significant operating leverage to expand their businesses globally. However, technology and digitalization open up opportunities in other fields as well: from smart manufacturing, to smart homes, smart grids, smart cities, etc. For instance, the progressive diffusion of smart cities as a potential model for sustainable development leads us to rethink the role of energy utilities as economic actors active in the urban context. Other beneficiaries of this trend are companies addressing the big data and business intelligence markets and vendors of semiconductors that provide the needed processing power for big data management in data centers.

Alongside this transformation, data theft and data protection are becoming key areas of development. Cybersecurity is expected to be among the most resilient areas of IT spending as the number of digital threats continues to rise (Willis Towers Watson 2017; Pfeifer et al. 2018). Until recently, the primary targets of cyberattacks were financial firms and governments. Today, the threat is universal, for companies and customers alike. Little wonder that risk managers now consider cyber-risk the biggest threat to their business and that some companies are investing up to $500 million on cybersecurity. Indeed, according to a survey by McKinsey (Poppensieker and Riemenschnitter 2018), 75% of experts consider cybersecurity to be a top priority. Yet only 16% say their companies are well prepared to deal with an attack. A report by Citi (Khorana et al. 2018) indicates that weaknesses in protecting digital assets have caused both significant direct financial damage and a negative investor response. As cyberattacks have become more severe, markets have responded more negatively, with average short-term excess stock returns of -6.8% in 2017. In the most severe breaches, short-term excess returns were -14%, bottoming out at -36% for the Equifax breach that was announced on September 7th, 2017. Institutional investors increasingly see cyber-attacks as a credible threat to their portfolio. As a result, they are ready to reduce investments in companies that are vulnerable, while buying stakes in firms providing cybersecurity solutions (Palma 2018).

Data storage is another area of interest. The Veritas Global Databerg Report (2016) reveals that 52% of all information stored and processed by organizations around the world is considered dark data of unknown value. Just 15% of corporate data is business critical, another 33% of data is considered redundant, obsolete or trivial. These findings confirm the huge amounts of dark data companies have, with little knowledge of relative content, and highlight the issues and risks associated with allowing data growth to continue unabated. Estimates show that, if left untamed, business data could cost organizations around the world a cumulative $3.3 trillion to manage by the year 2020. This could be a new business area that is on the rise for companies that help to qualify, manage and clean data storage.

Finally, burgeoning technology can transform some industries through the emergence of new services complementary to traditional ones. One example is the use of artificial intelligence and distributed ledger (blockchain) technology to inform business decisions and make transactions more efficient in the financial services industry. Specific cases could include insurers using machine learning to calculate premiums; clearing houses using blockchain to make settlements of securities and derivatives quicker and cheaper; lenders using big data to manage credit risk; and regulatory authorities using digital tools for supervision. Another example is the use of virtual reality in child care [see Venzin and Konert (2020) in Chap. 5], or digital tools to better access patients when providing healthcare services. In the latter case, better patient outcomes can be obtained through remote patient monitoring solutions, telehealth offerings, as well as health education and health management portals. With healthcare costs on the rise in developed countries, and infrastructure investors who are already invested in social infrastructure like hospitals, elderly houses and care services via PPPs, digitalization is offering new opportunities.

6.3.6   Mapping the Impact of Megatrends on Infrastructure Investment

We conclude our discussion of the technological and socio-cultural trends with the strongest potential impact on infrastructure investment by mapping them across different investment styles, geographical areas and sectors, in Table 6.2. The goal

Table 6.2 Map of the impact of megatrends on infrastructure investment

	Style				Region				Industry						
	Core	Core-Plus	Value Added	Opportunistic	North America	Europe	Asia	Rest of the World	Renewable Energy	Energy	Transport	Utilities	Water/Sanitation	Healthcare	Housing
Sustainability and the environment	●	●	●	●	●	●	●	●	●	●	●	●	●		●
Inequal, angry and scared societies	●				●	●						●			●
Demographic change and demography trends	●	●			●	●	●		●		●			●	●
Urbanization, transportation and smart cities	●	●	●	●	●	●	●		●		●	●			●
Digitalization and the shared economy		●	●		●	●	●	●	●	●		●		●	●

is to provide asset managers and investors a map they can use to identify new investment opportunities that open up as these trends influence the way infrastructure assets are built and operated.

Digitalization and the transition towards a more sustainable, green economy are the two megatrends with the widest implications, in terms of industries and regions. In our view, the former will open up investment opportunities in the renewable and traditional energy sectors (e.g., smart grids), in the way utilities provide their services, in social infrastructure to support the internet of things and services (e.g., data centers, data storage, data analytics and cybersecurity), healthcare (e.g., artificial intelligence, virtual reality and remote patient monitoring) and housing (e.g., smart cities). The transition toward a more sustainable green economy instead will have a deeper impact on renewable and traditional energy production (e.g., photovoltaic, wind) and distribution (e.g., batteries), transportation (e.g., electric vehicles), downstream expansion of the business model of utilities as they become more service intensive, with regard to water and sanitation (e.g. sewage treatment and desalinization plants), and energy efficient housing. However, while the transition towards a more sustainable, green economy is expected to generate new opportunities across the entire spectrum of investment styles, we think that the impact of digitalization will be more concentrated on core-plus and value-added investment styles.

We believe the impact of increasingly inequal, angry and scared societies will be especially severe in the developed economies of North America and Europe, and will be confined to core infrastructure assets. In particular, as political risk threatens private rents from public concessions, our view is that the most significant effect will be on utilities. We expect instead new opportunities opening up in the sector of social infrastructure in affordable housing and in response to the growing sense of insecurity (e.g., artificial intelligence, drones, robotics, cybersecurity).

With respect to demographic trends we anticipate that the following sectors will be most deeply affected: renewable energy (e.g., green power), transport (e.g., electric vehicles, assisted transportation, shared economy), social infrastructure (e.g., connectivity, fiber networks and towers, data treatment, data storage, data protection), healthcare (e.g., residential care facilities, assisted living services) and housing (e.g., senior housing, smart home devices). In our view, the impact of demographic changes will be stronger in core and core-plus investment styles.

Furthermore, we expect increased urbanization, higher traffic volumes of goods and services, and the transition towards smart cities will have a greater impact on renewable energy (e.g., smart grids), transportation and delivery logistics for goods (e.g., autonomous electric vehicles, drones), service provision by utilities, and green housing.

Remarkably, Table 6.2 shows that each sector is affected by multiple megatrends at the same time. This implies that the traditional business model of infrastructure asset managers, based on sectorial specialization, may become inefficient. Indeed, this model may even prove incapable of fully capturing those transformative trends that would guarantee investors long-term sustainable returns.

6.4   The Changes Ahead: Megatrends and the Infrastructure Universe

Our discussion of the implications of all this for investors and asset managers starts with an assessment of the status quo and then moves on to recommend possible actions that can be implemented to face the changes ahead.

6.4.1   The Status Quo

To get a sense of the status quo we begin by analyzing the largest asset managers and investors in the market, trying to map their approach to infrastructure and their investment styles.

Table 6.3 lists the top 20 infrastructure asset managers by assets under management at the end of June 2018. On aggregate, they account for approximately €465 billion of infrastructure assets under management, ranging from €7.4 billion to €86.6

Table 6.3 Top 20 Asset Managers by Infrastructure Assets Under Management, as of end of June 2018

		Infrastructure AUM (€m)	Total AUM (€m)	(%)
1.	Macquire Infrastructure and Real Assets	86,639	92,433	93.7
2.	Brookfield Asset Management	69,280	237,888	29.1
3.	M&G Investments	55,050	336,170	16.4
4.	Global Infrastructure Partners	37,773	37,773	100.0
5.	IFM Investors	32,159	65,594	49.0
6.	The Carlyle Group	21,247	171,754	12.4
7.	DWS	17,913	73,376	24.4
8.	BlackRock	16,015	4,979,701	0.3
9.	Energy Capital Partners	15,702	15,702	100.0
10.	EIG Global Energy Partners	14,774	14,774	100.0
11.	AMP Capital Investors	13,948	122,274	11.4
12.	Nuveen	11,593	808,402	1.4
13.	Allianz Global Investors	11,417	498,000	2.3
14.	Lazard Asset Management	11,155	185,183	6.0
15.	I Squared Capital	10,190	10,190	100.0
16.	Amber Infrastructure Group	9010	9010	100.0
17.	Partners Group	8314	61,963	13.4
18.	First State Investments	7706	142,121	5.4
19.	Ardian	7600	60,000	12.7
20.	JP Morgan Asset Management	7430	1,427,930	0.5
	Total	464,915	9,350,238	5.0

Source: Authors' elaboration of data provided by Investment and Pensions Europe (IPE Real Assets 2018b)

billion in individual holdings. We consider these firms to be fairly representative of the whole infrastructure asset management industry, which proves to be highly concentrated. In fact, the asset managers in question account for more than 76% of the total infrastructure assets under management of the top 50 asset managers.

The infrastructure asset management industry has advanced by following a specialization approach, be it either sectorial, geographical, dependent on their risk and return characteristics, or related to the development stage of the assets (i.e., brownfield vs. greenfield). To get a better picture of the variety of approaches to infrastructure and the different investment styles, we then classify the top 20 asset managers according to a set of non-mutually-exclusive categories based on the information available on their webpages. In particular, concerning geographical focus, we distinguish between domestic and emerging economies, while in terms of investment styles we differentiate among core, core-plus and value added/oppor-tunistic. Unfortunately, we do not have data that allow us to classify asset managers based on the stage of development of the assets in question, nor their allocations to economic vs. social infrastructure. Figure 6.9 shows that while the dominant focus tends towards core assets and developed economies, the investment style is drifting towards non-core and emerging economies. Indeed, as returns are being compressed,

Fig. 6.9 Investment Styles of Top 20 Asset Managers (Source: Authors' elaboration of data provided by Investments and Pensions Europe and Asset Managers' websites)

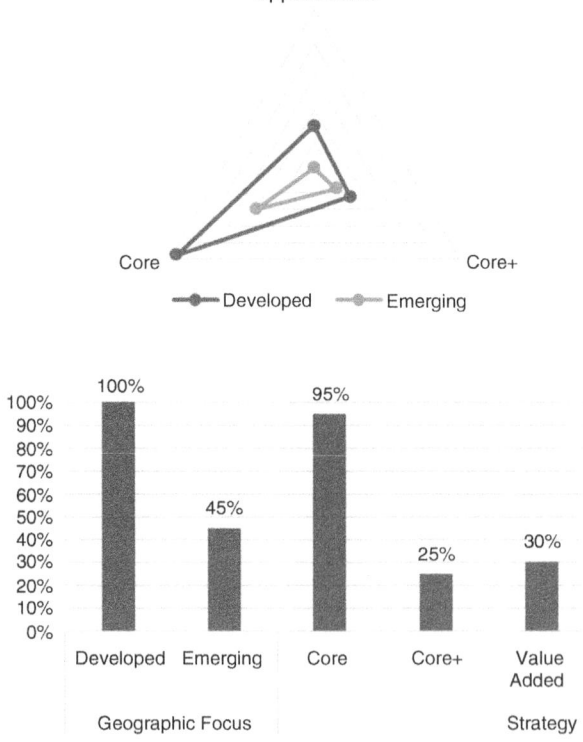

Table 6.4   Top 20 Investors by Infrastructure Asset Holdings, as of end of June 2018

		Country	Infra. (€m)	Total (€m)	(%)
1.	China Investment Corporation	China	40,676	813,513	5.0
2.	Abu Dhabi Investment Authority	UAE	24,840	828,000	3.0
3.	CPP Investment Board	Canada	18,235	237,802	7.7
4.	National Pension Service	South Korea	16,020	498,004	3.2
5.	Ontario Teachers' Pension Plan	Canada	13,215	130,368	10.1
6.	OMERS	Canada	13,025	79,826	16.3
7.	APG	Netherlands	12,851	51,4021	2.1
8.	Legal & General	UK	12,302	575,535	2.5
9.	CDPQ	Canada	10,914	154,199	7.1
10.	AustralianSuper	Australia	8617	81,245	10.6
11.	PSP Investments	Canada	8330	101,754	8.2
12.	bcIMC	Canada	8254	101,679	8.1
13.	Future Fund	Australia	8210	102,265	8.0
14.	PGGM	Netherlands	7902	26,823	3.6
15.	China Life	China	7703	352,445	2.9
16.	TRS Texas	US	7646	152,926	5.0
17.	UniSuper	Australia	7336	42,881	17.1
18.	Allianz	Germany	6960	741,605	0.9
19.	PKA	Denmark	6290	37,894	16.6
20.	USS	UK	4981	78,382	6.4
		Total	244,305	5,841,166	4.2

Source: Authors' elaboration of data provided by Investment and Pensions Europe (IPE Real Assets 2018a)

managers are now seeking riskier transactions to meet stated returns targets. This is consistent with the trend observed at the industry level for the evolution of fundraising, as shown in Fig. 6.4.

On the investor side, we focus on the top 20 investors ranked by infrastructure asset holdings at the end of June 2018. Table 6.4 reports for each investor its total asset holdings and compares this with its infrastructure assets. Also in this case, we consider the top 20 investors as being fairly representative of the whole market. Indeed, taken together they account for approximately €244 billion of infrastructure assets holdings, which corresponds to 67.8% of the infrastructure assets held by the top 100 investors.

Investors' allocations to infrastructure range from 0.9% to 17.1%, and for any two out of three investors this figure is below 10%, as shown in Fig. 6.10. Yet these allocations are polarized, with relatively smaller investors allocating proportionally more. Among investors with total asset holdings in excess of €150 billion, the maximum allocation to infrastructure is 7.7%, while for relatively smaller investors the minimum allocation to infrastructure is 6.4%. We interpret this as an indication of the fact that, for the costs of developing infrastructure-specific investment skills to be justified and for diversification benefits to materialize, the allocation to

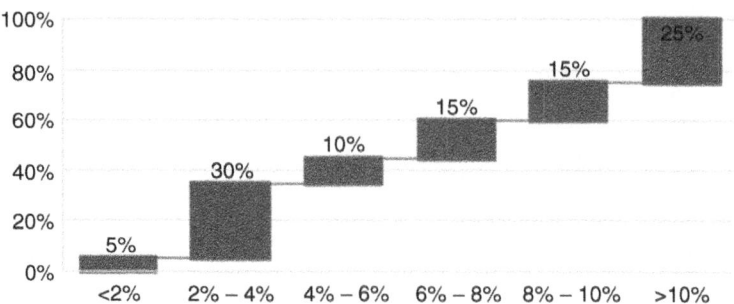

Fig. 6.10 Allocations by Top 20 Investors to Infrastructure, as % Total Asset Holdings at end of June 2018 (Source: Authors' elaboration of data provided by Investment and Pensions Europe)

infrastructure needs to be sizable. Consistently, we find that 80% of the top 20 investors have in-house specialized teams dedicated to infrastructure assets.

6.4.2   The Changes Ahead

As a result of the macrotrends reshaping the way society works and lives, we expect infrastructure will no longer be the safe harbor of alternative investments. More specifically, our view is that the emerging trends, which have consequences within and across infrastructure sectors, have five main implications for the asset management industry:

- Infrastructure is not the monolith of the past and not necessarily even a physical asset anymore. Under the pressure of social and technological disrupting forces, the boundaries between different segments of the infrastructure ecosystem are rapidly blurring at the aggregate level, as documented by Venzin and Konert (2020) in Chap. 5. Di Castelnuovo and Biancardi (2020) in Chap. 2, Baccelli (2020) in Chap. 3 and Sacco (2020) in Chap. 4 investigate the same phenomenon for energy, transportation and telecom, respectively. Moreover, as the predominant investment style drifts towards more risky strategies, contamination with private equity will eventually make the returns for infrastructure more closely correlated with other asset classes.
- Barriers of entry have become weaker than in the past, attracting new private equity competitors to challenge the incumbents. Indeed, according to Preqin data, 80% of fund managers report that competition for both assets and investor capital has increased in 2017.
- Asset managers are no longer monopolists in the market. The biggest investors are showing signs of internalizing investment capabilities and are more and more often co-investing with industrial developers. Indeed, 80% of the top 20 investors we studied in the previous section report having specialized in-house teams

dedicated to infrastructure assets. This way they side-step infrastructure asset managers and avoid paying management fees and carried interest.

- Megatrends challenge the traditional business model of infrastructure asset managers, based on the excellence of industry-specific skills combined with a deep knowledge of particular geographical areas, sectors and subsectors. To capture the benefits of intersectoral megatrends and spot emerging investment areas, infrastructure asset managers must adopt a broader and more forward-looking investment philosophy, grounded on a principle-based approach or eligibility tests based on the features of the needs served by the infrastructure, as discussed by Venzin and Konert (2020) in Chap. 5. Among these, we expect embedded flexibility to play a key role for adapting to the disruptive forces of technological and social changes.
- As a result of the intensified competition for infrastructure assets and the surging overpayment risk, we believe asset managers will start to pay more attention to the quality of management teams in investee firms. Indeed, we expect revenue growth and cost optimization through well designed strategic rethinking, which have been so far largely unexploited, will become increasingly important components of the long-term yields offered to investors. In contrast, other traditional private-equity value drivers (i.e., leverage and arbitrage) in our view will continue to play only a minor role.

To asset managers facing these challenges we recommend two complementary courses of action. The first one is more oriented to the short-term and more in line with the investment style of private equity; it involves actions aimed at enhancing performance while maintaining long-term strategic views. We refer to this course of action as tactical optimization. The second one, which is instead has a long-term orientation, requires recognizing current trends and positioning oneself to exploit long-term strategic opportunities. We refer to this second course of action as theme investing.

6.4.3   Action 1: Tactical Optimization

A natural way to enhance performance in the short-term while leaving long-term strategic views intact is to borrow from the private equity toolkit. In this respect, we identify three levers of tactical optimization that infrastructure asset managers can work on:

- strengthening their ability to spot undervalued assets;
- modifying their risk profile across sectors, geographical areas, and the lifecycle to adapt to emerging and changing risk; and
- increasing revenues and squeezing margins to create value.

In order to assess the viability of enhancing performance by spotting sectors and regions with some untapped potential left, we have collected data on the price-to-book ratio, the price-earnings multiple and the enterprise value to EBITDA multiple for a broad set of listed companies, operating all over the world in sectors closely related with infrastructure. Regrettably, the structural lack of data on the valuations of private infrastructure assets does not allow us to realize a more comprehensive assessment. Still, we believe that the results which emerge from our analysis of listed companies can be largely generalized to private infrastructure assets. Figure 6.11 reports boxplots for the distribution of the median price-earnings ratio over the

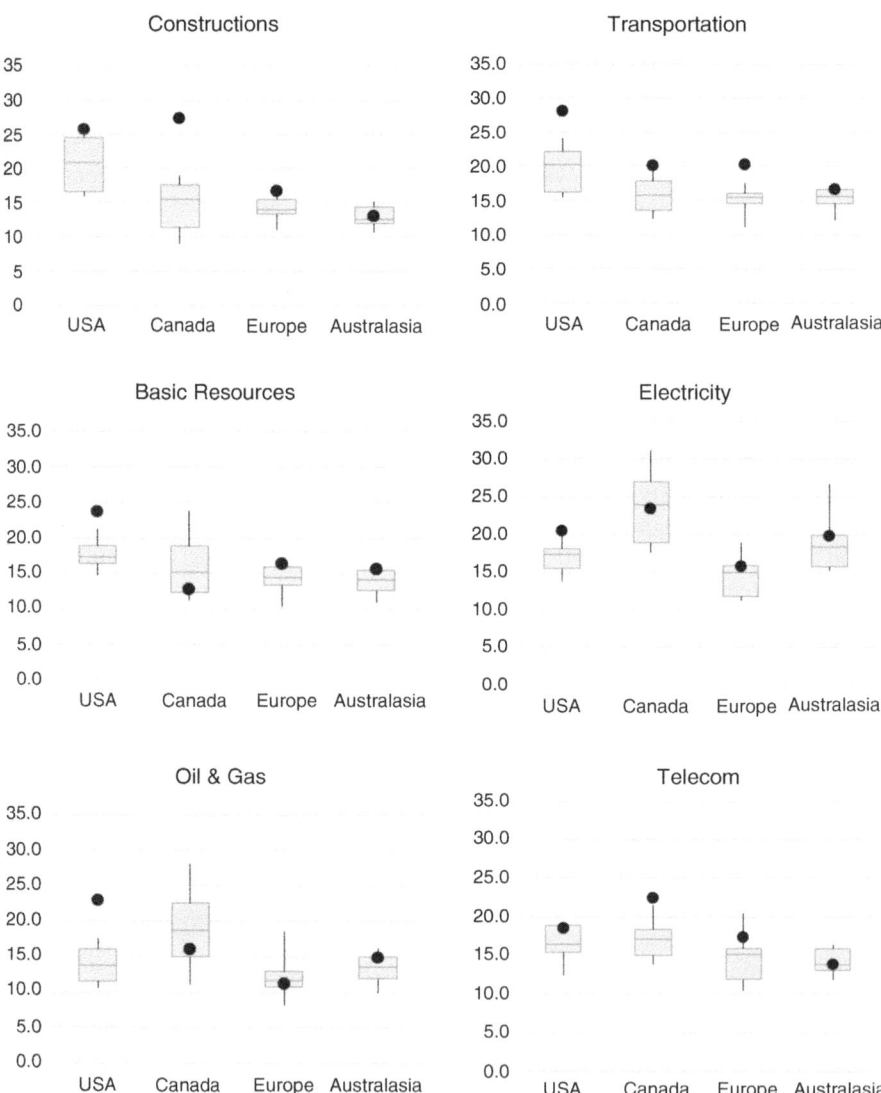

Fig. 6.11 Valuations Heatmap: Median PE Ratios from 2004 to 2017 (blue dot) (Source: Authors' elaboration of data provided by Thomson Reuters Datastream)

period from 2004 to 2017. For the majority of sectors and regions, the most recent valuations are at the highest end of the distribution, raising red flags for the risk of overpayment. Yet, not all sectors and regions are equally overheated. For example, taking a closer look at Europe, untapped potential could be found in the Electricity and the Oil & Gas sectors, where valuations are well below the 75th percentile of the historical distribution.

The ability to modify the risk profile of the investments in the portfolio moving across sectors, regions and the lifecycle is another important tool for enhancing and protecting performances.

- Moving across sectors to embrace more risky investment styles, such as core-plus or value added, would imply becoming more like private equity. On the positive side, the more forward-looking approach typical of private equity could help performances. Such contamination, though, involves a more active management of the investee firm and more uncertain long-term performance, which can determine an overall rise in the risk of the infrastructure asset class and an increase in its correlation with other asset classes, potentially undermining its appeal to more risk-averse investors.
- Analogously, performances could be enhanced by moving along the lifecycle of infrastructure assets from brownfield to greenfield. Indeed, according to Partners Group (2018), building core assets or investing in fragmented markets that have the potential for consolidation and platform-building can result in a IRR increase of 300–500 bps, depending on the sector and geographic location of the asset.
- Alternatively, the move in search of enhanced performances can occur across regions, from developed economies to emerging ones, all the while paying close attention to the underlying political risk.

To support this claim, we focus on the threat of political risk that is emerging prominently even in developed economies with a long-standing tradition of privatization. To assess whether infrastructure investors recognize emerging political risk as a relevant threat to the prospects of this asset class, which is highly concentrated in regulated industries, we analyze the market reaction to a speech delivered by John McDonnell at the 2017 annual conference of the UK Labour Party. On September 25th 2017, as Shadow Chancellor of the Exchequer, McDonnell criticized the excessive private rents from public concessions and argued in favor of nationalizations. Figure 6.12 shows the cumulative abnormal returns over the FTSE 100 index of two (equally weighted) baskets of listed UK water utilities and listed UK infrastructure funds (with substantial PFI exposure). The first includes Pennon Group, Severn Trent and United Utilities Group. The latter counts John Laing Infrastructure Fund, BBGI, HICL Infrastructure, International PBPART and 3i Infrastructure. We observe that, as a result of enhanced political risk, investors update their valuations of UK water utilities and listed infrastructure funds. The cumulative underperformance with respect to the FTSE 100 reached −6% in the days immediately following the speech. Interestingly, underperformance of UK water utilities, which was addressed directly in speech, is of the same order of

Fig. 6.12 Political Risk, Cumulative Abnormal Returns for Listed UK Water Utilities and UK Listed Infrastructure Funds with PFI Exposure (Source: Authors' elaboration of data provided by Thomson Reuters Datastream)

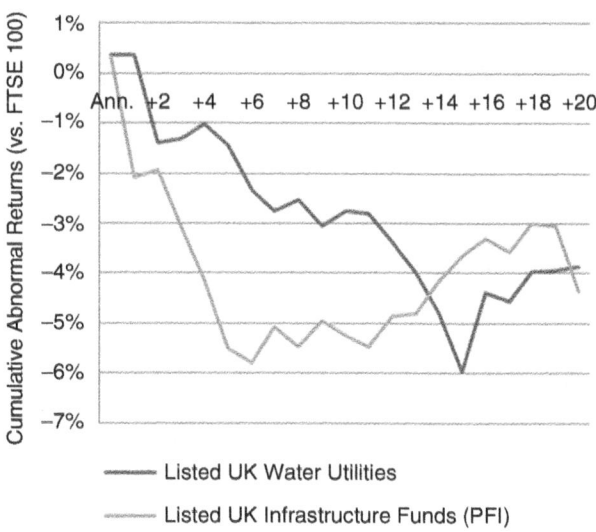

——— Listed UK Water Utilities

········· Listed UK Infrastructure Funds (PFI)

Table 6.5 Sample summary statistics

	Deal value ($ mil.)	EV/EBITDA (Entry)	PB (Entry)	PE (Entry)
Mean	1257	7.5	1.8	21.3
St. Dev.	1518	3.7	0.9	18.6

Source: Bloomberg

magnitude as listed infrastructure funds. This suggests that investors have adjusted their valuations to reflect a higher level of political risk across the board, since it is hardly diversifiable across sectors at the portfolio level. Consistently, the adjustment period is relatively shorter for listed infrastructure funds. In this case, therefore, the ability to recognize emerging political risk and to modify the risk profile of the investments in the portfolio accordingly, by means of geographical diversification, would prove extremely valuable for enhancing and protecting performances.

Enhancing performance through value creation in investee firms by upping revenues and squeezing margins is a typical lever of private equity returns. Yet its upfront applicability in the infrastructure asset class is not straightforward. To assess its viability, we collected data on 22 completed deals for listed infrastructure or real asset targets in the period from 2002 to 2015. Table 6.5 provides a few summary statistics on the deals included in our sample. The average deal size was $1.3 billion, ranging from $21.7 million to $3.7 billion. Targets encompassed airports, railway stations, parking lots, highways, logistic centers, water utilities, power plants and distribution networks.

We then formed a panel of financial data for the investee firms in the years following the entry to track their evolution over time. Figure 6.13 shows their average annual change over a three-year investment horizon. The results that emerge

Fig. 6.13 Changes in Financials of Investee Firms over a Three-Year Investment Horizon from Entry (Source: Authors' elaboration of data provided by Bloomberg)

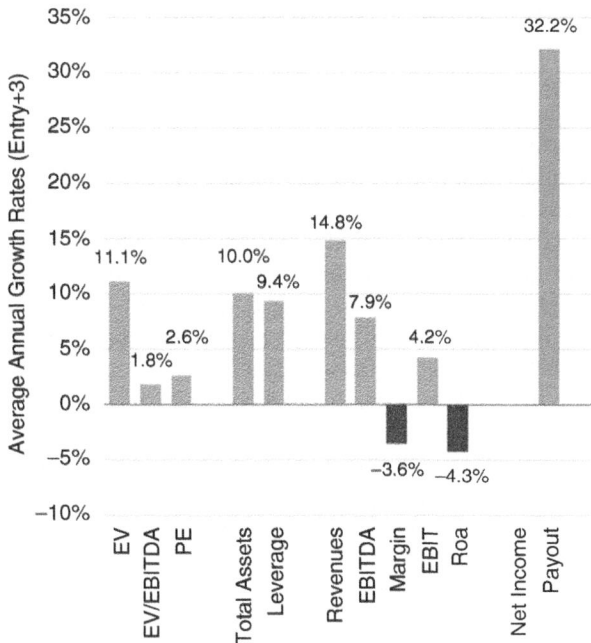

from this analysis need to be interpreted with due caution, given the small sample size. Yet, they provide some consistent indications. The operational improvements achieved over the period are prevalently directed to support income returns by means of larger payouts to investors rather than capital gains. Indeed, the average annual growth in PE and EV/EBITDA multiples is modest, only +2.6% and +1.8%, respectively, while payouts to investors almost double over the 3-year horizon (+32.2%). In short, investee firms grow in size but not in value. The increment in EV (+11.1%) is mostly explained by a growth in terms of total assets (+10%), fueled mainly by debt (+9.4). However, such growth in size is not accompanied by commensurate gains in earnings. Higher revenues (+14.8%), EBITDA (+7.9%) and EBIT (+4.2) do not translate into higher margins (−3.6%) or returns on assets (−4.3%). We conclude that the active management of investee firms to create value is therefore a largely unexplored tool to enhance performance, leaving ample margins for improvement through tactical optimization. Revenue growth and cost optimization through well-designed strategic rethinking are becoming the keys to ensuring good sustainable long-term yields despite intensified competition and higher prices. At the same time, asset managers need to pay more attention to the quality of management teams in investee firms. In this respect, good investment opportunities could emerge from spotting underperforming assets that industrial companies could divest.

6.4.4   Action 2: Theme Investing

Enhancing performance in the long-term requires identifying sectors that are supported by transformative trends which drive demand for new and better infrastructure. This is contingent on analyzing trends within and across industries to highlight disruptive business models or essential assets where new infrastructure needs are emerging.

To capture the benefits of intersectoral trends and spot emerging areas of investments, asset managers need to abandon their traditional business model based on specialization. Instead they must adopt a broader and more forward-looking investment philosophy, grounded on a principle-based approach or eligibility tests based on the features of the needs served by the infrastructure. This is in line with the work by Venzin and Konert (2020) in Chap. 5, who propose mapping the infrastructure ecosystem, its actors and their roles, to come up with a fundamental tool for adapting to the disruptive changes affecting the asset class. More specifically, theme investing requires a reorganization of the entire screening process of infrastructure investment opportunities, in order to combine each trend with the sectors it is expected to transform and with specific asset eligibility criteria (i.e., a set of criteria that, if met, qualify the asset as infrastructure). Table 6.6 provides an example of this approach. Under this more forward-looking investment philosophy, future-proof infrastructure assets are those with embedded flexibility rather than those with a proven track record.

In this respect, we provide two examples of theme investing:

- sustainability and the environment; and
- intangible infrastructure: the power of data.

Sustainability and environmental issues have never been so central to the public debate as they are today. What's more, they are becoming high priorities on the political agenda, as seen in Sect. 6.3.1 and thoroughly discussed by Di Castelnuovo and Biancardi (2020) in Chap. 2. But will these issues have the force to reshape entire sectors of our economy? Investors think so. Indeed, to assess the viability of a theme investment strategy related to sustainability and the environment, we

Table 6.6 Theme investing investment process matrix

	Theme I			Theme II	
	Sector A	Sector B	Sector C	Sector D	Sector E
Asset eligibility criteria	Essential asset, inelastic demand				
	High barriers to entry				
	Stable cash flow, long term contracts				
	Inflation link				
	Embedded flexibility				
	Downside protection				
	Etc.				

Table 6.7 News on data electric vehicles and bans to carbon emissions

Date	News
2/10/2017	General Motors announces new investments in electric vehicles. General Motors vs. S&P500 Automobile Manufacturer
5/7/2017	Volvo Motors announces new investments in electric vehicles. Volvo vs. MSCI Europe Automobiles
15/1/2018	Ford announces new investments in electric vehicles. Ford vs. S&P500 Automobile Manufacturers
28/6/2018	BP announces acquisition of electric vehicle charging network. BP vs. FTSE 100
18/7/2018	Renault announces new investments in electric vehicles. Renault vs. MSCI Europe Automobiles
16/12/2017	The World Bank announces plans to end support for fossil fuels from 2020. MSCI World Oil, Gas, and Consumable vs. MSCI World
13/4/2018	Britain announces new biofuel targets to reduce diesel reliance. MSCI World Oil, Gas, and Consumable vs. MSCI World
21/4/2018	HSBC announces stop funding fossil fuel industries. MSCI World Oil, Gas, and Consumable vs. MSCI World
5/7/2018	Shell says firm carbon emissions targets are superfluous. MSCI World Oil, Gas, and Consumable vs. MSCI World
12/7/2018	Irish parliament passes bill to force sovereign fund to divest from fossil fuels. MSCI World Oil, Gas, and Consumable vs. MSCI World
13/7/2018	Exxon CEO announces reduction in spending on fossil fuels. MSCI World Oil, Gas, and Consumable vs. MSCI World

Source: Authors' elaboration of data provided by Factiva

conducted an event study of the market reaction upon the release of different news items regarding electric vehicles or carbon emissions. We find that investors react positively to the launch of new electric vehicles or related investment programs, while they penalize oil and gas companies when news is released on new bans on fossil fuels or restrictions on carbon emissions. Table 6.7 provides a description of the news we considered in our analysis, while Fig. 6.14 shows the corresponding cumulative abnormal returns along a 5-day window around the date in which the news became public.

The average announcement-day abnormal return for automakers following new launches or investments in electric vehicles is +2.1%, while Oil & Gas stocks underperform the market on average by −0.9% upon reports of caps on carbon emissions or investments in fossil fuels. These results reflect investors' belief that sustainability and environmental issues will reshape different sectors in the long-term, including transportation and energy. This shows that sustainability and the environment are appropriate cornerstones upon which to build an intersectoral investment theme.

Nevertheless, upon recognizing a trend, determining a positioning to exploit its long-term strategic opportunities may not be straightforward. Not all assets are equally affected; returns can vary substantially within industry groups. Indeed, following the sustainability and environmental themes, we conducted an analysis

Fig. 6.14 Announcement Effect of Investments in Electric Vehicles and Bans on Fossil Fuels (Source: Authors' elaboration of data provided by Factiva and Thomson Reuters Datastream)

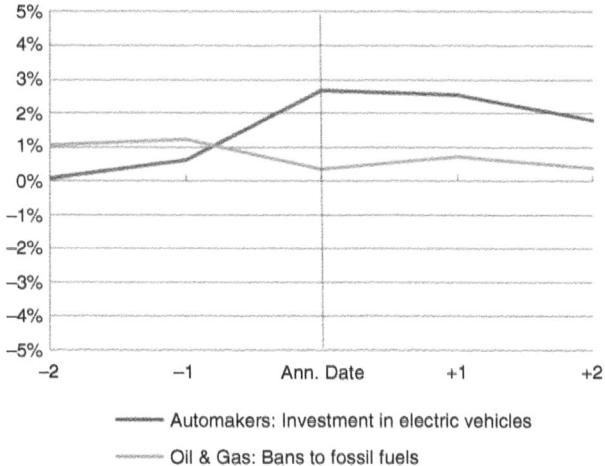

Fig. 6.15 Distribution of 3-Year Total Returns (as computed at end of June 2018) (Source: Authors' elaboration of data provided by Thomson Reuters Datastream)

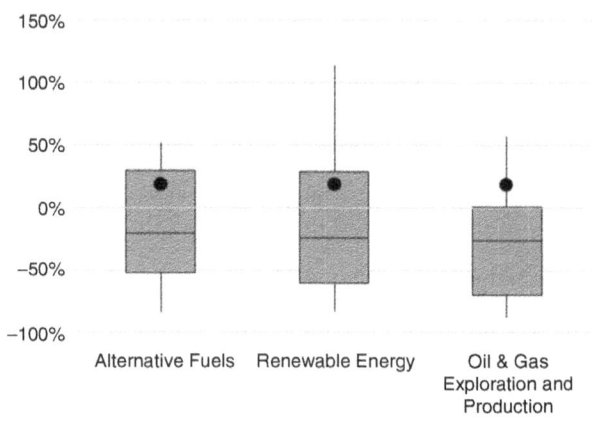

of the energy sector to compare the performances of 544 globally listed companies clustered in the following three industry groups: alternative fuels (33), renewable energy (50), and oil and gas exploration and production (471). Figure 6.15 reports the distribution of the 3-year total returns (as computed at the end of June 2018) for the companies belonging to each industry group, and compares their performance with that of a broad energy market index. What becomes clear is that theme investing is not without its perils. While the proportion of companies that delivered positive returns is relatively larger among the alternative fuels and renewable energy industry groups, their performances show notable variations within each group.

Other long-term strategic opportunities may originate from technological advances. As disruptive business models open the way to new essential products and services, novel types of infrastructure emerge to serve new consumer needs. Here we may not even necessarily refer to physical infrastructures, as is the case for example of intangible infrastructures related to digitalization and the power of data. Taking the topic cybersecurity, in order to assess its viability as an investment theme, we conducted an event study of the market reaction upon release of different reports regarding data breaches or improper use of data. We find that investors react negatively to this news. Table 6.8 provides a description of the news we considered in our analysis, while Fig. 6.16 shows the corresponding cumulative abnormal returns along a 5-day window around the date in which the public announcement was made.

The average announcement-day abnormal return for IT companies is -7% following news of a data breach and -5.8% after a report of improper use of data. These results reflect the value that investors give to cybersecurity, showing its suitability as the cornerstone upon which to build an intersectoral investment theme. This as companies' business models across different sectors increasingly rely on the use of data.

Table 6.8 News on data breaches and improper use of data

Date	News
22/9/2016	Yahoo announces data breach. S&P500 IT vs. S&P500
7/9/2017	Equifax announces data breach. Equifax vs. S&P500
13/6/2018	Dixons Carphone announces data breach. Dixons Carphone vs. S&P500
17/3/2018	Facebook acknowledges Cambridge Analytica scandal. Facebook vs. S&P500

Source: Authors' elaboration of data provided by Factiva

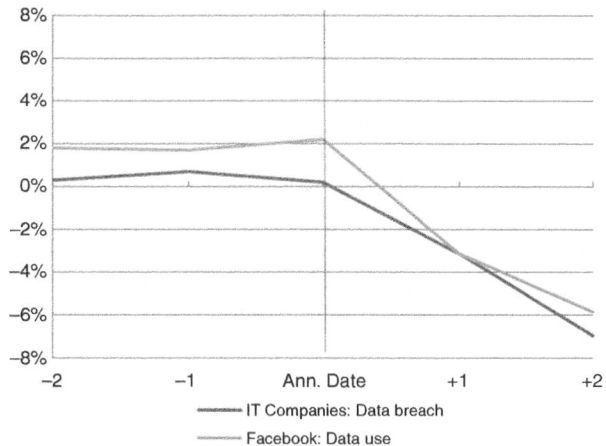

Fig. 6.16 Announcement Effect of Data Breaches and Improper Use of Data (Source: Authors' elaboration of data provided by Factiva, Thomson Reuters Datastream)

6.5   Conclusion

With public finances already stretched, private investors are called to fill the gap between historical infrastructure spending and greater infrastructure needs that will emerge through 2035. This poses important questions to investors and asset managers about the long-term changes that the infrastructure asset class will experience in the next few years, as it matures.

Historically, infrastructure has been viewed as one of the safest harbors in the universe of alternative investments. The regulation of the various sectors, high barriers to entry, rigid demand, and hedges against inflation were factors that allowed investors to benefit from stable and inflation-linked cash flows for extended periods of time. This might not continue to hold true looking ahead. On one hand, with opportunities in core infrastructure becoming scarcer and more expensive, asset managers face a new landscape characterized by compressed yields, risk of over-payment and an investment style drift towards higher-return strategies. On the other, technological and socio-cultural trends are rapidly reshaping the way society works and lives, calling for new and better infrastructures to serve new essential consumer needs.

To asset managers facing these challenges, we recommend two complementary courses of action. The first one is oriented more toward the short term and more in line with the investment style of private equity. It involves actions aimed at enhancing performance but not changing long-term strategic views. In this respect, borrowing from the private equity toolkit, we identify three levers of tactical optimization. First, infrastructure asset managers can work on strengthening their ability to spot undervalued assets. Then, they should modify their risk profile across sectors, geographical areas, and the lifecycle to adapt to emerging and changing risks. Finally, they can obtain enhanced performances by creating value in investee firms, paying more attention to the management of investee firms.

The second course of action that we recommend, which instead has a long-term orientation, requires recognizing sectors that are supported by transformative trends that drive demand for new and better infrastructure. This means analyzing trends within and across industries to identify disruptive business models or essential assets where new infrastructure needs are emerging. We refer to this as theme investing. To follow this course of action, asset managers need to abandon their traditional business model based on specialization. Instead they must adopt a broader and more forward-looking investment philosophy, grounded on a principle-based approach or eligibility tests based on the features of the needs served by the infrastructure. More specifically, to this end, we propose a reorganization of the entire screening process of infrastructure investment opportunities. The key is to combine each trend with the sectors it is expected to transform and with specific asset eligibility criteria (i.e., a set of criteria that, if met, qualify the asset as infrastructure).

References

Baccelli, O. (2020). Future developments in the European transport infrastructure sector. In S. Gatti & C. Chiarella (Eds.), *Disruption in the infrastructure sector - challenges and opportunities for developers, investors and asset managers*. Heidelberg: Springer.

Beal, D., Eccles, R., Hansell, G., Lesser, R., Unnikirshnan, S., Woods, W., & Young, D. (2017). *Total societal impact: A new lens for strategy*. BCG - Boston Consulting Group. Retrieved from https://www.bcg.com/publications/2017/total-societal-impact-new-lens-strategy.aspx

Bokkerink, M., Charlin, G., Sajdeh, R., & Wald, D. (2017). *How big consumer companies can fight back*. BCG - Boston Consulting Group. Retrieved from https://www.bcg.com/publications/2017/strategy-products-how-big-consumer-companies-can-fight-back.aspx

Carney, M. (2018, April 6). *A transition in thinking and action - Remarks given by the Governor of the Bank of England Mark Carney*. Bank of England. Retrieved from https://www.bankofengland.co.uk/speech/2018/mark-carney-speech-at-international-climate-risk-conference-for-supervisors

Chong, F. (2018). *Should global infrastructure investors worry about Australian protectionism?* IPE Real Assets. Retrieved from https://realassets.ipe.com/regulation/should-global-infrastructure-investors-worry-about-australian-protectionism/10023063.article

CISCO. (2017). *Visual Networking Index (VNI) Global Mobile Data Forecast Update – 2016-2021*. Retrieved from https://www.cisco.com/c/en/us/solutions/collateral/service-provider/visual-networking-index-vni/white-paper-c11-738429.html

Cox, W., & Pavletich, H. (2018). *14th Annual Demographia International Housing Affordability Survey*. Retrieved from http://www.demographia.com/dhi2018.pdf

Credit Suisse. (2017). *Supertrends – One year on, The future now – Investing for the long term*. Retrieved from https://www.credit-suisse.com/about-us-news/en/articles/news-and-expertise/supertrends-one-year-on-201806.html

Deloitte. (2016). *European infrastructure investors survey 2016 – A positive horizon on the road ahead?* Retrieved from https://www2.deloitte.com/content/dam/Deloitte/uk/Documents/infrastructure-and-capital-projects/deloitte-uk-european-infrastructure-investors-survey-2016.pdf

Di Castelnuovo, M., & Biancardi, A. (2020). The future of energy infrastructures: Brace yourself for a bumpy ride! In S. Gatti & C. Chiarella (Eds.), *Disruption in the infrastructure sector - Challenges and opportunities for developers, investors and asset managers*. Heidelberg: Springer.

DLA Piper. (2018). *UK Infrasturcture – Defining the future*. Retrieved from https://www.dlapiper.com/~/media/files/insights/publications/2018/07/dla-piper%2D%2D-uk-infrastructure-report%2D%2D-defining-the-future-0718.pdf

Emsden, C. (2018). *How e-commerce is changing logistics and transportation systems*. The Infrastructure Channel. Retrieved from https://www.infrastructure-channel.com/mobility/how-e-commerce-is-changing-logistics-and-transportation-systems/

Fixsen, R. (2018). *Demographics Europe: An age-old problem*. IPE Real Assets. Retrieved from https://realassets.ipe.com/real-estate/demographics-europe-an-age-old-problem/10023522.article

Ford, J., & Plimmer, G. (2018, January 22). Pioneering Britain has a rethink on privatization. *Financial Times*. Retrieved from https://www.ft.com/content/b7e28a58-f7ba-11e7-88f7-5465a6ce1a00

Gapper, J. (2018, June 6). How millennials became the world's most powerful consumers. *Financial Times*. Retrieved from https://www.ft.com/content/194cd1c8-6583-11e8-a39d-4df188287fff

Gurria, A. (2017, April 24). Putting water at the centre of the global agenda – Speech by OECD Secretary General Angel Gurría. *OECD*. Retrieved from https://www.oecd.org/about/secretary-general/putting-water-at-the-centre-of-the-global-agenda-remarks-a-gurria.htm

Hechler-Fayd'herbe, N. (2017). Silver economy – Investing for population aging. *Credit Suisse*. Retrieved from https://www.credit-suisse.com/about-us-news/en/articles/news-and-expertise/silver-economy-investing-for-population-aging-201707.html

Hofrichter, S. (2017). The economics of populism: Why populism matters to growth and markets –
    Update. *Allianz Global Investors.* Retrieved from https://www.allianzglobalinvestors.de/
    MDBWS/doc/AllianzGI+-+Stefan+Hofrichter+-+The+Economics+of+Populism.pdf?
    022932e0cd78ed7743f7efafcfbfa396b38e2e9e

International Energy Agency. (2017). *Renewables 2017.* Retrieved from https://www.iea.org/
    reports/renewables-2017

IPE Real Assets. (2018a). Top 100 infrastructure investors 2018. *Investment and Pensions Europe.*
    Retrieved   from   https://realassets.ipe.com/surveys/top-100-infrastructure-investors-2018/
    10026765.article

IPE Real Assets. (2018b). Top 50 infrastructure investment managers 2018. *Investment and
    Pensions Europe.* Retrieved from https://realassets.ipe.com/infrastructure/top-50-infrastruc
    ture-investment-managers-2018/10025380.article

Jenkins, P. (2018, January 24). City continues to back PFI deals despite Carillion's collapse.
    Financial Times. Retrieved from https://www.ft.com/content/eb993f02-00ea-11e8-9650-
    9c0ad2d7c5b5

JP Morgan. (2015). *Infrastructure Investing – Key benefits and risks.* Retrieved from https://careers.
    jpmorganchase.com/jpmpdf/1158630194855.pdf

Khorana, A., Shivdasani, A., & Kimyagarov, G. (2018). *2018 Corporate finance priorities.* Citi
    GPS: Global   Perspectives   &   Solutions.   Retrieved   from   https://www.citibank.com/
    commercialbank/insights/assets/docs/2018/2018-Corporate-Finance-Priorties/2/

Marketsandmarkets. (2018). *Cybersecurity Market - Global Forecast to 2023.* Retrieved from
    https://www.marketsandmarkets.com/Market-Reports/cyber-security-market-505.html

McDonnell, J. (2017, September 25). *Speech by UK Shadow Chancellor John McDonnell to
    Labour Party Conference.* Labour. Retrieved from https://labour.org.uk/press/shadow-chancel
    lor-john-mcdonnell-speech-to-labour/

Megaw, N. (2018, January 23). National Grid hits out at Ofgem over Hinkley Point proposal.
    Financial Times. Retrieved from https://www.ft.com/content/baa21606-0010-11e8-9650-
    9c0ad2d7c5b5

Meggiolaro, M. (2017). A clean disruption of energy and transportation is around the corner. *The
    Infrastructure Channel.* Retrieved from https://www.infrastructure-channel.com/sustainability/
    a-clean-disruption-of-energy-and-transportation-is-around-the-corner/

Meggiolaro, M. (2018). The future of logistics. *The Infrastructure Channel.* Retrieved from https://
    www.infrastructure-channel.com/infrastructure/the-future-of-logistics/

Palma, S. (2018, July 12). Cyber security is biggest worry for GIC chief executive. *Financial Times.*
    Retrieved from https://www.ft.com/content/7f167cc8-85c9-11e8-96dd-fa565ec55929

Partners Group. (2018). *Leveraging the winds of change, Private Markets Navigator Outlook 2018.*
    Retrieved from https://www.partnersgroup.com/en/news-views/corporate-news/archive/detail/
    article/partners-group-publishes-market-outlook-for-2018-leveraging-the-winds-of-change/

Pfeifer S., Fildes N., & Ram A. (2018, April 18). Energy sector on alert for cyber-attacks on UK
    power network. *Financial Times.* Retrieved from https://www.ft.com/content/d2b2aaec-4252-
    11e8-93cf-67ac3a6482fd

Poppensieker, T., & Riemenschnitter, R. (2018). *A new posture for cybersecurity in a networked
    world.* McKinsey & Company. Retrieved from https://www.mckinsey.com/business-functions/
    risk/our-insights/a-new-posture-for-cybersecurity-in-a-networked-world

Preqin. (2018a, January). *Real Assets Spotlight.* Retrieved from https://docs.preqin.com/
    newsletters/ra/2018-Preqin-Global-Real-Assets-Report-Spotlight.pdf

Preqin. (2018b, February). *Real Assets Spotlight.* Retrieved from https://docs.preqin.com/
    newsletters/ra/Preqin-Real-Assets-Spotlight-February-2017.pdf

Preqin. (2018c). *Quarterly infrastructure update – Q1.* Retrieved from https://docs.preqin.com/
    quarterly/inf/Preqin-Quarterly-Infrastructure-Update-Q1-2018.pdf

Preqin. (2018d). *Infrastructure fund manager outlook – H1.* Retrieved from https://docs.preqin.
    com/reports/Preqin-Special-Report-Infrastructure-Fund-Manager-Outlook-H1-2018.pdf

Pressi, F. (2018). Big data and automotive. *The Infrastructure Channel*. Retrieved from https://www.infrastructure-channel.com/digitalization/big-data-and-automotive/

Sacco, F. (2020). The future of telecom. In S. Gatti & C. Chiarella (Eds.), *Disruption in the infrastructure sector - Challenges and opportunities for developers, investors and asset managers*. Heidelberg: Springer.

United Nations. (2018). *World urbanization prospects: The 2018 Revision*. Retrieved from https://population.un.org/wup/Publications/

Venzin, M., & Konert, E. (2020). The disruption of the infrastructure industry: How investment decisions in the infrastructure industry are expected to change and how to prepare. In S. Gatti & C. Chiarella (Eds.), *Disruption in the infrastructure sector - Challenges and opportunities for developers, investors and asset managers*. Heidelberg: Springer.

Veritas. (2016). *The Global Databerg Report – See what others don't*. Retrieved from http://images.info.veritas.com/Web/Veritas/%7B364a7ca5-e05c-4fce-971b-88e18c62eafb%7D_45145_EMEA_Veritas_Strike_Report_Gulf.pdf

Willis Towers Watson and PRI Global Investment. (2017). *Responding to Megatrends*. Retrieved from https://www.willistowerswatson.com/-/media/WTW/Insights/2017/12/Responding-to-megatrends.pdf

Woetzel, J., Garemo, N., Mischke, J., Hjerpe, M., & Palter, R. (2016). *Bridging global infrastructure gaps*. McKinsey Global Institute. Retrieved from https://www.mckinsey.com/industries/capital-projects-and-infrastructure/our-insights/bridging-global-infrastructure-gaps

Woetzel, J., Garemo, N., Mischke, J., Hjerpe, M., & Palter, R. (2017). *Bridging global infrastructure gaps: Has the world made progress?* McKinsey Global Institute. Retrieved from https://www.mckinsey.com/industries/capital-projects-and-infrastructure/our-insights/bridging-infrastructure-gaps-has-the-world-made-progress

Conclusions

Stefano Gatti and Carlo Chiarella

The contributions in this book provide very specific insights for the future of infrastructure, as perceived across different sectors and from diverse points of view. The findings of the authors have clear implications for incumbents, disruptors, regulators, policymakers, investors and asset managers. This final section summarizes the results of the various analyses conducted in the previous chapters, highlighting the key outcomes and connecting them in a unified framework from the standpoint of investors and asset managers.

For them, three key takeaways emerge.

First, asset managers and investors must recognize that the transformation of the infrastructure sector is a reality, one that will continue to exist in the years to come. New ecosystems are coming into existence, spawned by sectors that are very far away from the traditional concept of infrastructure. Indeed, from the picture that emerges from the analysis by Markus Venzin and Emilia Konert on the evolution of the infrastructure industry and its profitability (Chap. 5), we can see that technological advancement is reshaping competition across all sectors, increasingly favoring synergies across energy, transportation and telecom infrastructures. As soon as one disruptive business model or product emerges, another one is developed, and new industry or outside disruptors disrupt the former disruptors.

As far as the energy sector is concerned, the analysis conducted by Matteo Di Castenuovo and Andrea Biancardi in Chap. 2 shows that the industry is currently undergoing an unprecedented revolution characterized by six major underlying forces: decarbonization, decentralization, electrification, digitalization, custom activation and convergence of industries. This *new normal* represents a paradigm shift in

S. Gatti (✉)
Department of Finance, Bocconi University, Milano, Italy
e-mail: stefano.gatti@unibocconi.it

C. Chiarella (✉)
Colegio Universitario de Estudios Financieros, Madrid, Spain
e-mail: carlo.chiarella@cunef.edu

© Springer Nature Switzerland AG 2020
S. Gatti, C. Chiarella (eds.), *Disruption in the Infrastructure Sector*, Future of Business and Finance, https://doi.org/10.1007/978-3-030-44667-3_7

the energy industry across its value chain, with massive implications in terms of economic fundamentals, investment opportunities and business strategies. In particular, the electricity industry is experiencing a transformation that seriously threatens to disrupt the status quo of its players within the next few years. However, according to the analysis of these authors, Europe's largest utilities are responding with different business models to the challenges and opportunities provided by the six drivers mentioned above. So, it is not yet clear which of these models, if any, will prove to be better suited to adapt to changes in climate policy (e.g. carbon target), market design (e.g. capacity mechanisms) and regulation (e.g. network pricing), or better positioned to compete against newcomers from inside and outside the sector. In any case, a few key outcomes emerge from this analysis. The expected growth in corporate renewable procurement opens valuable investment opportunities in clean energy portfolios, including less mature technologies. However, natural gas cannot be written off yet because of its role in balancing renewables, thanks to its flexibility, and because of its uses in sectors other than electricity. Finally, electricity networks together with electrical energy storage represent the key enablers of the paradigm shift in the energy industry.

In a similar vein, in his analysis of the transportation sector in Chap. 3 Oliviero Baccelli identifies demographic changes and widespread adoption of new technologies as the key drivers of mobility trends in major metropolitan areas. His analysis also emphasizes how stronger demand for intra- and extra-EU mobility for both passengers and freight is leading to an increased demand for new infrastructure, especially at international gates: airports, terminals at major ports (for containers, dry bulk and cruise ships), and intermodal links to the main nodes. As a result, specific investments are called for to boost capacity and improve environmental performance, to respond to the competition and to comply with new EU and international regulation. This means that the evolution of the industry in the years to come and its rate of change still depend crucially on the trajectory of oil prices, fuel efficiency programs and the costs of emission compliance. Nonetheless, two key drivers of value creation emerge from the analysis. The first is the enhanced operational efficiency at both node and link level thanks to opportunities stemming from the technological and organizational innovations triggered by automation and digitalization. The second is the expanded spectrum of services offered by transport infrastructure operators to capture new sources of revenue from value added services offered at transportation nodes.

Continuing on, according to the analysis by Francesco Sacco in Chap. 4, the telecommunication sector is evolving in two main directions. In the first, technological innovations and changes in working and living habits have given rise to a great number and variety of new assets that extend the definition of the telecom asset base. The second is the transformation of basic telecom assets already in place by using software to create different business models and potential disruptions. At the origin of both these trends is the exponential growth in connected devices and transmitted data, as well as the geopolitical interests of regulators, which all call for an evolution of the network and related services. The analysis in this chapter shows how increased network capacity in terms of throughput, and network quality in terms of latency and reliability, can be obtained through a fiber-based evolution involving fiber densification, access network simplification and the development of proximity data centers. All this necessitates much deeper pockets than in the past, but incumbents seem unable to keep up with the investment required by the market and the regulators, as their average revenues are on the decline. Still, the analysis in question emphasizes that network evolution is expected to form different layers of telecom infrastructure, favoring the emergence of new business models and thus new opportunities for investors. However, the monetization of innovation is not an intrinsic implication of innovation itself. In particular, assets that have a software component are more prone to be disrupted by new business models, new evolutions, or new combinations of assets. Instead in the more complex space of more traditional and essential assets the evolution is still based on solid, even if minimal, cornerstones.

The book's second key takeaway is that such a transformation of the infrastructure industry ecosystem calls for investors and asset managers to adopt a more flexible approach to investments, in which the definition of infrastructure is stretched beyond its current boundaries. Instead of a strictly sectorial definition, in fact, eligibility criteria should apply and the sources of value for investors would be rebalanced, from income streams to capital gains, more in line with a private equity investment style.

With this in mind, in Chap. 6, Stefano Gatti and Carlo Chiarella recommend two complementary courses of action for investors and asset managers. The first, which is more short-term oriented and more in line with the investment style of private equity, involves actions aimed at enhancing performance while leaving long-term strategic views intact. In this respect, borrowing from the private equity toolkit, three levers of tactical optimization are identified. Infrastructure asset managers can initially work on honing their ability to spot undervalued assets. Then, they should modify their risk profile across sectors, geographical areas, and the lifecycle to adapt to emerging and changing risks. Finally, they can upgrade performances by creating value in investee firms, by paying more attention to their management. The analysis presented here shows that these are as of yet largely unexplored levers of value creation, leaving ample margins for improvement through tactical optimization.

The second recommended course of action is instead long-term oriented and requires recognizing sectors that are supported by transformative trends that drive demand for new and better infrastructure. This means analyzing trends within and across industries to identify disruptive business models or essential assets where new infrastructure needs are emerging, a strategy referred to as theme investing. To follow this course of action, asset managers need to abandon their traditional business model, structured on specialization, and adopt a broader more forward-looking investment philosophy, grounded on a principle-based approach or eligibility tests that assess the features of the needs served by the infrastructure. More specifically, to this end, the authors propose a reorganization of the entire screening process of infrastructure investment opportunities, in order to match each trend with the sectors it is expected to transform and with specific asset eligibility criteria. In fact, their analysis shows that as disruptive business models pave the way for new essential products and services, new types of infrastructure emerge to serve new consumer needs, originating new long-term strategic opportunities. Yet, they also warn that upon recognizing a trend, positioning to exploit its long-term strategic opportunities may not be straightforward. Not all assets are equally affected, and returns can vary substantially within industry groups. A scrupulous and diligent assessment of asset-specific characteristics remains a driver of performance.

The natural consequence of such a renewed investment approach, and the third key takeaway from this book, is that asset managers and investors must spend more time and effort on market analysis and market screening, adopting advisory boards, think-tank teams and rigorous methodologies to analyze evolutionary trends and the potential impacts on their current and future investments. First movers will create a durable competitive advantage vis-à-vis less established asset managers.

In this respect, while recognizing that there is no standard formula for industry incumbents to respond to a rapidly evolving infrastructure ecosystem, Markus Venzin and Emilia Konert in Chap. 5 identify adaptability as the key to dealing successfully with disruption. In particular, they highlight the importance of adopting a more dynamic and intelligence-based approach to investing by continuously tracking, studying and investing in the companies driving the change. To do so, they suggest that investors and asset managers should create an infrastructure radar to map disruptive companies, analyze their business models and assess their impact on the industry as well as on investee companies or assets. As this analysis shows, this approach would help investors and asset managers thrive through changes in the infrastructure ecosystem by protecting, complementing and enhancing their investments.

The manufacturer's authorised representative in the EU is Springer
Nature Customer Service Centre GmbH, Europaplatz 3, 69115 Heidelberg,
Germany. If you have any concerns regarding our products, please
contact ProductSafety@springernature.com

Printed and bound by CPI Group (UK) Ltd, Croydon, CR0 4YY
24/04/2026
02096308-0003